CW01064895

HOUSING, COMMUNITY CARE AND SUPPORTED HOUSING
RESOLVING CONTRADICTIONS

Edited by Mark Foord and Paul Simic

Chartered Institute of Housing
Policy and Practice Series
in collaboration with the
Housing Studies Association

The Chartered Institute of Housing
The Chartered Institute of Housing is the professional organisation for people who work in housing. Its purpose is to maximise the contribution housing professionals make to the well-being of communities. The Institute has 19,000 members across the UK and the Asian Pacific working in a range of organisations, including housing associations, local authorities, the private sector and educational institutions.

Chartered Institute of Housing
Octavia House, Westwood Way
Coventry CV4 8JP
Telephone: 024 7685 1700
Fax: 024 7669 5110
Website: www.cih.org

The Housing Studies Association
The Housing Studies Association promotes the study of housing by bringing together housing researchers with others interested in housing research in the housing policy and practitioner communities. It acts as a voice for housing research by organising conferences and seminars, lobbying government and other agencies and providing services to members.

The CIH Housing Policy and Practice Series is published in collaboration with the Housing Studies Association and aims to provide important and valuable material and insights for housing managers, staff, students, trainers and policy-makers. Books in the series are designed to promote debate, but the contents do not necessarily reflect the views of the CIH or the HSA. The Editorial Team for the series is: General Editors: Dr. Peter Williams, John Perry and Professor Peter Malpass, and Production Editor: Alan Dearling.

Cover photographs © Stonham 2005

This publication has been sponsored by Home Group

ISBN 1 903208 39 4

Housing, community care and supported housing: resolving contradictions
Edited by Mark Foord and Paul Simic
Published by the Chartered Institute of Housing © 2005

Printed by Hobbs The Printers, Totton

Contents

Foreword by Malcolm Levi, Chief Executive of Home Group Ltd.   **v**

Acknowledgements   **vi**

PART ONE: **Housing, care, and support – setting the context**   **1**

CHAPTER 1:   Introduction: supported housing and community care – towards a new landscape of precariousness?   2
Mark Foord

CHAPTER 2:   Housing and community care in its historical and political context   20
Murray Hawtin

CHAPTER 3:   Working in partnership for 'joined up' housing and community care   41
Julie Savory

CHAPTER 4:   Scoping the supported housing sector – the funding and regulatory framework   62
Deborah Bennett

CHAPTER 5:   Involving users and carers in housing and social care planning – the rhetoric of 'user empowerment'   75
Charlie Cooper

CHAPTER 6:   Housing needs assessments: time to move on?   88
Bogusia Temple

PART TWO: **Housing, care and support: key user groups**   **99**

CHAPTER 7:   Learning disability, housing and community care   100
David Race

CHAPTER 8:   Adapting to life – are adaptations a remedy for disability?   113
Pam Thomas and Marcus Ormerod

CHAPTER 9:   *'He went berserk and stabbed his mother 43 times ...'* Thinking in headlines: mental health and housing   126
Paul Simic

CHAPTER 10:   Supported housing and frail older people – towards whole systems approaches?   142
Mark Foord

PART THREE: **Looking to the future**   **163**

CHAPTER 11:   Contested communities? Homelessness, substance
              misuse and regeneration policy   164
              Anya Ahmed and Julia Lucas

CHAPTER 12:   Housing and community care: a comparative perspective   175
              Tim Brown and Nichola Yates

CHAPTER 13:   Not another policy plan: Supporting People strategies
              and community care   188
              Tim Brown, Jo Richardson and Jackie Thompson-Ercan

CHAPTER 14:   'Social capital': a systems approach to housing and
              community care   201
              Paul Simic

Contributors   **223**

Bibliography   **227**

Index   **255**

Foreword

Social policy discourse since 1945 has been driven by what some have termed the post war consensus. Yet it is three successive New Labour governments that have challenged the orthodoxy of Beveridge's welfare state, with Labour's emphasis on rights and duties, value for money and targeting. However, the number of people in need of housing, support and community care provision is increasing.

Beveridge's world of the five giants has changed markedly - people with mental health needs are no longer routinely locked away in long stay institutions; the homeless no longer fester in Poor Law era 'doss houses' and ex-offenders are being offered alternatives to incarceration. There is now an expectation of improved service levels but this is tinged with public anxiety about living next door to many service users.

All this is in the context of a key government tenet - that of the laudable aim of joined up thinking between government departments which is easy to say but so hard to achieve. Emphasis on partnership working and the clear recognition that a civilised society has duties to its citizens, particularly those who are vulnerable, sets the context for this book.

Stonham, a division of Home Group, is the largest provider of supported housing in the UK with circa £50 million of Supporting People funding. Now more than ever we need to focus on providing high quality, value for money services, whilst reshaping our organisation in response to Supporting People cuts. Government has always found supported housing a difficult area, and its agencies equally so. There cannot be many social funding programmes which, having been completely restructured, are then expected to implement what are effectively three years of cuts.

This book is a valuable contribution, setting out the development of housing and community care in the UK today. The history, funding mechanisms, work with Black and Minority Ethnic communities, the specific needs of people with mental illness and those with a learning disability are charted, as are links with the elderly and frail. The intention is both to inform and to provoke.

This is a challenging subject and the authors are to be commended for a timely contribution to the ongoing debate. They remind us of the benefits of joint working and collaboration, but by concentrating on the problems as they see them, they do not shirk from telling us how it is. Practitioners will find it of real value.

Malcolm Levi
Chief Executive
Home Group

Acknowledgements

Mark Foord

I am grateful to those friends and colleagues who read sections of the book and made helpful suggestions and criticisms, especially Frances Young, Jane Heyes, Dawn Judd, Mary Drummond and Michelle Cornes. To my partner Uschi Muller for patiently enduring the traumas of academic life. And finally to the staff at Exchange Coffee Shop in Clitheroe, for providing an environment more conducive to writing, thinking and reflection than the University!

Paul Simic

To my father (Jovan) who died recently and my mother. To my wife (Ann) who has had to listen to me going on about this book for so long. To my children (Jonathan, Anna and Misha) who care not a fig, but are equally dear to me. However expensive they may be, though, I love them too (ho, ho!). To my co-editor, for carrying so much of the burden of putting this together.

The editors wish to thank Alan Dearling for his constant patience and good humour, John Perry for his sound thoughts and encouragement, the referees for their advice and comments, and finally the Home Group for their generous sponsorship of the book.

PART ONE

Housing, care and support – setting the context

CHAPTER 1:
Introduction: supported housing and community care – towards a new landscape of precariousness?

Mark Foord

Introduction

In April 2004, the government announced that it would develop a new 'vision' for adult social care. The resulting green paper, *Independence, Well-being and Choice – Our vision for the future of social care for adults in England* (Department of Health, 2005) sets out a number of key proposals to deliver this 'vision':

- A wider use of direct payments and the piloting of individual care budgets to stimulate the development of services, delivered in ways that people want.
- A greater focus on preventative services to allow for early, targeted intervention and the use of a local 'well-being' agenda to ensure greater social inclusion and an improved quality of life.
- A strong strategic and leadership role for local government, working in partnership with other agencies, especially the NHS.
- Encouraging the development of new models of service delivery, particularly harnessing new technology and forms of telecare.
- Users and carers will be placed at the centre of needs assessments.
- The creation a new local government post – the Director of Adult Social Services.
- *Connected Care Centres* providing NHS, social care and other community professionals around the clock will be strongly supported.
- The paper also raised the possibility of a registration scheme covering those working with vulnerable adults (this would, we can presume, include many staff working in supported housing).

The green paper contains the now familiar range of New Labour discourses around *choice, citizenship, community, modernisation, community leadership, value for money* etc., and is underpinned by a strong hint that natural selection will weed out social care providers not delivering consumer demands. Despite few explicit references to the housing role in community care, many of the key themes: preventative services, telecare, extra care sheltered housing, good residential care and bad, will resonate with housing providers.

What doesn't appear is any sense of how Supporting People and the new support role carved out for housing providers will dovetail with the government's vision for community care. There is in fact, little sense of any strategic role for housing authorities. It appears that the housing role in community care is once again in transition and flux. The green paper will steer the development of community care for the foreseeable future, which will be built around an axis of social services and primary care trusts. Hanging in the air is a growing question mark over the future of Supporting People and the destination of many supported housing projects.

The crisis around Supporting People, its place in the landscape of housing and community care, and the uncertainty this crisis engenders for supported housing providers is a key theme in this introductory chapter, which attempts to provide a context for the discussion of housing and community care contained in the remainder of the book.

Supporting People: transition and change

So, what's new? Talk of '*crisis*' and '*retrenchment*' is in the air, as the supported housing sector is said to be facing '*massive upheaval*' (Cooper, 2004). Housing associations are now laying off staff as the Supporting People budget cuts begin to bite. Stonham which received £50 million of Supporting People money each year is to cut 250 jobs (Rickets, 2005). Nigel Rogers, Director of the advice agency SITRA said,

> '... this is a hugely significant moment in Supporting People's evolution. If the largest provider of support services can't sustain its existing range of jobs, what hope is there for others?'(Rickets, 2005).

As sceptics anticipated, the transition from a largely open ended funding system, to one that is cash limited, has placed enormous strain on the willingness of the Treasury, to fund the ambitions of local authorities to provide supported housing. The catalyst was the Robson Rhodes review of Supporting People, instigated after the bill for Supporting People was pushed up to £2.8 billion in April 2003. This they argued was '*too much to pay*' for housing-related support services, and suggested funding should quickly be released from the historical 'legacy' provision; redistributed according to need, and that services should be developed on the basis of evidenced need. They suggested remedies to the problems they identified in the Supporting People programme:

At a local level:
- Strategic reviews based around client groups.
- Pool expertise across administering authorities by developing specialist strategic teams for reviews.
- Strengthen the decision-making process through supporting the capacity of commissioning bodies.

At a national level:
- Client group reviews to identify where needs are being met, where non-housing-related support is included looking at how to integrate funding sources appropriately.
- Focus on high cost authorities identified through strategic reviews, inspection and value for money reviews.

Moving with telling speed, the government suggested that the method for distributing Supporting People would be radically overhauled, and all monies allocated according to a needs-based formula. In August 2004 the government announced that the Supporting People budget would be cut by £80 million to £1.8 billion (in 2005/6). For the following two years the budget would be held around £1.7 billion. In December 2004, the Office of the Deputy Prime Minister announced a three year programme of budget cuts. Every local authority has seen it budget slashed for 2005/6, with average cuts of 5 per cent. Over the following two years cuts will be limited to 5 per cent, and budget increases to authorities who have been deemed to require more funding will be limited to 10 per cent. The formula sought to identify the 55 'outlying' councils who will face the biggest and smallest cuts in the future. Local authorities are expected to make savings following wide ranging service reviews. Alan Hagger of Hampshire County Council argued the three year programme of cuts would *'blow its business plan out of the water'*. SITRA said the allocation made *'grim reading'* (*Inside Housing*, 10th December 2004, p.7).

For readers with long memories, Supporting People is following an uncannily similar path to the implementation of community care in 1993: a generous initial budget, followed by a radical paring back, leading to means-testing, the application of harsh eligibility criteria and year on year efficiency savings. Martin, Phelps and Katbamna (2004) point out:

> '... *cost containment was arguably an overriding aim of the community care reforms of the early 1990s, and so to this extent it should come as no surprise that its effect has pervaded all aspects of the conduct of community care practitioners'*.

The contradiction between 'value for money', rationalising provision and the needs of users will become starkly apparent in the coming years. As with community care, there will be role conflict for professionals as the custodian of resources and guardians of their client's interests.

Supported People and community care – a symbiotic relationship?

Supporting People provides the 'sceptre at the feast' in this book – it the latest attempt to redesign how aspects of housing and social care can be reshaped to form a closer functional fit, in order to deliver the seamless services talked about since the Seebohm and Cullingworth reports in the 1960s. A number of chapters explore in detail the impact of Supporting People on aspects of the relationship between housing and care providers. Where previously housing was largely tangential to the organisation of community care, Supporting People gives local authorities a pivotal role in the management and distribution of supported housing revenue funding, with the intention that such services, will form a 'bridge' between general housing services and community care.

Research suggests that the programme has resulted in benefits to users and the Treasury, as its focus on preventative services has allowed benefits to accrue 'downstream' in crime reduction, community care and homelessness (Office of the Deputy Prime Minister, 2004d). However, in delineating a new housing sphere of control, an additional boundary with care providers has been created, when agencies are enjoined to develop seamlessness. Ironically, the criticisms of made by Robson Rhodes are strikingly reminiscent of those levelled at the previous funding system: criticism which itself provided the rationale for developing Supporting People. Only time will tell whether the problems of Supporting People are based in flawed implementation or, relate to systemic problems accruing from the artificial separation of support and care in budgeting and planning, to the detriment of person centred, whole systems approaches.

The uncertain place of housing in community care

Despite the essentially unplanned growth of the housing role in community care, it is now a key player. It provides a growth area for housing associations, at a time when it has become difficult for many smaller associations to access capital grants. In 1998, the Audit Commission identified that there are least 1.3 million tenants and home owners receiving housing-related community care services, at a cost of more than £2 billion pounds per annum (Audit Commission, 1998). Now there are around 250,000 units of housing support (excluding sheltered housing and community alarms) compared to fewer than 100,000 in 2000 (Office of the Deputy Prime Minister, 2004c). The principal client groups being older people, people with mental health problems, people with a learning disability and those with physical disabilities. In recent years the sector has developed projects and floating support schemes for homeless people, people with a substance abuse problem, lone teenage parents, asylum seekers, refugees, etc.. The unclear nature of 'housing support' has allowed many 'new' needs groups to be incorporated into the 'official' list of groups who might benefit from supported housing, leading to accusations of 'budget shifting' (from care resources to housing) in recent Supporting People reviews.

At the heart of government's approach to public policy is a belief in the idea of enhanced partnerships infusing every aspect of policy (Powell, 2000). The call has been for the range of housing, social care and health agencies to work together, plan strategically and think holistically in a policy arena where competitive working has so far been privileged above collaboration. The New Labour modernisation agenda has had a major impact on housing and community care services. There are a number of key aims running through the 'modernisation' programme for the public services:

- The reduction of inequalities.
- The promotion of active citizenship and the promotion of an agenda based on the rights and responsibilities of the citizens to help themselves.
- The pursuit of equity in the provision and supply of services.
- Greater attention to outcomes based on measurable standards and evidence that the most effective service approach is being used.
  (Spencer and Fletcher, 2002)

As part of this agenda, the government has attempted to transform the architecture of health, housing and social care; Supporting People is a major part of that transformation. Yet, whilst government has often repeated that, *'housing is a vital component of community care and is often the key to independent living'* (Department of Health, 1989a), the housing role has been marginalised within joint planning, whilst the exact terrain of the housing role in community care has been hard to define or specify. In the past, the absence of a whole systems approach to housing and care; 'supported housing' has effectively formed a parallel support sector alongside social care and health systems. 'Hard to reach' (homeless people, ex-offenders etc.) or 'unpopular' groups (substance misusers for example) have struggled to receive a holistic service which met their housing, care and health needs, and have increasingly been 'hived off' to the supported housing sector. Cameron, Harrison, Burton, and Marsh (2001) point to the dominant themes around the relationship between housing and community care:

- The need to integrate housing and support into mainstream local services.
- The necessity of placing users at the centre of community care and for care plans to be developed from the user perspective.
- The need to develop mechanisms which provide users and carers with opportunities to express views about the services they receive.
- The future role of sheltered housing in the context of community care.
- Social services eligibility criteria were having a deleterious effect on the capacity of housing providers to play a preventative role in community care.
- Strategic weaknesses in terms of local planning and financial frameworks.
- Research suggested that there were professional stereotypes and differences between housing and social care staff.
- There was tension between three elements of policy: the policy emphasis of ensuring that everyone should be able to live in their own home with

support; community care not providing new entitlements to housing, and finally, social service's departments cutting back on resources going into low level or medium cared needs.
• Housing residualisation and stigma on social housing estates, as *'right to buy'* removed the best stock and the most economically active tenants from the social housing sector.

Supporting People: promoting a whole systems approach?

The role of housing providers in the recent past has been expanded and transformed in response to a number of key drivers: firstly, the growing numbers of people with support needs as more people are living to an older age and expressing a preference for independent living. Secondly, the NHS has shifted its role away from long term care, towards primary care, whilst social services have refocused resources on higher level needs and crisis intervention, leaving housing providers to meet the needs of tenants requiring low level support. Thirdly, financial systems and the signals these provide to agencies. In the mid-1980s the residential care bill rose in response to the Thatcher government's encouragement of the residential care sector, so supported housing grew in the 1990s as housing benefit was allowed to take the strain of the developing market for supported housing. Repeating the pattern of previous government attempts to control public spending on residential care payments, the government sought to ring-fence housing benefit to its core purpose of paying for accommodation. In 1998, expenditure on housing benefits reached £11 billion per annum and a series of court cases determined that mainstream housing benefit should not be used to meet the costs of housing-related support. The judgement crystallised debates that had been rumbling for years in the Department of the Environment, Transport and the Regions (as was). The government's response to the outcome was affected by three factors:

• A belief that there was much unmet need in the supported housing sector.
• Systems for meeting supported housing needs should move to a cash limited basis as a means of managing unmet need.
• That the quality of services delivery and management could be improved. (Office of the Deputy Prime Minister, 2004d)

Mechanisms for developing supported housing were seen to be unco-ordinated, unrelated to local priorities and frequently provider and funding driven. There were built in resource incentives which encouraged the development of outdated models of institutional, 'hostel' provision which no longer met the aspirations of users. But as part of their service charge tenants were required to pay for a range of support services for which they often had no need (for example in sheltered housing). Whilst others lingered in supported housing, waiting for 'move on' rehousing long after the need for crisis intervention or support had ended. The planning, provision and funding of supported housing was seen as chaotic and wasteful, with little sense of being 'joined up' to other health and social care priorities. As the Joseph Rowntree Foundation (1999b) commented during the Supporting People consultation period:

> '... the development of Supporting People has come as a result of the "confusion and complexity of the current labyrinth of funding mechanisms", whose fragmentation and lack of transparency lend themselves neither to coherent cost-appraisal of options nor to quality-driven services'.

The government's response came with the publication of *Supporting People – a new policy and funding framework for support services* (Department of Social Security, 1999). This proposed bringing together several funding streams into a single resource pot aimed at providing support to people who need help to find or settle into stable accommodation, and learn to live independently. The focus was on *'housing-related support'*, enabling individuals to obtain suitable housing, sustain their tenancy, and develop skills and self confidence (Watson, *et al.*, 2003). Supporting People aimed to deliver a systemic approach to the provision of supported housing. Local authorities were to become 'commissioners' of housing support. The government believed that this would provide resource incentives for housing and social services to work effectively in partnership with other agencies. The key objectives of Supporting People are:

- *Prevention:* sustain people in the community and pick up problems before they become a crisis.
- *Promote independence:* support people to make decisions and live their own lives.
- *Alleviate crisis:* support people through crises in their lives.
- *Resettlement:* help people to establish themselves in their homes and in the community.
- *Inclusion:* Supporting People who may have difficult behaviour or unconventional lifestyles or multiple needs which fall outside traditional client groups.
- *A focus on people:* providing flexible services moulded on people and the way they chose to live their lives.
  (Department of the Environment, Transport and the Regions, 1998)

It had the objective of improving the quality and effectiveness of support services by:

- *Focusing on local need:* by introducing a systematic and strategic process to assess needs within and across local authority areas in order to supply relevant support services.

- *Improving the range and quality of services:* by promoting the development of a wider range of support services geared to the needs of people receiving support. In particular, breaking the link between tenure and support, and promoting the development of floating support schemes.
- *Integrating 'support' with wider local strategies:* with health, social services, housing, neighbourhood renewal and community safety.
- *Monitoring and inspecting quality and effectiveness:* through integration with Best Value, introducing more effective decision-making, changing the arrangements for funding, and developing more transparent and cost effective administration.
 (Department of the Environment, Transport and the Regions, 2000b)

The 1990 NHS and Community Care Act and Supporting People share a number of key themes: a focus on needs assessment at the level of individual and population needs; joint strategy making; planning; joint purchasing and evaluation and an enhanced voice for service users. Supporting People set out to end a disaggregated approach to the development of supported housing, and replace it with a planned system, based on the strategic enabling role of local authorities. Hence the local Supporting People strategy must set out how the programme can 'join up with', and complement broader government policies around tackling social exclusion and helping vulnerable people live independently, prevent homelessness, improve services for older people, help vulnerable young people make the transition to adulthood, assist women experiencing domestic violence, promote community safety and take a risk management approach for people at risk of re-offending, and complement policies to support people who misuse drugs and/or alcohol (Housing Corporation/Anchor Housing, 2002).

Supporting People straddles a number of government concerns; acting as the 'glue' that integrates services for users with needs that are not quite care and not quite housing management. Supporting People is intended,

'... to be an integral element of the emerging strategies for modernising social services, for crime prevention and community safety, for combating social exclusion, and for the development of housing services in line with the Housing Green Paper. The provision of housing can play an important part in the delivery of each of these programmes, and each authority will be expected to identify how best to ensure that the provision of support and supported housing under the Supporting People programme can complement them' (Department of the Environment Transport and the Regions, 2000b).

Whilst Supporting People cannot be used to fund health and social care, it was believed it would lead to a wider acknowledgement of the role of housing support services in contributing to the wider determinants of health and social care and might provider greater flexibility to fund services across tenures and enable closer working between health, housing and care services.

Supported housing and community care border conflicts

The early optimism around Supporting People has evaporated. Parallels with the implementation of community care look inescapable. Robson Rhodes identified four key problems with Supporting People:

- Much of the provision was *provider* rather than *commissioner* led.
- New services were not necessarily *strategically relevant*.
- The range of unit costings raise questions about *value for money*.
- Services provided *more than housing support alone*.

The critical issue may not lie with the programme itself (Supporting People is merely a device for allocating resources) but the ideas underpinning it, particularly the demarcation between personal *care* and housing *support*, and the implications that flow from organising systems around that fulcrum point.

Secondly, the idea that funding streams, strategic planning and the rational distribution of resources can be made to work through partnership and 'community of interest' appears flawed.

Thirdly, it raises questions about the coherence and identity of supported housing itself. What is it? What are its goals? Is it intellectually/practically conceivable that we can design housing support that is qualitatively different from environments where 'care' is delivered?

Fourthly, when government policy is promoting whole systems working, does the creation of a new demarcation line make sense for users? It seems to us that there are a number of issues of concern to the future direction of Supporting People and its relationship with community care provision:

The amorphous identity of supported housing

The identity and purpose of supported housing has never been entirely clear. Hence its amorphous nature has meant that the sector could be called upon to support groups the government deems cannot be allocated independent accommodation, without first being filtered through supported accommodation (for example, lone parents under 18). The sector also supports groups perceived to be a 'risk' or 'deviant' (for example, substance misusers) and supported housing plus low level policing (for example the 'Dundee Project' which works with families at risk of eviction due to anti-social behaviour). Supported housing also provides a locale in which support can take place. The growth in extra care sheltered housing, intermediate care, and the Single Assessment Process, further align housing with care provision. These functions entail solidifying relationships of inter-dependency with health and social care providers, and blur the edges between housing and social care.

The eligibility criteria for Supporting People grant makes clear that there is a statutory requirement that funds are not used to discharge a statutory duty (for example, community care). Supporting People teams are required to ensure that statutory care is paid for out of funding sources other than Supporting People. The key distinction appears to relate to the difference between a highly individualised package which outlines care activities, and housing-related support which enables a service user to maintain a tenancy. The Supporting People grant conditions refer to eligible services in the following way:

> *'Housing-related support is about promoting independence by sustaining people in the community. This can be about providing immediate refuge to homeless people or those at risk of violence. It entails enabling, reminding or assisting service users to live independently and maintain their accommodation'.*

The purpose of housing-related support is therefore, to enable people to live in a more independent environment than they might otherwise have had, provide services to maintain their accommodation, and help them develop the skills to live independently.

Whilst the Office of the Deputy Prime Minister have provided a list of excluded services (nursing; personal care; social care services; psychological therapy; intensive counselling services; treatment services for offenders imposed by the courts; general housing management, and services provided within a residential care establishment) there is no definition of housing support in statute.

The difference is one based on *enabling* rather than *providing services*. For example, explaining to users *how* to maintain the cleanliness of their accommodation, rather than *doing* the cleaning. The aim of housing support would be to facilitate the development of greater independence. Although a social care perspective will also aim to enhance independence, it relates to all aspects of life rather than simply maintaining accommodation. A definition of care is laid down in the *National Care Standards* as follows:

> *'Personal care is defined as assisting people with bodily functions. These types of services are usually provided in registered care homes or by domiciliary care services. Where those services are provided they must be funded from a source other than Supporting People'.*

> *'General social care services are intended to help people with their day to day lives. These types of services are not primarily intended to assist people gain access to accommodation, or to maintain their accommodation. Where those services are provided they must be funded from another source'.*

As such Supporting People can be seen as cement filling the cracks left by other funding streams as it: provides services to a range of previously excluded individuals; provides an alternative to more expensive and intensive forms of support (for example, sheltered housing rather than residential care); and as a complementary service for health and social care (for example a stable regime in which drug treatment services can be delivered).

Housing support, personal care and cost-shunting

The 2004 review of Supporting People noted there was 'strong circumstantial evidence' that councils had plundered the Supporting People budget to fund care services. Further,

> '... one of the key problems facing policy-makers both within the Office of the Deputy Prime Minister and the Department of Work and Pensions, has been the difficulty in distinguishing between housing-related support and personal care, particularly in relation to clients with behavioural problems. The Department of Work and Pensions reported that they were keen to avoid being too prescriptive because of problems of definition and potential challenges' (Office of the Deputy Prime Minister, 2004d).

They reported that 4 per cent of services funded from Supporting People had been inappropriately allocated. In a further 28 per cent of services, councils were 'confused' as to whether these were housing-related services or not. The government has tried (perhaps not too hard?) to articulate the difference between community *care* and housing *support*. As a result of uncertainty about what can/should be funded, local services were,

> '... redefined, re-purposed and re-positioned. This has enabled local delivery agencies to increase, change or stabilise the level of funding for services, increase the number of individual clients receiving service provision and improve the quality and choice of such services' (Office of the Deputy Prime Minister, 2004d).

Service reviews are seen as the key mechanism for exploring the eligibility of services for Supporting People funding and maintaining the emphasis upon 'eligible housing-related services'.

Cost-shunting took place in three key ways: deregistration – the voluntary cancelling of the registered status of facilities formerly registered as care homes; the funding of projects through transitional housing benefit that might once have been funded through care funding; the withdrawal of 'top up' grants. The Audit Commission have suggested that they found evidence of deregistered homes providing high levels of non-housing-related care (Kumar, 2004b). A recent report from Sainsbury Centre for Mental Health (2004b) argues for the positive benefits of deregistration. In a review of ten deregistered schemes they found:

- Greater flexibility in staffing levels depending on levels of need.
- New legal rights for residents who became tenants and have additional personal income to spend for themselves.

- New types of support that aim to encourage greater independence and encourage people to take more responsibility for their lives and offer more freedom to make building changes and refurbish accommodation.

As care budgets have been stretched, local authorities have established clear hierarchies of need, effectively limiting the level of care packages that can be delivered. In 2003 the government issued guidance on *Fair Access to Care Services*, formalising a hierarchy of need by requiring each local authority to decide the extent to which it had financial resources to fund different levels of care. Four levels were created – *critical, substantial, moderate and low*. The majority of local authorities decided that their resources would only allow them to meet critical and substantial levels of need. There was an imperative to move users on the outer margins of the care budget into the less stringently policed and more loosely defined domain of 'support'. Inevitably, some users are lost in the middle of two funding regimes.

There is evidence from Audit Commission Supporting People reviews that people with complex needs have had their cases closed by social services due to their support being funded from the Supporting People grant (Audit Commission, 2004b).

Person centred planning and Supporting People

Supporting People leaves considerable scope to deliver support in innovative ways (particularly to those with complex and multiple needs), but appears to contradict the thrust of government policy towards *person centred planning* and *person centred services* (see for example the 2005 green paper *Independence, Well-being and Choice – Our vision for the future of social care for adults in England*). Person centred planning can be defined as a group of techniques for working with individuals which:

- Focus around the concerns of individuals, families or carers, and are concerned with life not services.
- Imply a different working relationship between professionals and the people who use services (working with rather than 'doing to').
- Seeking to set the individual firmly in the context of their community.
- Are orientated to what is possible not simply what is available.
- To try and balance ambition with the need to produce support that is competent, reliable and sustainable through developing 'problem solving' strategies.
  (Simons, 2001)

The government has promoted care management that aspires to be responsive to person centred planning, and should be experienced as seamless by users. This suggests that housing and care should provide a combination of interventions that enable individuals to live in ways they choose and in places of their own choosing.

Yet, Supporting People funds are still overwhelmingly locked into accommodation based support. The flexibility we were promised would enable users to disaggregate housing support from accommodation is as yet illusory. By these measures many of the supported housing services we now have are not person centred. Other long standing barriers to seamlessness are also re-appearing, as the Matrix research argued – *'think of the package of care and support, the higher the care the more social services and primary care trusts need to contribute'* (Kumar, 2004a), but for many social services and primary care trusts, the focus of Supporting People is not a priority in their commissioning strategies.

Central control v local autonomy?

Broader government policy initiatives have influenced the development of Supporting People and the way administrating authorities might develop their priorities. These include the Homelessness Act 2002 (which extended the definition of priority need status to 16-17 year olds, and people considered vulnerable who are fleeing domestic violence); the objective that all under 18 year old lone parents should be offered supported accommodation; the role of Local Community Safety Boards; and other more general strategies such as the *National Service Framework for People with Mental Health Problems*; and the white paper *Valuing People: a new Strategy for Learning Disability*. The growth in floating support services has begun to address the needs of users who fall between funding sources and needs groups, for example pre-existing tenants.

The amorphous nature of the supported housing sector allows the government great freedom to include/exclude new groups defined as eligible for housing support. These have been described as *'unfunded mandates chasing uncapped benefit based funding streams'* (Office of the Deputy Prime Minister, 2004d) and were greatly expanded during the development of transitional housing benefit. There is a danger that in times of retraction, these 'mandates' will direct and distort the strategic decisions of local administrating authorities.

Devolution issues

The introduction of devolution was the 1997 Labour government's most important constitutional reform. Devolution has added an important new dimension to discussions about the future of health, housing and care in the UK. The different pathways being followed by Scotland (and to a lesser extent Wales) indicate that *'British Social Policy'* can no longer be assumed to be *'English Social Policy'* (Ellison, Bauld and Powell, 2004). Post devolution Britain will experience considerable policy divergence, although the impact of this on housing and community care is little understood.

Scotland and devolution: the 1998 Scotland Act created the architecture for devolution and laid the ground for a Scottish Parliament. However, Westminster retains sovereign control and can overrule the Scottish Parliament. These devolved powers have been characterised by Parry (2002) as *'a policy system with incomplete responsibilities'* concerned with non-cash social services such as health, education and housing, whilst macro economic powers such as tax and social security transfers remain with Westminster. The Scottish Parliament can also marginally change the level of taxation. Historically, Scotland has spent more on health and social care than the rest of the UK through the 'Barnett Formula'. Stewart (2004) notes that Scottish health and social welfare policy can be characterised as pursuing: a cross departmental approach to the development of services; a greater emphasis upon social inclusion (rather than exclusion) championed by a minister for communities who has a brief to drive social justice issues; and finally, a conscious effort to re-build the NHS. The Community Care and Health Act (Scotland) 2002 introduced free personal and nursing care for the elderly; a measure intended to facilitate the closer integration of health and social care in Scotland. A bold decision as Westminster had previously rejected the findings of the Sutherland Commission on Long Term Care.

The divergence of UK health and social care policies, and the tension it engenders, raises questions about the direction of the welfare state both north and south of the border (Stewart, 2004). The reaction to cuts in the Scottish Supporting People grant (following the Scottish Executive decision to cut the Supporting People budget from £422.5 million 2004/5 to £406 million in 2005-6), gives an indication of these tensions. After a fierce campaign led by housing providers and local authorities, the Executive agreed to slow the introduction of the new formula to prevent a dramatic funding cut. Malcolm Chisholm, the Communities Minister, said *'I have slowed down the rate of change so that those who were going to lose the most under the original announcement will lose significantly less over the next few years'* (*Inside Housing*, 3rd December 2004). It is hard to envisage a similar ministerial response south of the border.

Wales and devolution: the Welsh Assembly has significantly fewer legislative powers than the Scottish Parliament. However it has been characterised by Chaney and Drakeford (2004) as a body dominated by social policy issues, with a distinctive set of ideological principles. The assembly lacks tax raising powers and primary legislative capacities, but has responsibilities for housing, health, education and social services. This has enabled a distinctly Welsh social policy to develop, based on 'collectivist' principles. Chaney and Drakeford (2004) point to three drivers behind Welsh social policy: universalism and unconditional citizenship rights; a concern for *'equality of outcome'* as opposed to approaches based on *'equality of opportunity'*, and hence suspicion around the role of markets in welfare, and co-operative approaches to the delivery of collective consumption goods such as health and social care.

This qualitatively different approach is illustrated by the document *A Better Country* (Welsh Assembly Government, 2003a) which restated the ideological beliefs underpinning its policy preferences:

> '*To care for those in need by providing a strategic context in which the care and support of vulnerable groups is delivered to improve their comfort and well-being; to support elderly people and facilitate independent living; to get services to work together in an inclusive, partnership way; to provide an appropriate level of funding and ensure that it is used to optimum effect*'.

The *Strategy for Older People in Wales* (Welsh Assembly Group, 2003b) has attempted to put these principles into action, setting out a three year programme consonant with its universalist and non-market preferences. It has the following aims: the pursuit of older people's health and well-being integrated in planning and service delivery; to promote high quality services which support people to live independently; and to promote effective planning for an ageing population. From 2001, all nursing home residents in Wales received free care, rather than being subject to the banding system which takes place in England.

Where does this leave health and social care in the UK? With better funded care for older people, higher levels of hospital spending and staffing, based on collective, inclusive styles of policy-making, health, housing and social care professionals will surely be rushing to the borders. However, Mooney and Poole (2004) argue that notions of a distinctly different policy direction based on Scottish distinctiveness are largely mythical, and that in reality the Scottish Executive is keen to challenge these ideas as they undermine the Scottish Executive's goal of transforming Scotland into a flexible, enterprise economy. None-the-less, the developing policy divergence does indicate that there are alternative discourses to the market driven policies of New Labour.

Housing and community care looking to the future

A key theme of this book is to draw attention to the dislocations and transformations the housing sector is encountering. 'Transformations' that appear not to have challenged the artificiality of the terms 'care' and 'support', as they are applied to the domain of housing. These are boundary faultlines which mean little to service users. Funding streams based on sectors (housing, health etc.) perpetuate the erroneous idea that support and care can be 'boxed off' as qualitatively different activities.

Yet government policy is steeped in the language and discourse of whole systems working and functional integration. A more flexible approach to funding might allow providers to agree joint funding options needed to develop holistic care and housing services, the composition of which might change with the recipient's needs. This is close to the model recommended in the Robson Rhodes review, and the 'care navigator' role outlined in the recent government green paper (DoH, 2005).

However, the government seems set on a programme of retraction in the Supporting People budget, through the development of market testing and the re-tendering of existing services – we might be seeing a decisive shift from partnership and commissioning to procurement and contract. Such a shift would raise questions around how the stability of providers can be maintained; whose interests come first – the procurer, the agency or the user, and indeed whether local authorities have the capacity and needs data to develop contracts and ensure quality.

Despite the widespread acceptance among practitioners of the importance of the dismantling a range of 'Berlin Walls', it's far from clear that progress has been made in developing seamless services. Indeed the hazy nature of taken for granted concepts in the government lexicon, such as 'partnership', 'collaboration' and 'joined up working' may be hindering the development of action on the ground. The biggest challenges facing local authorities remain those identified in previous research: working in partnership; the joint commissioning of services for vulnerable adults, and the involvement of users in planning and developing services.

Transformation and dislocation are words that encapsulate the experience of working in supported housing or community care. Despite the good things in Supporting People, it has further solidified the artificial divide between care and support. Other problems with Supporting People are becoming apparent. A glimpse at a selection of Audit Commission Supporting People reviews, illustrates: the limited involvement of service users; concerns around social services closing the cases of people receiving Supporting People funding; significant gaps in services for single homeless people, rough sleepers, people with HIV/AIDS, people with drug and alcohol problems; the poor strategic leadership and limited integration into corporate strategies; weaknesses in strategic planning and commissioning; inconsistent application of grant eligibility criteria; insufficiently robust shadow strategies; a lack of integrated working and planning between housing and social services; and weak service monitoring.

Budget cuts might well undermine the new provision funded by Supporting People. As the House of Commons select committee suggested (House of Commons Select Committee, 2004):

> '... real cuts in annual provision applied blindly to each authority could damage services for vulnerable people in an unacceptable way', further that 'for the next few years there is a danger that, in an attempt to deal with the elements of the legacy provision valuable services for the vulnerable may suffer from undue financial constraints curing the disease but killing the patient'.

The Select Committee called for the ring fencing of funding for less popular needs groups, a call taken up by the Audit Commission who suggested that local authorities should prove they are not discriminating against groups such as ex-offenders. This will be tested by a new performance indicator on fair access to be introduced in 2005. These are some of the issues that are played out in the forthcoming chapters.

Our aim in this book

The contributors to this text approach housing and community care from different perspectives and with wide variations in focus. Housing and community care provision represents a complex mosaic, whose development reflects broader ideological, social and political tensions. It is intended here to provide an introduction to issues surrounding the development of housing and community care in the UK today. Throughout the book, we signpost non-specialist readers who wish to explore issues in further detail towards books, articles and websites.

Our aims are to:

- Arrive at an understanding of the issues surrounding the housing contribution to community care.
- Help practitioners locate the changes they are experiencing in a theoretical context.
- Build bridges across the housing and social care divide.
- Enable readers to ask 'how' and 'why' questions in relation to policy change.

The book is divided into three main parts:

Part One explores the historical and policy context within which the housing role in community care has developed, and explores some of the key issues and arguments exercising the sector today. In Chapter 2, Murray Hawtin looks at the history and development of the housing role in community care, identifying themes which recur in many of the following chapters; in Chapter 3, Julie Savory explores issues around joint working and the development of 'whole systems' approaches to social policy; in Chapter 4, Deborah Bennett outlines issues around the funding, regulation and scope of the housing role in community care; in Chapter 5, Bogusia Temple looks at problematic issues around needs analysis and service planning in the context of Black and Minority Ethnic communities; in Chapter 6, Charlie Cooper sets out how housing and care agencies can work more effectively to include users as partners.

Part Two picks up many of the themes developed in Part One and applies these to particular user groups. We are aware of the deficiencies of this approach; many of the groups we discuss share commonalities (such as access to resources, stigmatisation etc.). However, users are still largely defined and categorised by their primary user group. Whilst interventions are defined by where and how users are 'filtered' into health, social care and housing services. This inhibits the development of person centred approaches that meet the unique needs of each person. In Chapter 7, Pam Thomas and Marcus Ormerod, explore the struggles faced by disabled people in accessing accessible housing, particularly in the owner occupied sector; in Chapter 8, Mark Foord looks at the increasing functional integration between housing and care providers around the development of supported housing for frail older people; in Chapter 9, Paul Simic looks at the development of services for people with a mental illness, and in particular the increasing concentration on 'risk' and 'danger' in policy development; in Chapter 10, David Race reflects on the transformation of housing and care services for people with a learning disability and changing notions of 'normalisation' and 'role valorisation'.

Part Three of the book draws together themes outlined in the previous sections and looks to the future of housing contribution to community care; Chapter 11 by Tim Brown, Jo Richardson and Jackie Thompson-Ercan explores Supporting People strategies and questions whether they can ensure the development of more appropriate housing with support. They outline the tension between strategic planning and the pragmatic responses required to respond to changing funding structures and government demands; in Chapter 12, Anya Ahmed and Julia Lucas explore notions of 'urban renaissance' and community sustainability, and question whether there can be tensions between the ambitions of developing sustainable communities, and the development of housing for groups such as homeless people and substance misusers; in Chapter 13, Tim Brown and Nicola Yates provide a comparative view of housing and community care in Europe; and in Chapter 14, Paul Simic draws diverse strands together in a challenging and provocative conclusion.

CHAPTER 2:
Housing and community care in its historical and political context

Murray Hawtin

Introduction

Until the 20th century the predominant belief was that welfare provision should be met by families, and where that was not possible, from philanthropic sources. State involvement in welfare was reluctantly acknowledged when all other sources failed. Industrialisation brought widespread prosperity, but at the price of greater suffering for those at the bottom of society. By the 19th century, institutions such as workhouses and asylums mirrored the values of Victorian society itself, and were disciplinarian and intimidating. They represented the ultimate badge of stigma where the infirm, sick and aged were punished and monitored. With the growing complexity of industrial society, the enormity of caring for the 'economically inactive' became apparent. Poverty and vulnerability began to be seen less as a result of moral judgement visited upon individual miscreants, but rather as social ills requiring state funded solutions. The development of community care policies evolved in the 20th century largely as a failure of health, housing and care policies to meet the needs of vulnerable people; such policies have had a low priority and their implementation has consistently been underfunded.

This chapter aims to provide a review of the historical linkages between poverty and state involvement in housing, health and social care, in particular the development of a 'housing role' in social care. It chronicles the development of key policies from the origins of the poor laws through to 1979 – when Margaret Thatcher's seminal 'New Right' government came to power. The chapter explores two main phases of historic development: *before* and *after* the close of the Victorian era. These are identified as periods in which the social and political ideologies that underpin contemporary housing and care policies were developed. It then goes on to explore the drivers behind the development of the community care agenda from the end of the Second War to the 1970s, in particular the range of accommodation and domiciliary care services that arose to help shape the emerging care in the community project. The concluding section summarises key issues in the unfolding context of housing support and community care that link this historic review to the current policy and practice examined in the remainder of this book. The analytic approach of this chapter is that policy responses to social concerns have been far from planned, but rather pragmatic, ad-hoc reactions to economic and social issues.

Before the end of the Victorian era

The impact of poor housing on people needing care

Housing 'policy' was unknown before the middle of the 19th century, by which time rapid urbanisation had resulted in concentrations of unplanned, speculatively built homes that were poorly designed, small and unsanitary. The link between housing and health was recognised by the Victorians who expanded the role of the state in housing based on 'sanitary approaches'. It was not until after the First World War that councils began to build and own property in any quantity; as general housing standards improved and major epidemics were eliminated, housing developed as a separate area of public policy, but its role in health and social care were largely underplayed. By the late 20th century, the majority of social work service users lived in poorer areas, often characterised by 'difficult to let' housing estates and areas that exacerbate as much as enhance support needs. In the sections below a number of housing themes are used to demonstrate the historic interconnection between ill health, poverty, housing and social care.

The importance of environment

Where housing is situated is of crucial importance to people with impairments. Living in unsatisfactory environments has been shown to lead to mental distress, as do fear of crime, harassment and powerlessness. Lack of accessible transport facilities and access to public and recreational services can also limit opportunities for independent living, conversely, sensitive infrastructure planning (particularly transport), enhances greater freedom.

Tenure change

Patterns of housing tenure were transformed in the 20th century. Initially the majority of the population rented from small-scale private landlords. With decreasing profits from property rental and higher expectations, the local state assumed the role of landlord for the working classes, whilst owner occupation gradually became the norm for others. The state also took on the responsibility for the support and care of those judged unable to care for themselves, for example local authorities have had a statutory responsibility since the 1970 Chronically Sick and Disabled Persons Act for the 'special needs' of people with impairments. As a result many disabled people have been housed in council housing. Capital spending cuts and residualisation have therefore, had a disproportionate impact on the housing experience and opportunities of this group.

Access to housing

Central and local housing policies resulted in unequal access to housing leading to discrimination on the basis of disability, ethnicity and gender. Community care policies depend upon vulnerable people being able to live in healthy homes, but local authorities were often only able to provide accommodation on unpopular, poor quality estates which were neither healthy nor safe. People with impairments live disproportionately in less desirable areas, most often associated with 'post code discrimination'. Access to 'desirable districts' may help to break the cycle of poverty through greater access to services and employment.

Housing conditions

Housing standards are of special concern to older people and people with impairments. Such conditions have a significant effect on the quality of life. The main cause of home accidents are falls, which account for around 80 per cent of all fatal accidents in the home for people aged over 75. Fires and hypothermia also kill many older people each year. Dampness is a common problem in poorer housing and has been shown to correlate with a range of debilitating illnesses and conditions especially bronchial and chest problems. Poor conditions and certain types of housing (such as mass-produced deck-access or tower blocks) have also been associated with other physical and mental health problems (Arblaster and Hawtin, 1993). Slum clearance, improved house building regulations, and aids and adaptations have contributed significantly to addressing poor housing conditions. However, many older and disabled people still live in the poorest, unmodernised accommodation. Although councils had been able to control the quality of new building since 1858, it was not until 1957 that housing law embraced an 'unfitness standard' (based on a 1919 manual!).

Housing shortage

Housing shortage can lead to those most marginalised living in the poorest quality dwellings or becoming homeless. Overcrowding has been closely linked to mental distress and poor physical health, as well as leading to high levels of accident and fire. When housing policy addresses this issue it is generally formulated as providing housing for 'able-bodied' families. Sufficient accommodation of suitable size, quality and type and in the right environment to enable those with impairments and their carers to live a 'normal' life is an ideal that has not yet been achieved.

Homelessness

Homelessness as a shortage of suitable accommodation is the most extreme form of debilitating housing conditions. In previous centuries, poverty drove large numbers to leave their homes to find better wages, giving rise to fear of beggars and vagabonds roaming the countryside for assistance. After the 1977 Housing (Homeless Persons) Act vulnerable people who were 'unintentionally homeless' and had a local connection were eligible for council housing. This included those vulnerable due to old age, mental illness or learning disabilities, or people leaving long stay institutions; very few single people were eligible. Homeless people still have very poor access to welfare and especially health services (Fisher and Collins, 1993).

Special needs and housing construction

Even 'normal' housing can become disabling to people with impairments, and exclude them from the homes of their family and friends. The effects of this may be minimised through design centred on the needs of the resident and their carers. Housing agencies have sought solutions to the needs of disabled people, particularly since the late 1960s. However, that contribution has been mainly through 'special schemes' such as group homes or hostels or rather than the 'ordinary' housing that community care promotes. By 1979 housing departments were building nearly 6,000 mobility and 600 wheelchair homes per year. Special needs housing has been criticised for reinforcing issues of stigma and increasing marginalisation, other solutions including 'Lifetime' homes were later proposed (Cooper and Watson, 1995).

The development of the poor law

Prior to the 19th century welfare provision was rudimentary. Over the course of time pressures emerged to force the state to face welfare obligations. The following sections trace the development of key policies related to housing and social care and the philosophy underpinning these decisions.

Box 2.1: Relevant dominant ideology 18th-19th century

The Industrial Revolution at the end of the 18th century brought prosperity, but also served to intensify divisions in society. Increasing numbers of labour migrants flocked to urban areas which became dangerously overcrowded and unsanitary with resulting high levels of illness, disease and infant mortality. Industrialisation exploited labour and the traditional social relations of mutual obligation and care disintegrated. The ability of families to support and care for the vulnerable became difficult to sustain and those more severely impaired became more reliant upon help from outside the family to avoid the spectre of the workhouse. In his attempts to understand these economic and social changes, Adam Smith developed the notion of society as a collection of individuals and social structure as the relationship between them. He believed economic growth would only achieve its full potential if individuals were allowed to pursue their own self interest and that the pursuance of individual interest would lead to the welfare of all. Throughout the Victorian years the middle classes prospered under this 'laissez-faire' ideology developing a moral code of work, thrift, respectability and self-help. The philosopher Jeremy Bentham recognised that individualism and collective provision are not mutually exclusive, and that minimal state intervention could be justified in providing basic public services, to be tested on grounds of utility: i.e. efficient, economical and conducive *'to the greatest happiness of the greatest number'*.

The dominant social concern of the period was poverty, seen as closely related to if not the cause of ignorance, immorality and apathy. The poor law was largely driven by the common belief in the centrality of the market and the necessity to avoid dependency on the state. The 1832 Royal Commission on the Poor Law introduced two key principles:

* The pauper must be *'less eligible'* than the independent labourer. Therefore workhouse conditions had to be lower than *'an independent labourer of the lowest class'*.
* Outdoor relief should be ended and only given if the pauper was prepared to enter the workhouse. The *workhouse test* distinguished the deserving from the undeserving poor in that anyone prepared to accept relief in a repugnant workhouse must be lacking the moral character to live independently.

The primary principle was to force the 'lower classes' into self reliance and gain support through the family and charitable organisations. The 1834 Poor Law Amendment Act signified a defining moment between the previous 'benevolent' religious based system which believed that disability was a consequence of sin or divine ordination, to the more 'enlightened' scientific system determined to rid society of the 'moral scourge' of poverty.

19th century developments of care and housing

By the end of the 19th century the use of general mixed workhouses was still commonplace. The growth of asylums for people with mental health problems were initially seen as a positive development. However, the brutality of the system was recognised from the start and an anti poor law movement soon took hold as scandals emerged. Despite attempts in England to abolish outdoor relief for the able-bodied from 1832, older people continued to receive such assistance. In addition voluntary agencies developed residential care for older or disabled people with the older almshouses continuing provision for the respectable aged.

Although custody was the main driver of institutions, they were usually considered only as part of a continuum of care and the majority of vulnerable adults below 60 years old lived in 'the community', typically with family carers. As early as 1850, medical professionals were suggesting that rather than providing large 'warehouses' for the insane, a combination of institutional and community care should be adopted (Scull, MacKensie and Hervey, 1996). It was recognised that people with a high degree of impairment would require long term care; one of the functions of the institution was to enable their 'moral treatment', and involved short term periods within the institution. Such periods were intended to improve behaviour and 'cure'. Research demonstrated,

'... the persistence of extramural care, control, treatment and supervision during the so-called asylum "era" ... Care outside the walls of the asylum was therefore a reality, not only for those suffering madness who were never admitted at all, but also for patients who were confined in mental hospitals for only short periods of their illness' (Bartlett and Wright, 1999 p.3).

The belief in the 'evils' of state dependency and a genuine concern about poverty and destitution drove many middle class reformers to seek alternative housing and social care provision. Octavia Hill, Dr Barnardo, General Booth, Edwin Chadwick, Lord Shaftsbury, Elizabeth Fry, Florence Nightingale and other Victorians were instrumental in the rise in charitable organisations. In 1869 the Charity Organisation Society was established, in part as a response to the proliferation of charities and to administer charity to those who were seen as 'deserving'. The organisation was convinced that solutions to public ills lay in educating the working classes and developing moral character: *'the proletariat may strangle us, unless we teach it the same virtues which have elevated other classes of society'* (Samuel Smiles, 1885, quoted by Stedman Jones, 1971). Such charitable organisations may have slowed the encroachment of the centralised state. By the second half of the century, laissez-faire was gradually giving way to an acceptance of a mixed economy based on a new form of 'social liberalism'. Self-help and voluntary assistance were still seen as the 'correct' means of addressing care issues; however, groups of vulnerable people began to be seen as needing state support rather than private charity. For example, Booth, in recording the extent of poverty in old age called for the establishment of a state pension.

In housing, a growing lobby for state intervention was supported by evidence of the impact of rapidly changing urban localities on disease and sanitary conditions. Outbreaks of cholera and other diseases led to a substantial rise in morbidity rates. The medical profession spearheaded campaigns for public action (Gauldie, 1974). When the epidemics began to affect the middle and ruling classes, parliament was finally moved to regulate the conditions in working class urban areas.

Newly emerging local authorities were seen as vehicles able to assist the commercial sector, which remained the main housing provider. However, the Labouring Classes Lodging Act 1851 allowed councils to build accommodation, whilst legislation in 1868 and 1879 empowered councils to remove slums and require their replacement with housing. Of greater significance was the 1875 Public Health Act which led many councils to commandeer unfit dwellings, enforce standards on new properties and plan urban development. Thousands of terraced houses were built and standards for the majority of the working class rose significantly; as a result it may be argued that improvements in housing and the environment have had a far greater effect on general health of than any medical advances.

Box 2.2: 19th century initiatives to address care and housing issues

Charitable sector

The activities of charitable organisations included not only the disbursement of charitable funds but also the development of the 'mission worker'. This was the early beginnings of professional social work. Care was provided by the *After-care Association for Poor and Friendless Female Convalescents on Leaving Asylums for the Insane* in 1879, now more succinctly called the *Mental Aftercare Association*. By 1889 the Association had inspected 143 cottage homes and about 50 people a year were helped, from 18 asylums in England and Scotland. The Association also placed 'people at risk of becoming insane' in cottage homes, and established the first residential care home in England for people with mental health problems in 1893.

Private sector

The Housing of the Working Classes Act 1890 was designed to encourage councils to build 'model dwellings' and enable private developers to follow with commercially viable developments. By 1914, 20,000 local authority dwellings had been developed. Even where benevolent investors required only a 5 percent return on new developments the resulting rent was beyond the income of the poorest people including those who were disabled.

Philanthropic concern

In attempting to meet the housing and welfare needs of the labour force, Robert Owen developed an experimental utopian community established around a New Lanark cotton mill in Scotland between 1800 and 1829; based on tight management coupled with social welfare and education. As well as quality housing he provided pensions, early forms of sheltered housing, a school and recreation centre, and adult education. Several other employers later established 'model villages' for their labour force (for example Lord Lever in Port Sunlight).

Octavia Hill sought to renovate decrepit properties to a basic standard and rent to those who could keep up regular payments on an affordable (low-profit) basis. She believed poor conditions *'are tenfold worse because the tenants' habits and lives are what they are'*, so her approach was to combine efficient management principles with the reforming of tenants' character through case-work.

Self-help

A variety of initiatives and organisations were developed by the working class themselves as an answer to poor housing. These included individual-focused forms of housing, health and welfare provision to elevate the poor from hardship and provide local support. Friendly societies and savings banks helped provide people with sustainable forms of welfare, social insurance, medical care, and even housing loans. Also housing and worker co-operatives were developed, initially with the Rochdale Pioneers in 1823, based on Robert Owen's enlightening belief in co-operation between workers and the possible reform of human nature.

Post-Victorian era

20th century developments

Although it has been argued that serious public unrest in the late 19th century was largely contained through the 'embourgeoisement' of the working classes (working class people attempting to assert 'middle class values' of self-help and betterment) there were still real threats of revolution from the political far left.

With the onset of World War One, housing shortage and private sector rents soared. Rent strikes were organised, supported by a growing women's movement, which led to the government introducing national rent controls in 1915. Some felt that this parliamentary act was instrumental in controlling unrest and instilling compliance in British society. A Royal Commission on the Poor Law was appointed in 1905, the most extensive investigation since the Royal Commission of 1832. Its 18 members took four years to complete their findings, but ultimately were split in their views, and two reports were published:

- The *Majority Report*, informed by the Charity Organisation Society was based on a modified deterrent poor law and recommended creating a new poor law authority in each county and replacing workhouses by institutions catering for separate categories of people such as children, older people, unemployed, and the mentally ill.
- The *Minority Report* advocated the abolition of the poor law and its replacement with comprehensive health and education services.

Neither report led to new poor law legislation, but the commission signified the growth of divergent discourses around social welfare. The Fabian Society organised a popular campaign in support of the Minority Report. The much hated term 'workhouse' was later replaced in official documents by *'Poor Law Institution'* (1913) although in public perception they remained substantially similar. Significant pieces of social legislation were passed prefiguring the modern welfare state; old age pensions in 1909; the National Insurance Act initiating a partial form of unemployment and health insurance in 1911; the Housing and Town Planning etc., Act 1919 (Addison Act) offered central government subsidies to councils to address local housing shortage.

Box 2.3: Dominant ideologies – the early 20th century

The inherent tensions between capitalist production and labour exploitation was hidden beneath the benefits of rapid economic change in the 19th century, although anti-capitalist theories had been developing since Thomas Paine published *The Rights of Man* (1791) and was taken up by the Chartists, and later by Marxist and Fabian socialists. By the latter half of the nineteenth century, the British socialist movement was a broad-based coalition of groups, many based on ideas of state welfarism, collectivism and the centralisation of power. These emerging ideas had a significant impact not only on the Labour movement but also on housing, and welfare policy.

The Fabian society was one of the most influential organisations on social policy; they believed that the root of individual ills lay in the detrimental consequences of capitalism, and could only be addressed through the provision of public welfare. Incremental and rational reform was needed to redistribute resources and provide an adequate welfare system. Although a counter argument suggested that the state adopting responsibility for welfare undermined working class self-help. Fabian views gathered support and public acceptance of the need for state intervention increased steadily after the First World War. Attitudes towards poverty, mental and physical illness and 'mental deficiency, changed from the Victorian discourse (based on moral causation) to a greater emphasis on scientific reason and medical science

After the war, sufficient housing of a decent quality was needed if Lloyd George's 'land fit for heroes' (many of whom were in poor physical and mental health) was to become reality. Unlike other European countries, myriad small-scale landlords were not up to the task and so local government was given the duty and subsidy to develop adequate housing. Over the next quarter of a century housing conditions improved immeasurably; four million homes were built, 1,330,000 in the public sector, 470,000 in the private sector with state aid and 2.5 million by private enterprise. A quarter of a million unfit dwellings were demolished. The most significant trend was the change in the tenure structure; rented housing in the private sector represented 90 per cent of the stock in 1914 and only 58 per cent by 1938, owner occupation rose from 10 per cent to 32 per cent.

The Local Government Act 1929 transferred the responsibilities and powers of Boards of Guardians to councils who were required to submit schemes to end poor relief. Responsibility for acute and chronic patients was split between two committees; a health committee covering curable acute illnesses, and a public assistance committee for those deemed to have long term dependency (including the elderly and disabled). In detaching those with long term care needs from mainstream health services, a 'warehousing' rather than rehabilitative care model developed. Workhouse conditions improved a little, although the majority of 'inmates' continued to be older people, people with mental health problems, unmarried mothers, and vagrants. Poor law hospitals were renamed public health hospitals (under the local authority health committees) and were no longer part of the poor law. The new hospitals freed the bed spaces of the chronically sick and those with long term health needs by sending them to other institutions (McEwan and Laverty, 1949). The 1930 Poor Law Act reasserted the liability of near relations of the poor *'if possessed of sufficient means, to relieve and maintain that person not able to work'* and restored outdoor relief, restricting admission to the Public Assistance Institutions to the aged and infirm.

Post war developments

The culmination of Fabian and other philosophies supporting direct state provision was the Beveridge Report (1942) which proposed establishing a fully comprehensive, universal welfare state with a National Health Service as its centrepiece. During the Second World War many older people and people with impairments lived in Public Assistance Institutions, where conditions were little better than the workhouse. Pressure for change led to the National Health Service Act 1946, which reorganised public hospitals under Regional Health Boards into a comprehensive system of health care, free at the point of delivery. The overcrowded Public Assistance Institutions hospitals were reorganised and the overriding principle of family responsibility abolished. The National Assistance Act 1948 stated that *'it should be the responsibility of every local authority ... to provide residential accommodation for persons who are by reasons of age, infirmity or any other circumstances in need of care and attention which is not otherwise available to them'* (quoted in Means and Smith, 1994); it put a duty on councils to provide smaller, homely accommodation for people who were older and infirm or fund places in the independent sector. However, the act made no provision for domiciliary services.

After the Second World War there was a political consensus around the need for a massive house building programme, with an initial target of 240,000 dwellings per year. The bulk of this was undertaken by local authorities as the only developers able to meet such targets. After this time the proportion of tenants on low incomes increased significantly. Many of the mass dwellings erected in the 1960s proved disastrous especially for those who were mentally or physically impaired. By the end of the 1970s council housing had a reputation as 'residual' housing and was declining in popularity. However, it was often the only available tenure for many people with 'special needs'. Homelessness re-emerged as a political issue in the late 1960s after screening of the TV Drama, *Cathy Come Home*. The Seebohm, Cullingworth and Finer Reports all highlighted homelessness as a *housing*, rather than *social services* problem and recommended that statutory responsibility for homeless people be transferred to local authority housing departments. The 1977 (Homeless Persons Act) gave local authorities a new obligation to accommodate households classed as in priority need and unintentionally homeless, these included: vulnerable people such as the elderly or mentally ill. Most councils would only house those with a local connection, inviting parallels with the old poor laws.

Developing community care policy – competing drivers and ideologies

Before the First World War, care was the prime responsibility of families supported by voluntary contributions or the poor laws. Institutions were a last resort; their function was seen as a mixture of the custodial and therapeutic. The burden on institutions grew with insufficient social or affordable housing and the failure of successive policies to alleviate the plight of those with 'impairments' and the state began to experiment with alternative forms of care. However, the effect of institutions and their power came under considerable scrutiny. Community care was seized on as a solution able to counter the failures of housing and care policies.

Towards the end of the 19th century there was a 'moral panic' related to a fear of the racial stock degenerating (Jones, 1986). Darwin's theory of evolution was applied to human society with the fittest at the top and the most inferior at the bottom. Such ideas gave rise to the eugenics movement which argued 'inferior' people including the 'morally defective' and depraved, should be prevented from reproducing in order to reduce illegitimacy, criminality, mental deficiency, disease, alcoholism and prostitution. Moral education, sterilisation and incarceration were all believed to be means of minimising the risk of 'racial degeneracy'. Following a sustained campaign to promote institutional care, the

Mental Deficiency Act 1913 established machinery to identify those perceived to be 'mental defectives' (i.e. people with learning difficulties) and restrain their number by segregation. In 1927 Local authorities were given the duty to ensure training was provided, leading to the development of Occupation and Industrial Centres (later Adult Training Centres). The 1913 Act established three types of care:

- *Institutional care* to stabilise and socialise inmates and equip them for life outside through instruction and training.
- *Guardians* had such powers *'as could be exercised by the parent of a child of under fourteen years'* (Tredgold, 1947). Schemes such as the Scottish boarding out arrangements were established whereby local authorities were able to pay appointed guardians an allowance.
- *Supervision* entailed patients being seen in their homes by professionals such as health visitors, school nurses or voluntary organisations.

Licences to work or be cared for outside of institutions were conditional on good behaviour. Thus a formal community care framework was established, with individuals able to move from institutions to the community. The aim was to combine the protection of the community and the individual, but had the explicit intention of controlling 'mental defectives' (Thomson, 1996). This system of 'control in the community' also applied to those who were mentally ill. Among the recommendations from the 1926 Royal Commission on Lunacy and Mental Disorder was that patients should be treated in their own homes wherever possible; the key were community services based on prevention and treatment. It also recommended that local authorities should establish out-patient clinics, and fund voluntary agencies to run after-care services. Following the Mental Treatment Act of 1930, there was a radical increase in the number of out-patient clinics.

After 1948 and the establishment of the NHS, the plight of people incarcerated in long stay hospitals and asylums came into focus. A consensus around the concept of community care was gradually being adopted. The Ministry of Health in 1954 declared that *'the importance of enabling old people to go on living in their own homes where they most wish to be, and of delaying admission to residential care for as long as possible is now generally accepted'* (quoted in Means, 1992). The 1957 Royal Commission (The Percy Report), proposed a comprehensive mental health service which moved away from institutional care towards care in the community, and is credited with coining the term 'community care'. Community care was formally encouraged in the 1959 Mental Health Act although, it did not use the term 'community care'. In a speech in 1961 the Minister of Health, Enoch Powell, announced a 50 per cent reduction of the 150,000 mental hospital beds, by 1975, despite *'the defences we have to storm'*. Responsibility for residential and social care was shifted to local authorities. In 1963 the Ministry of Health published *Health and Welfare: The Development of Community Care*. In setting out the ten-year plans, the huge variation between local authorities in their provision and planning for these services was highlighted. The report proposed that future hospital provision would focus on acute care, with others treated in the community. Those affected the most would be older patients and people with physical and mental disabilities.

Financial drivers of community care

By the 1970s, commentators from all sides of the political spectrum agreed that the out of touch, hierarchical bureaucracies that had come to dominate local authority and other statutory organisations needed radical transformation. The monolithic welfare state had served a purpose but now needed to be modernised. The effects of increasing financial constraints had a considerable impact on the emerging community care policy, as did growing criticism of professionalisation and institutional care. In addition to these negative policy drivers, growing interest in community based alternatives offered a positive influence.

A fundamental driver of welfare policy has been the 'distributive dilemma' – societies need to reconcile the twin distributive systems, one based on work and the other on need, whilst not undermining the market economy (Stone, 1984). The importance of workhouses, asylums and other institutions was in influencing and controlling the beliefs and attitudes of people, towards becoming economically independent, and protecting society from the 'unproductive' and 'undesirable'. From the inception of the NHS the costs of hospitals and the bottomless demand for care became apparent, and necessitated a system for rationally distributing resources. The Guillebaud Report (1956) for example, acknowledged government's continuing concern for high and increasing hospital costs.

By the early 1960s the belief arose that community care would save resources, allowing more patients to be treated. Titmuss argued in 1961 that reductions in hospital beds and community care proposals were economically driven with no real intention to develop the community based services so essential to the effectiveness of community care. Domiciliary services were underfunded and lacked support at both national and local level (Younghusband, 1959). During the 1970s the post war era of expanding welfare services came to an end with economic recession and fiscal crisis. The debate shifted from demands for overall increases in spending on social care to more effective targeting and a greater balance between domiciliary and residential care provision. Care for vulnerable people remained a significantly lower priority than child care, and the bulk of the decreasing resources continued to go to residential services.

Critique of institutions

Public pressure sustained since the 19th century demanded that large institutions (especially mental hospitals) were closed and patients discharged into 'the community'. This was intensified by the middle of the 20th century with some of the most robust criticism emanating from social scientists and health professionals. Barton (1959) wrote of the adverse effects institutions had on their inmates. In his seminal work *Asylums*, Goffman (1961) developed the idea of the 'total institution' cut off from the outside world and leading to institutionalisation. Drawing on Goffman's findings, Townsend in his influential *Last Refuge* (1962) (a study of elderly people in residential care) portrayed institutions as authoritarian and little better than workhouses. Rather than merely improving conditions, Townsend argued people should be prevented from being admitted to institutions by developing adequate community based services. Similar studies were made of hospitals for 'mentally handicapped people' in *Put Away* (Morris, 1969); Miller and Gwynne (1971) of provision for the physically disabled (from which they developed the idea of 'warehouse' versus 'horticultural' models of care); and King, Raynes and Tizard (1971) of homes for 'mentally handicapped' children, who argued that when they were given identical living and learning opportunities as 'normal' children in children's homes they improved in individual and social capacity; from this they developed the theory of *'normalisation'* (see the chapter by David Race in this volume).

Criticism of institutions was not confined to academia; condemnation of psychiatric hospitals took on a more public aspect in the 1970s. In response to a letter in *The Times* in 1967, patients, relatives, nurses and social workers wrote of the neglect and squalor existing in such places. The resulting book, *Sans Everything* (Robb, 1967) led to a public outcry with dozens of cases of cruelty and ill treatment coming to light. In addition, groups such as the National Association for Mental Health (MIND) and the Campaign for Mentally Handicapped People lobbied vociferously against large-scale institutions and the lack of speed in their replacement under emerging community care policies.

However, many of the premises of the anti-institutional movement have been challenged, not least using the recent accumulation of evidence of care outside institutions (Bartlett and Wright, 1999) suggested that the relationships between different care arrangement and locations (i.e. institutions/community services) are far more complex than have been previously characterised.

Critique of professional care

The case against institutional care was advocated at the time when a new wave of psychotropic drugs was introduced. The chlorpromazine drug group (or tranquillizers) were developed in 1952, and the therapeutic effects of these and other drugs changed the focus on control to allowing patients to be treated more easily outside instructional settings (Davis, 1980). Although the drugs were successful in suppressing the more alarming symptoms of mental illness, there was not a clear consensus as to whether they also contributed to recovery. The commonly held belief that innovations in drug use in the 1950s and 1960s contributed to community care policies is not held by everyone, Goodwin (1989) argued that they may have actually be a factor in maintaining the use of hospitalisation and treatment to a wide number of patients. Others such as R.D. Laing and Ivan Illich suggested that social rather than medical reasons were responsible for schizophrenia and that professional treatment for mental illness may add to the illness. They therefore opposed many standard treatments, including electro-convulsive therapy and hospitalisation. Although some analysts saw Victorian asylums as a reflection of a new humanitarianism and the embodiment of the state's recognition of its responsibility for vulnerable people, others took a critical view. Theorists such as Foucault (1972), Scull (1996) and Ryan and Thomas (1980) perceived the motivation of the developing psychiatric profession as 'professional imperialism' rather than philanthropy. The care of people with learning disabilities and mental health issues became the sole concern of the 'medical entrepreneur'. Their expert knowledge in the treatment of madness was closely related to institutional treatment and their own professional advancement. Furthermore, the development of different techniques applied by the 'medical model' of care was often regarded as serving only to keep control over the inmates of institutions and support professional power.

Care, it is argued, has always been used overtly and covertly to control behaviour. Although institutions are useful in achieving this aim through segregating those labelled as undesirable or of little economic use, in the 1960s community care was used as an extension of professional and ideological desires to control deviance (Goodwin, 1990). Recent mental health care developments have reintroduced the practice of surveillance as an element of community care (Brindle, 1998). Whereas in the early 20th century 'mental defectives' represented dangerousness, now it is people with mental illness. Issues of control outside the institutional context have also been raised in relation to the role of health visitors in policing the family (Abbott and Wallace, 1990) and case-work more generally.

People who are disabled are among the most marginalised and powerless in society lack collective political representation. The civil rights campaigns of the 1960s gave a voice to disabled people, and condemned social perceptions of disability and welfare policies. They challenged the traditional *'medical model'* of disability that stigmatises people by their disability and introduced an alternative *'social model'*. The Independent Living Movement in the USA highlighted the observation that the main obstacles to full independence and participation in society were *'hostile physical and social environments, and the operation of medical and rehabilitation services'* (Barnes and Mercer, 1995). But it was not until the 1980s that Centres for Independent Living, based on these principles were established in Britain.

Developing an accommodation and domiciliary support infrastructure

Prefiguring the New Right experiment of the 1980s with its emphasis on a mixed economy of care (focused on private sector provision); a range of care and support initiatives began to emerge alongside the development of community care policies. Institutions themselves were becoming more 'open' and integrated in the community, and a range of means to keep people out of institutions were developed, using less 'institutional' accommodation with built in support and care, or domiciliary support services to enable people in their own home.

Box 2.4: Post war care alternatives to closed institutions

- Dingleton Hospital in Melrose pioneered an 'open-door' policy from 1948, whereby hospitals and asylums developed open wards, parole systems and open days. In 1953 the World Health Organisation published a report advocating open-door developments in mental health services including out-patient, day care, domiciliary care, hostel and other related community services (World Health Organisation, 1953).
- With improved medical understanding, therapeutic communities (as they later became known) were developed such as 'the Northfield experiments' from 1942 (Jones, 1968).
- After the war the newly formed National Association for Mental Health ran 11 agricultural hostels for 'mentally handicapped men', two homes for 'mentally defective children', two holiday homes for 'mental defectives' and mental hospital patients, and a convalescent home for epileptics.
- The increase in homelessness after the war was partly addressed through under the 1948 National Assistance Act which turned workhouse casual wards into 'reception centres' (later renamed 'resettlement units') and hostels for homeless single people. The centres offered board and lodging with compulsory counselling and 'case-work'.
- Government policies throughout the 1960s and 1970s gradually encouraged the development of a range of community care-oriented treatment and rehabilitation services primarily run by social services. These included: day hospitals, out-patient clinics, and social after-care services (Jones, 1972).

Despite a long history, initiatives such as those outlined in Box 2.4 led to the perception that institutions had a therapeutic and beneficial role rather than just a custodial one, and raised the possibility of further treatment outside hospitals. However, in addition to specific care and rehabilitation centres, a range of accommodation facilities linked to care were seen to be needed if institutions were no longer to house people. The stakeholders in the emerging community care agenda became involved in developing accommodation including: hostels with care staff, residential care homes, shared living schemes (which include people with and without 'special' needs), clusters of warden accommodation and sometimes with communal facilities and more recently, dispersed accommodation to which 'floating support' is delivered. Despite this diverse range of facilities, it was not until the early 1970s that administrative mechanisms for developing care in the community began to evolve systematically including:

- Establishing joint planning arrangements between local and health authorities.
- Fixing national targets for the level of provision.
- Establishing a system of joint financing.

In the 1970s, housing agencies recognised the need for houses adapted for use by people with impairments. However, the main contribution of local authority housing departments in the management of care and accommodation of older people (and to a lesser extent younger people with physical disabilities) in the 1960s and 1970s, was through the provision of 'special needs' housing (including sheltered housing). Following the Housing Act 1974, housing associations also became involved in developing special needs housing, often in conjunction with specialist organisations. There were two main categories of sheltered housing (later increased to four) both with wardens, one category without communal facilities and the other with, they were designed to cater for both older people who were fit and active to very frail people. In practice a significant proportion of those accommodated in sheltered housing had limited levels of need. In addition to sheltered housing, housing agencies started to build properties designed for physically disabled people.

Domiciliary care services aimed at keeping people in their own home may be traced back to the Second World War when in the early stages people who were older or impaired were seen as presenting a problem; left in the community they, *'placed pressure on women needed in the munitions factory or they "cluttered up" public air raid shelters'* (Means, 1992) and in hospitals they blocked beds reserved for war casualties.

Box 2.5: Post war domiciliary services

- The home help service was extended in 1944 to families with frail or sick older members.
- Mobile meals services were initiated to help alleviate the need for frail people to queue for food rations.
- Organisations such as Women's Royal Voluntary Service developed a range of services including day centres and visiting schemes
- In 1946 the government asked the National Association for Mental Health to provide a national after-care service for people discharged from military service on psychiatric grounds; extended later to civilians it was the foundation of community mental health care.

The Ministry of Health supported the voluntary sector as the main provider of domiciliary and community based services, during and after World War Two, holding the view that state provided services would undermine people's (i.e. women's) care of elderly or infirm relatives. This *'belief that support in the home should only be offered by relatives or voluntary workers'* (Means, 1992), was maintained into the 1960s. However, from the 1950s, a growing range of domiciliary support services were developed by agencies. Although voluntary organisations were keen to develop such services, most were not up to the formidable task this presented. Local authorities were able to provide their own meals on wheels service in 1962, The Health Services and Public Health Act 1968 gave local authorities the statutory duty to provide a home help service, and the 1970 Chronically Sick and Disabled Persons Act obliged councils to assess for home adaptations. The expansion of care, accommodation and domiciliary services represented a determined step away from institutions; however, provision was underfunded, unplanned and insufficient. It was provided by a mix of sectors – statutory, voluntary, and to a lesser extent, the independent sector. Towards the end of the 1970s and early 1980s demands were being made for greater pluralism in welfare provision, all political factions were calling for a mixed economy of welfare; the left wanting to involve the voluntary sector (to counter problems associated with the inflexible bureaucratic provision of local authorities) (Hadley and Hatch, 1981), whilst the right wanted greater provision by the private sector.

Emerging community care issues

The criticisms of professionals, institutions and the state coupled with financial crisis and subsequent reductions in welfare spending led to the need to reappraise the welfare state more generally. The welfare consensus of the previous two decades gave way at the end of the 1970s to divergent views of the solution. In relation to housing and community care, this chapter concludes by outlining four inter-related issues that came to the fore during the 1960s and 1970s:

1. Lead co-ordinating role

Whilst the medical profession within the newly-established NHS, dominated institutional care for people with learning difficulties and mental health problems; the lead role for older people and people with physical disabilities was more contentious. In the 1960s the family doctor and the medical officer of health (responsible to local authority health departments) disputed the role with welfare services (including the chief welfare officer, responsible to the local authority). New broad-based generic social service departments were created by the Local Authority Social Services Act 1970 based on recommendations in the Younghusband and Seebohm reports. The act merged children's departments with welfare and mental health departments, and included social work, home help and occupational therapy under a single director of social services. Under the 1974 health care reforms, the health care services (including health visitor, district nurse and GP services) were separated and placed within newly formed district health authorities.

However, this separation of responsibility for home care and district nursing left unanswered the question of who was to co-ordinate the now disjointed domiciliary care team. Furthermore, not everyone was in favour of generic social work. A report by the committee that brought together the Royal College of Psychiatrists, the Society of Medical Officers of Health and the British Medical Association in 1972, wrote that their most important conclusion,

> *'... is the necessity for compulsory provision for liaison between the National Health Service and local authorities at all levels ... We strongly support the concept of community care, both for the mentally ill and the mentally subnormal, but it is still too rudimentary in some local authorities; the task of providing it adequately will be immense ... We have no faith in the idea that a so-called generic social worker could replace a specialised worker. We are*

sure that special training is necessary, and we recommend that appropriate clinical training should be organised as a matter of urgency' (Royal College of Psychiatrists, The British Medical Association and the Society of Medical Officers of Health, 1972).

A more general criticism of community care was that it consisted largely of trying to find provision that most suited clients, within an inflexible and limited range of choices. Care services were organised around providers' needs. Therefore, alongside calls for a more pluralistic care system, a model of local government as contractor of care provision, alongside a monitoring and inspection role was conceived. In his study of *Mental Handicap and Community Care* (1973), Michael Bayley introduced the concept of 'a structure for coping' whereby services for people who were disabled should be an arrangement of services using all available resources in the community including the family, statutory and voluntary agencies. Meanwhile, case management was being developed as an approach within a mixed economy of provision where clients were guided to develop a package of care that suited their needs by a worker who acted as a service broker. The approach was piloted in Thanet (Kent) and Gateshead (Challis and Davies, 1986) in the late 1970s; the trial was later extended through the Department of Health and Social Security Care in the Community Project in 1983. *Care management* as it became known, was seen as an effective use of scarce resources where a range of services were available.

2. Community approach

Part of the analysis of the failure of managing the welfare state was that local authorities had become centralised, functionally managed and lacked contact with localities. A solution developed in the late 1970s was to increase accountability and quality by decentralising service delivery through 'patch based' area offices or 'community social work'. Community development was seen by many as an integral aspect of welfare and had taken root in parts of Scotland after the Social Work Scotland Act 1968 gave social work departments the power and duty to,

> *'... promote social welfare by making available advice, guidance and assistance on such a scale as may be appropriate for their area ... and provide ... such facilities ... as they may consider suitable and adequate'* (Ministry of Health, 1968).

Community development had a range of functions including involving users of services in their planning and delivery as well as enabling collective identification of needs and issues and taking action to address them including redistributing wealth in areas of urban deprivation (for example under the Community Development Projects). Community care as a paradigm became a contested issue, was it care 'in' the community or 'by' the community? The 1963 Ministry of Health *Community Care Blue Book* focused on care in the community and by professionals, but by the 1980s policy appeared to centre on care by the community, i.e. by family and carers. The white paper *Growing Older* stated that *'care in the community must increasingly mean care by the community'* (Department of Health and Social Security, 1981). This statement however, may be interpreted as either the state playing a minimal role whilst primary care is provided by family and friends, or that the state should maintain the foremost responsibility but engage family, friends and the 'community' in the process. (Clapham, Kemp and Smith, 1990). Not everyone saw communities as a utopian alternative to institutional care; this required a view of communities not as a collection of self-interested individuals, but one where social interaction is based on social exchange and the capacity of giving and receiving services freely.

Rather, many communities into which ex-psychiatric hospital patients were placed may be seen as uncaring, hostile and lacking the resources to build understanding and capacity. It was also demonstrated that small 'community based' shared accommodation and support initiatives such as hostels did not meet the values of the normalisation philosophy and were just as able to produce depersonalised and harsh environments as larger institutions, with less opportunities for stimulation (Apte, 1968).

3. The housing role

The role of housing in health and welfare issues has always been complex. As we have seen a discourse within housing circles about whether it is concerned more with peoples' 'problems' than property, stems from the origins of the profession in the mid-19th century, when it first adopted the dual aspects of 'caring' and 'bricks and mortar'. Managerial and professional practices and government policy urged local authorities towards a more restricted approach. Prior to the 1980s structural, professional and implementational links between community care and housing policies were limited (with notable exceptions such as special needs housing). Housing, if considered at all, was only regarded as providing the bricks and mortar for living space (British Association of Social Work, 1985) and not in terms of shaping the inhabitants' worldview or empowering individuals. As this book demonstrates however, housing policy has had a significant impact on community care, indeed the Seebohm Committee (Seebohm, 1968) acknowledged the link between services provided by housing departments and community care groups and recommended that housing became more involved in *'households containing mentally or physically handicapped members as well as old people'*.

With the emphasis on accommodating people with special needs in the community, a discourse arose as to whether sheltered housing was primarily an alternative to residential institutions or was redirecting resources away from 'general needs' housing. Debates therefore focused on the use of wardens, as well as the need to fully subsidise mainstream housing, which if made appropriate and flexible enough could meet the 'normalised' needs of people with impairments. The independent living movement emphasised the importance of enabling people to live independently in accommodation without the stigma of living in 'special' accommodation – a label Clapham and Smith (1990) argue is a technical and political term used to discriminate between groups when allocating scarce welfare funding. A similar perspective was articulated by the Union of the Physically Impaired Against Segregation:

> *'In our view it is society which disables physically impaired people. Disability is something imposed on top of impairments by the way we are unnecessarily isolated and excluded from full participation in society. Disabled people are therefore an oppressed group in society'* (Union of the Physically Impaired Against Segregation, 1976).

However, sufficient resources were not available to provide 'social housing' to meet the needs of those requiring it, despite this being where the majority of people needing care in the community live. The demand for affordable accommodation had been masked by the effect of large long stay institutions, and the pressures grew as the number of those people increased with demographic changes, medical advances and community care policies. This was at the time when the role of general needs housing was under question and the trend was towards targeted provision. Tenants' needs cannot be neatly compartmentalised into organisationally or professionally defined spheres and housing authorities had to deal increasingly with highly vulnerable tenants. Housing officers could not easily ignore these social problems as *'unmet social care and support needs are soon encountered as housing management problems'* (Arnold and Page, 1992) leading to a more socially oriented role for housing authorities and pressure to provide intensive management. The terms 'care' and 'support' are often loosely used interchangeably in the housing context, but are rarely defined (Franklin, 1998). Finkelstein (1998) identified two concerns of those offering assistance before residential and institutional forms of care had developed: *'"caring" for those deemed unable to manage and "supporting" those who can manage with assistance'*. This undifferentiated mixture of 'care' and 'support' he contends, was later separated by those managing institutions, appropriating and professionalising the care role, which was transferred to the 'community' setting. In her attempts to distinguish care from support, Anderson (1994) argues housing should not be involved with care, but rather should be concerned with support. 'Care' is often qualified, as, 'health care'; 'social care'; 'residential, nursing or hospital care'; Barnes asks, *'does this imply that care is whatever action is carried out, or whatever services are provided by the qualifier?'* (Barnes, 1997).

4. Inter-agency co-operation

We have seen that the growing complexity of local and central government and the diverse range of service providers led to overlap and competing claims for responsibility for managing care. Statutory agencies managed and funded independent structures, and had distinct geographic boundaries. Each responded to their own priorities founded on shifting national guidelines, professional philosophies, accumulated areas of expertise, and spatially defined needs.

Not only did implementation of policy, services and expenditure vary considerably geographically (Hunter and Wistow, 1987), but it was little wonder that *'inter-agency collaboration between housing, health and social care agencies is difficult to achieve'* (Arblaster *et al.*, 1996).

Longstanding rivalry between housing and social services stems partly from this very different cultural and professional backgrounds – with the dual (care/bricks and mortar) role of housing adding to the confusion. In 1982 the Institute of Housing commented that *'unfortunately, in many cases the working relationships between housing officers and social workers are not good ... Generally speaking they view each other with considerable scepticism'* (British Association of Social Work, 1985). Lack of co-operation between those services was confirmed by a number of subsequent studies (Arblaster *et al.*, 1996). Collaboration was necessary between health and social services if the policy of running down long stay hospitals was to continue, joint care planning was therefore introduced in the mid-1970s, however, *real* joint arrangements rarely took place. Arrangements were complex and managers in both services did not find time to undertake the necessary joint work. Professional jealousies and loss of control also resulted in lack of joint working.

Conclusion

This chapter began by demonstrating areas in which housing plays a critical role in welfare, and indicated that a sensitive, well funded housing policy may enhance the lives of vulnerable service users. However, in practice the history of the last two centuries has rather been one of oppression and control for such people, with poverty and a lack of suitable housing, leading many into institutional care. Once major public health issues had been addressed, the central role of suitable housing in care and support of vulnerable people had all but been lost, and the connection barely made before the 1980s. However, if state intervention in housing was made grudgingly, its underpinning of care and support was even more reluctant, as it took half a century of campaigning and two world wars before the idea that the state should take collective responsibility for its most vulnerable members took root. Even then this was almost overridden by fiscal concerns of providing care as cheaply as possible. A major saving was seen possible through the closure of long stay institutions, although because of cultural incompatibilities between agencies this policy was only partially implemented before 1980. Meanwhile, domiciliary services and support for carers was being developed slowly and patchily within growing financial constraints.

CHAPTER 3:
Working in partnership for 'joined up' housing and community care

Julie Savory

Introduction

In 2001 the Department of Health stated that *'a whole systems approach across social care, health and housing that recognises the impact of changes in one sector on others'* (2001d) is essential. Key terms in the public service 'modernisation agenda' developed by the Labour government since 1997, are partnership and collaborative working with great emphasis on agencies working together, and with individuals and communities, to ensure services provide choice, satisfaction and quality of life outcomes. This stems from a recognition of *'collaborative advantage'* (Huxham, 1996), meaning that the outcomes sought by service users and communities cannot be met by individual agencies working in isolation. Other advantages of collaborative working include the potential to make better use of resources, prevent duplication and gaps in service provision and generate new insights and solutions (Department of Health 1998a). This is particularly true in the field of health and social welfare where the activities of health, housing, social care and voluntary agencies all interact to provide support. In practice, the contribution of housing agencies has tended to be seen as subsidiary to the need to ensure effective joint working between health and social services. However, there are many links between housing provision and health and social care (see Box 3.1 below), and as the government has acknowledged adequate housing and support is *'the key to independent living'* (Department of Health, 1989a). Yet, as many commentators have noted, despite policy exhortations, achieving collaboration and partnership in practice has proved elusive (Audit Commission 1998; Means, Richards and Smith, 2003).

Box 3.1: Links between housing, health and social welfare

- NHS: The links between poor housing and poor health and the new emphasis on health gain and prevention should encourage health authorities to consider links with housing in their health strategies to avoid extra health care costs falling on the NHS.
- Social services: Inadequate housing provision can create extra support needs.
- Housing providers: Increasing numbers of vulnerable tenants within social housing creates pressures to ensure appropriate support is provided to avoid problems maintaining tenancies.
- Service users: It can be difficult to compartmentalise a complex mixture of health, housing and social care needs.

This chapter will review the role of, and developments in, joint working to meet community care and housing support needs over the past decade. It will explore: different definitions of partnership working; outline developments in the policy framework since 1990; explore factors contributing to success or failure in inter-agency working; and assess the implications of the current policy framework for housing providers and people with housing and support needs.

What's in a name?

The policy and practice literature for health and welfare support is infused with references to the following types of working: multi-agency; inter-professional; partnership; collaboration; co-operation and more recently whole systems .The terms are often used interchangeably but in reality refer to a range of practices and relationships. Unless differences are identified a lack of clarity and misunderstanding about the role of different professions and agencies can exist. A number of commentators have identified that working together exists along a continuum of different levels of involvement (Pratt *et al.*, 1998). As Balloch and Taylor note (2001) there are three levels of inter-agency working:

Co-operation: involving informal sharing of information and formal exchange of information; co-ordination: which takes account of the activities of other groups to achieve shared goals/tasks, and finally collaboration where agencies work together to achieve an outcome which neither could achieve alone.

An important consideration is the extent to which each agency retains its autonomy. Working together may consist of co-operating on an issue which is marginal to the main focus of each agency, joint commissioning of services or even an integration of service delivery, authority to deliver and funding. Recent policy guidance is seeking to place partnership working within the wider umbrella of *'whole systems working'*. Systems theory stems from the work of biologist Ludwig von Bertalanffy (1971) who was dissatisfied with reductionist explanations of living organisms and instead sought to explain the wholeness and interconnectedness of different parts. The concept has been applied to the social and behavioural sciences, defined by Loxley (1997) as *'wholes are more than the sum of their parts, interactions between entities are purposeful, boundaries between them are permeable and cause and effect are not linear but inter-dependent'*. The main features of whole system working as described by the Audit Commission (2002):

- Services are organised around the user.
- All of the players recognise that they are inter-dependent and understand that action in one part of the system has an impact elsewhere.
- There is a shared: vision, objectives, action, resources and risk.
- Users experience services as seamless and boundaries between organisations are not apparent to them.

Key elements are the emphasis on boundaries between services as well as services themselves, and recognition of the concept of 'interconnectedness', meaning that change in any one part of a system will bring change in others. The effectiveness of the system is determined by the service user's experience rather than organisational priorities.

Box 3.2: Comparison of a fragmented structure and a user centred whole systems approach

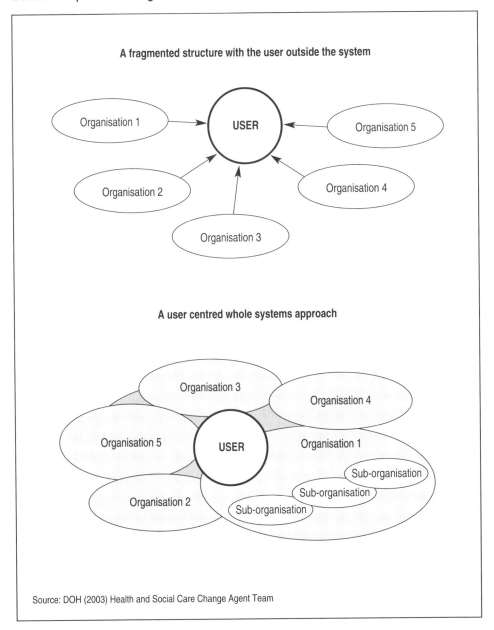

Source: DOH (2003) Health and Social Care Change Agent Team

Box 3.3: A whole systems approach in health and social care – who does what and where?

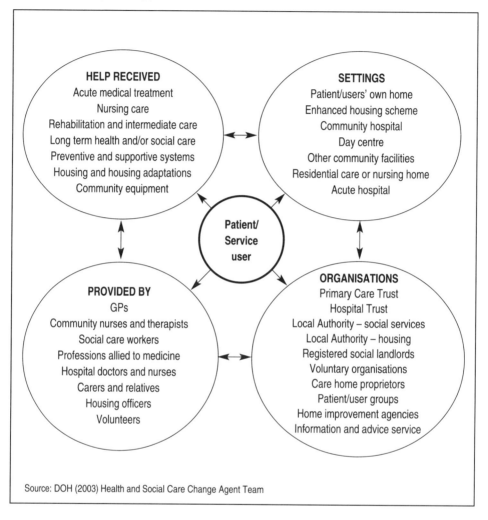

HELP RECEIVED
Acute medical treatment
Nursing care
Rehabilitation and intermediate care
Long term health and/or social care
Preventive and supportive systems
Housing and housing adaptations
Community equipment

SETTINGS
Patient/users' own home
Enhanced housing scheme
Community hospital
Day centre
Other community facilities
Residential care or nursing home
Acute hospital

Patient/ Service user

PROVIDED BY
GPs
Community nurses and therapists
Social care workers
Professions allied to medicine
Hospital doctors and nurses
Carers and relatives
Housing officers
Volunteers

ORGANISATIONS
Primary Care Trust
Hospital Trust
Local Authority – social services
Local Authority – housing
Registered social landlords
Voluntary organisations
Care home proprietors
Patient/user groups
Home improvement agencies
Information and advice service

Source: DOH (2003) Health and Social Care Change Agent Team

At strategic management and planning levels the arena usually consists of different agencies such as housing associations, primary care trusts and local authority social services departments working together to agree strategy and responsibility for funding and managing different activities. At operational levels the focus shifts to inter-professional work which can be defined as to *'how two or more people from different professions communicate and co-operate to achieve a common goal.'* (Ovretveit, Mathias and Thompson, 1997). This can range from making a referral, to needs assessment, or working as a service delivery team. In the provision of community care a wide range of professions could be involved including social workers, probation officers, GPs, health visitors, tenancy support workers and housing managers.

What is housing support?

Ambiguity in the past has contributed to lack of ownership for certain aspects of support and impeded joined up working. Recent policy developments have helped to clarify the differences and for the first time activities which can be funded as housing support have been identified. Housing support has been defined as support which develops an individual's capacity to live independently in the community or sustains their ability to do so (Department of Transport, Local Government and the Regions, 2001c). This document teases out the difference between housing support and intensive housing management. Housing management is defined as landlord activities which may include helping those who need support to sustain a tenancy, but also assistance provided to any tenant when a need arises. Housing support costs eligible for Supporting People funding are those which *'are provided as part of an agreed and planned package of support'*. Such activities differ from personal care and domiciliary care. Personal care has been defined by Department of Health (2001e) as the provision of assistance with bodily functions. Domiciliary care has been defined by the Care Standards Act 2000, *'as an undertaking which consists of or includes arranging the provision of personal care in their own homes for persons who by reasons of illness, infirmity or disability are unable to provide it themselves without assistance'*. In practice it often difficult for service users to make a clear demarcation between different types of activity. For example, when is taking a bath social care and when is it health care? The following sections will outline developments in joint working to meet community care and support needs between 1990 and 1997; and 1997 to 2005. A subsequent section will evaluate why successful inter-agency working to meet community care and support needs has been difficult to achieve and the implications of the new policy landscape with particular emphasis on the contribution of housing services.

The policy framework for joint working to meet community care and support needs: 1990-1997

The 1990 NHS and Community Care Act

During the 1980s there was recognition that the joint planning and finance arrangements, introduced in the mid-1970s, between the NHS and local authorities were ineffective. The NHS was unwilling to share resources with local authorities (Audit Commission, 1994) and this was combined with growing unease that long stay hospitals for those with mental health and learning disabilities were being closed without adequate alternative care arrangements being in place. In 1986 the Audit Commission published a report which was critical of existing arrangements for community care provision concluding, there is *'considerable organizational fragmentation and confusion, with responsibility for the introduction of community care divided between a variety of separately funded organizations who often fail to work together effectively'*. Of particular concern was a 'perverse incentive' in the social security regulations which made it financially advantageous for social services departments to place people in residential care which would be funded by the Department of Social Services budget rather than provide and fund community based domiciliary services. This resulted in a 'mushrooming' of the Department of Social Security bill for residential care from £10 million in 1979 to £1,872 million by 1991 (Means and Smith, 1994). In response, the then Conservative government commissioned Sir Roy Griffiths to undertake a review.

The main proposals of his 1988 report formed the basis of the 1989 white paper *Caring for People* and the subsequent 1990 NHS and Community Care Act. The objectives of the community care reforms were as follows:

- To promote the development of domiciliary, day and respite services to enable people to live in their own homes wherever feasible and sensible.
- To make proper assessment of need and good care management the cornerstone of high quality care.
- To promote the development of a flourishing independent sector alongside quality public services.
- To clarify the responsibilities of agencies and make them more accountable.
- To secure better value for taxpayers money by introducing a new funding structure for social care (Department of Health, 1989a).

The main features of the community care system introduced by the 1990 act were as follows:

- Local authority social services departments became the lead agency with responsibility for:
  - co-ordinating community care provision;
  - care management (assessing individual need, contracting care arrangements and securing their delivery within available resources;
  - producing annual community care plans after consultation with other agencies including health and the LA housing authority and service users and carers (Replaced by Joint Investment Plans in 1997).
- A special transitional grant, which included money previously spent by the Department of Social Security on residential care, was transferred to local authority social services departments in 1993, with a requirement that 85 per cent of the grant was spent on care provided by independent agencies. In 1996 this was incorporated into a fixed amount within local authorities' Revenue Support Grant.
- A specific grant for the development of mental health services (Mental Illness Specific Grant) was created, accessible upon evidence of collaboration between social services and district health authorities.

The 1990 NHS and Community Care Act was an 'enabling' piece of legislation. It did not require new services to be provided but introduced a new framework for the organisation and funding of existing care services, implemented in 2003. Key features were the introduction of a purchaser/provider split, the promotion of a mixed economy of welfare through the introduction of quasi markets and a contract culture. The act also introduced changes to the structure and funding of NHS services, the most significant being the creation of an 'internal market'. These changes formed part of a wider policy to break down public sector bureaucracies and replace them with 'government by the market' in line with the neo-liberal ideology of the Conservative administration (Hudson and Henwood, 2002). It was anticipated that competition resulting from the separation of purchasers/ commissioners/providers would result in greater responsiveness to user needs, and more cost effective, better quality services (Department of Health, 1991).

Box 3.4: Mixed economy of welfare

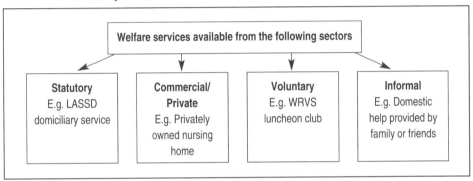

Box 3.5: Quasi market

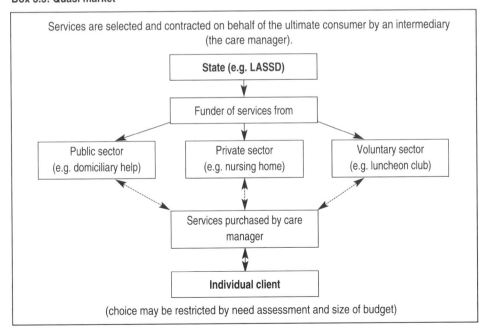

Despite a general concern to improve inter-agency working, a notable feature of the 1990 act was the lack of linkage between the NHS and community care reforms. The 1989 white paper *Caring for People* devoted a short chapter to the importance of collaborative working but gave no detailed guidance. Health agencies and local authority social services departments were exhorted to work together but apart from the incentive of the Mental Illness Specific Grant which required evidence of collaboration, there was no specific requirement. The main mechanism for bringing agencies together was the community care planning process. Government policy guidance and community care practice gave little consideration to the contribution that housing support could make. A joint Department of the Environment/Department of Health circular in 1992, provided the first policy guidance on the role of housing agencies in community care provision stating that housing and social services should adopt joint arrangements to deal with individual needs assessments where a housing need is involved and that housing strategies and community care plans should be consistent. However, Lund and Foord (1997) in a survey in 1995 of 120 housing strategies and corresponding community care plans found limited synergy between them. Other research has found little evidence that housing professionals are regularly involved in individual community care needs assessment (Foord and Simic, 2001). From the mid-1990s onwards there was growing concern that the new framework had not resolved the problem of agencies failing to work effectively together to meet the needs of vulnerable people. There were a number of high profile cases where failures in inter-agency working and gaps in provision resulted in tragedies (Ritchie, Dick and Lingham, 1994) plus a steady build up of concern about tightened eligibility for domiciliary services and the impact of this on the quality of life for older people and those vulnerable due to mental health or learning disabilities (Association of Directors of Social Services/Local Government Association, 2003). Media coverage of older people unable to be discharged from hospital due to lack of community care support introduced the term 'bedblocking' and highlighted the tensions that continued to exist at the interface of health and social care. An emerging concern for housing agencies was the development of a support gap for those with lower level support needs living in general needs housing (House of Commons Health Select Committee, 1994).

Research into the care needs of people living in ordinary housing identified serious shortfalls in care and health support exacerbated by lack of appropriate accommodation. It was found that: social services were increasingly only able to respond to the most severe needs; housing workers were struggling to respond to needs they were not trained or qualified to deal with; the missing services were relatively simple, for example befriending, weekend support, transport, basic skills training, budgeting and benefits advice'; lack of support resulted in crises and sometimes loss of accommodation (Arblaster, Conway, Foreman and Hawtin, 1996). They found that *'there were very few examples in which all agencies – health, housing and social care – worked together in a three way collaborative approach'*. A housing officer quoted in a London Federation of Housing Association publication (1995) suggested, *'it's like a merry go- round. Vulnerable people get evicted, the homeless persons unit picks them up, they get rehoused,*

*cause us difficulties, we haven't the support to deal with issues so there are
neighbour complaints and eventually the individual gets evicted again'.*
Housing agencies were responding to the support gap by the development of
tenancy support and resettlement services. However a complicated patchwork of
funding sources with different eligibility requirements and lack of clarity about
responsibility for different levels of support resulted in inconsistent access to
housing-related support between local authority areas and tenures and provision
which was often inflexible and inequitable in meeting the changing needs of people
with support needs (Department of the Environment, 1993; Oldman, Quilgers and
Oldfield, 1995; National Housing Federation, 1997). The Audit Commission (1998)
in a review of the role of housing in community care criticised:

- the fragmentation of services for health and social care and the lack of
  recognition of the potential role of housing agencies;
- the dominance of crisis response measures and the lack of preventative
  support;
- the lack of funding and responsibility for ensuring low intensity support is
  provided;
- a pattern of cost-shunting between health agencies and social services and
  between social services and housing authorities;
- a failure to maximise value for money.

The report concluded that *'some problems stem from constrained resources, but
there is evidence of poor collaboration between housing, social services and health
authorities that allows too many people in need to "fall through the net"'.*

The policy framework 1997 onwards – from contracts to partnership?

The New Labour government quickly made clear that it sought to raise standards in
public service provision and make services more accountable and responsive to
service users through what has been named 'the modernisation agenda'. It was
critical of the tendency for different agencies involved in public services to operate
in 'silos', which failed to take a holistic view of where their contribution fitted into
overall service outcomes for users, the gaps in provision and the inconsistency in
quality and standard of service provision between areas. A number of white papers
set out the government's agenda: *Modernising Government* (The Cabinet Office,
1999), *Modernising Social Services* (Department of Health, 1998b); *Modernising
Local Government: improving local services through Best Value* (Department of
the Environment Transport and the Regions, 1998a); *The NHS Plan* (Department of
Health, 2000) and the Housing green paper, *Quality and Choice: a decent home for
all* (Department of the Environment, Transport and the Regions, 2000a). The Local
Government Act 2000 placed a responsibility on local authorities to improve the
social, economic and environmental well-being of their areas, to achieve which
they are required to prepare community plans, in consultation with local citizens
about what is needed to enhance local well-being. To provide a framework for

drawing together stakeholders, most local authorities have established a Local Strategic Partnership to gather together the public, private, voluntary and community sectors. Into this overarching framework, are fed strategies addressing different aspects of service needs, including those developed with health agencies. 'Joined up working', by closer integration of services in terms of planning, commissioning and provision, is seen as a key means of achieving these aims and a raft of policies and initiatives have been introduced to facilitate this. The main measures have been directed at the political priority to *'bring down the Berlin Wall that can divide health and social services'* (Department of Health, 1998a).

Box 3.6: Main measures to improve inter-agency working between health agencies and local authority social services departments

---

Health Act 1999
- Introduced a duty of partnership and co-operation between NHS bodies and local authorities (replacing years of exhortation) and a number of measures to facilitate joint working.
- s29 gives health authorities and primary care trusts the ability to fund any function of a local authority which is connected to public health provision or the role of the NHS.
- s30 permits local authorities to transfer funds to health authorities for certain health-related functions, particularly activities which would avoid hospital admissions.
- s31 introduced three new 'flexibilities':
  - pooled budgets: health authorities and local authorities can now put resources into a single budget to fund services;
  - lead commissioning: either the local authority or the NHS can take the lead in commissioning services on behalf of both;
  - Integrated provision: the ability to merge service delivery.

The NHS Plan 2000
The 1999 act flexibilities would become mandatory unless local level progress in developing partnerships improved.

National Service Frameworks and the Single Assessment Process
For a number of vulnerable groups, the *National Service Frameworks* set out national standards and priorities for joint action by health and social services. The move to a Single Assessment Process aims to reduce the problem of multiple unco-ordinated assessments by health and social care agencies, with potential for the inclusion of housing needs.

Health and Social Care Act 2001
Permits the creation of Care Trusts which would use the 1999 act flexibilities to combine health and social care functions into a single organisation. These Care Trusts can cover a single geographic area and/or specialise in a single client group such as adults with learning disabilities. The partnership can include other service providers such as local authority housing providers, housing associations and voluntary agencies, raising the possibility of 'one stop shops' for all health, welfare and housing needs.

Community Care (Delayed Discharges) Act 2003
Since January 2004 local authorities can be required to reimburse the NHS when a patient's discharge is delayed by a lack of appropriate care in the community. The boundary between the NHS and local government with particular regard to hospital discharge and domiciliary and care home liaison is to be monitored by a National Director of Local Government and Social Care.

Although measures to promote better joint working between NHS agencies and social services departments have received most attention, the broader policy focus stresses the importance of rehabilitation, developing preventative services and promoting independence and health and reducing health inequalities (Department of Health, 1997; Department of Health, 1998d; Department of Health, 1999b). Several policy measures have been introduced linked to a key government commitment to reduce social exclusion and health inequalities. It is within this framework (see Box 3.7) that there are opportunities for housing agencies to work with social services and health agencies to meet health, community care and related support needs, by demonstrating how housing support can contribute to meeting the objectives of service commissioners.

Box: 3.7: Policy measures to reduce social exclusion and health inequalities

Health Improvement and Modernisation Plans (HImPs)
Introduced by the 1997 white paper *The New NHS*, HImPs are the overarching health improvement vision for the local NHS and its partners covering: tackling health inequalities, health improvement and modernisation of services.

Better Services for Vulnerable People Initiative 1997
Requires health agencies and local authorities to jointly develop 'Joint Investment Plans' for older people and those with mental health and/or learning disabilities. JIPs in effect are the action plan for the improvements identified in the Health Improvement and Modernisation Plans and replace the duty placed on local social services departments in 1990 to produce community care plans. Special grants were made available by the Social Services Modernisation Fund in 1997 to encourage partnership working to meet the aims of the Joint Investment Plans.

Promoting Independence: partnership grant
£650 million over three years to encourage the development of initiatives to improve rehabilitation services and measures to reduce unnecessary admissions to hospital or institutional care.

Promoting Independence: prevention grant
£100 million over three years. To encourage the development of preventative strategies and risk assessment to enable appropriate targeting of low level support.

Better Care, Higher Standards – a charter for long term care (DH 1999c)
By 2000 social services departments were required to take a lead role in developing long term care charters specifying standards adult service users can expect for help with social care, housing and health.

Health Action Zones
Since 1998, a number of health action zones have been established in areas of the country suffering from particularly high levels of deprivation with access to dedicated funds. Taking a holistic approach, including the use of financial resources, their aim is to tackle health inequalities at a local level by co-ordinating employment, education, housing, health and anti-poverty initiatives. The activities are co-ordinated by a partnership board, on which housing agencies can be represented.

→

The New Opportunities Fund 1998
Provides for the allocation of National Lottery money to establish Healthy Living Centres which can bring together a wide range of activities to tackle the social, economic and health impacts of deprivation. These centres can be developed and led by other agencies such as housing associations working in partnership with local health trusts.

Primary care trusts
Are separate statutory bodies accountable to the strategic health authority and the local community for developing the Local Delivery Plan and providing health services for their area. They hold over 75 per cent of the NHS budget and have the power to commission and provide hospital, primary and community health services from providers in the public, private or voluntary sectors. They are also able to commission non-health services which demonstrate ill health prevention or health gain, such as home insulation or handyperson schemes.

Building Care Capacity Grant 2001
Grant made available to health and social care agencies to further develop services to reduce delays in older people waiting to be discharged from hospital.

Quality and Choice for Older People's Housing (Department of Transport, Local Government and the Regions/Department of Health, 2001a)
Set out the government's strategic framework for older people's housing and emphasised the contribution housing and service models can provide to flexible service provision and the importance of joint working between health, housing and social care agencies to enhance independence and meaningful choice for older people.

Intermediate care funding
Funding available to primary care trusts to spend on developing measures to promote independence, prevent admissions to hospital and reduce delays in hospital discharge.

Extra Care Housing Fund 2003
To be jointly run by the Department of Health and the Housing Corporation, supported by the Office of the Deputy Prime Minister with the aim of developing innovative housing with care options, stimulating effective local partnerships in the interests of older people and piloting a number of supported living schemes for people with learning disabilities. To access the funding social services departments will have to show evidence of partnership with public and private sector bodies.

The primary focus of many of these initiatives has been to tackle the issue of older people taking up hospital bed spaces longer than necessary due to the lack of community rehabilitation and preventive support services and there is growing recognition of the contribution housing services can make to meeting this high political priority, by providing services such as community alarms, handyperson services, extra care housing, and the establishment of intermediate care beds in sheltered housing schemes. For housing agencies a number of other policy developments have recognised the preventative contribution their services can make to meeting and/or reducing health, care and support needs of those who do not fall into the traditional community care categories, and stressed the importance of inter-agency working.

New policy initiatives

*   The Homelessness Act 2002 which for the first time requires local housing authorities to develop a strategic response to the prevention of homelessness and the meeting of homeless people's needs. The Code of Guidance (Office of the Deputy Prime Minister, 2002c) recognises that meeting the needs of some homeless people will require input from a number of agencies including social services, health, education, environmental health, the voluntary sector and prison and probation services and that such agencies should be consulted in developing the homelessness strategy. Homelessness strategies are required to link in with other strategies, particularly the Supporting People strategy.

*   The Supporting People initiative (Department of Social Security, 1998) which came into effect in April 2003 provides a new policy, funding and monitoring framework for housing support services. At local level the commissioning body which consists of representatives from local housing and social services authorities, the local health authority and the probation service, develop the Supporting People strategy based on a joint mapping of supply and support needs in the local population and jointly agree which housing support services to fund and commission. Supporting People funding will cover a wide range of client groups including victims of domestic violence, ex-offenders, drug and alcohol abusers .The guidance (Department of Transport, Local Government and the Regions, 2001) stresses that the Supporting People strategy must link in with other relevant plans and programmes including: Health Improvement and Modernisation Plans, Joint Investment Programmes; Housing, Homelessness and Crime and Disorder Reduction strategies; Learning Disability Partnership Housing Strategy and the National Anti Drugs Strategy.

*   The neighbourhood renewal agenda (SEU, 2001) recognises that housing provision, housing management practices and housing support services have a significant contribution to make in tackling social exclusion and improving health. Initiatives such as the New Deal for Communities require collaboration between a wide range of agencies, including health, social care, housing, voluntary agencies, local businesses and partnership working with individuals and communities.

*   The Crime and Disorder Act 1998 s5 requires the establishment of local Crime and Disorder Reduction Partnerships. Police, Local Authorities and primary care trusts (England) and health authorities in Wales are required to work together to produce strategies for reducing crime and disorder and combating misuse of drugs and alcohol. It is expected that the housing association sector will be represented in the partnership.

*   The Anti-Social Behaviour Bill seeks to encourage stronger focus on the prevention of anti-social behaviour by targeting children at risk and encouraging improvement in partnerships between agencies such as housing and social services.

- Modernising Mental Health (Department of Health, 1998a) and the *National Service Framework for Mental Health* (1999) refers to housing authorities as key partners with health and other agencies in work to jointly assess needs, audit current provision and devise Joint Investment Plans for people with mental health needs.

- *Valuing People* (Department of Health, 2001c) provides the first major strategy for learning disability in 30 years. A key requirement is for local Learning Disability Partnership Boards to develop a housing strategy for people with learning disabilities.

Working together for housing and support

So far in this chapter, we have identified the different formats that partnership working take and outlined the policy developments affecting community care and housing support provision between 1990 and 2003. This section will identify factors which contribute to success or failure, and evaluate to what extent this affected the implementation of the 1990 NHS and Community Care Act. The prognosis for successful inter-agency working in the post 1997 policy framework will then be explored with particular reference to housing support needs. Drawing upon organisational theory, Hudson (1987) identified factors which predispose agencies to collaborate or result in tensions between them: funding constraints; lack of clarity and understanding about each agency's roles and responsibilities; different organisational structures and professional ideologies and values. Webb (1991) added 'trust' as another important factor.

Funding constraints

From its onset, there was criticism that the 1990 framework for community care was underfunded. Reforms were implemented during a time of considerable financial constraints for social services, health and housing agencies. All were under pressure to meet narrowly defined performance indicators based on the cost effectiveness of their core activities, which did not take account of wider cost benefits and inhibited the development of a holistic approach to support provision. Budgetary constraints, increased demand for services and political emphasis on NHS performance in acute areas of health provision contributed to pressures to tighten the boundaries between health and social care. Funding constraints on health and social care have impacted negatively on service boundaries. For health providers, in order to demonstrate efficiency gains, elements of post acute healthcare were carried out by community health service staff and social services increasingly provided care and support at home, which would previously have been the responsibility of district nursing services. This resulted in speedier hospital discharge but placed increased demands on local authority social services departments (Wistow, 1995). Whilst for local authority social service departments conflict with health authorities have arisen when a shortage of suitable care packages has delayed hospital discharge (Local Government Association, 1997). To avoid overspending, local authority social services departments increasingly found it necessary to tighten eligibility criteria for services, to focus on the most dependent people living in the community and to introduce or increase service charges. Preventative services were cut back to allow concentration on statutory duties and this reduced the scope of social services to meet less clearly defined lower level support needs (Department of Health, 1998a).

Hospital orientated health professionals remained reluctant to transfer their control over money obtained from the closure of long stay hospitals to community services provided by local authorities (Audit Commission, 1994). For local authorities there has been continuing pressure to define the 'landlord' role in a narrow way reducing the ability to charge low-key 'good neighbour' type support activities, traditionally associated with public sector housing provision, to the Housing Revenue Account (HRA). In 1992 a Court of Appeal judgement against the London Borough of Ealing found that Ealing were wrong to charge warden services with a social services character to the HRA. It was viewed that only services carried out for all tenants, and not just a sub-group, should be charged to the HRA. In view of widespread concern about disruption to sheltered housing provision, the Leasehold Reform, Housing and Urban Development Act 1993 s126 and s127 permitted such services to continue to be funded by the HRA provided that such services were not the dominant function of the housing staff concerned. In a foretaste of the Supporting People funding framework, government guidance stated that the long term policy objective was for the HRA to *'be strictly a landlord's account, and that welfare services should be accounted for elsewhere'* (Department of the Environment, 1993). The extension of compulsory competitive tendering by the Local Government Act 1992 resulted in housing management services being tightly specified leading to concerns that the welfare support role which is difficult to cost would be lost from mainstream housing management (Clapham and Franklin, 1994). Housing associations were, and continue to be, under similar pressures to reduce management costs. Increased demarcation of funding responsibilities is a particular concern for people with lower level support needs, who are not clearly the responsibility of any particular agency with no incentive for agencies to commit resources to services for which they are not statutorily accountable.

Lack of clarity and understanding about each agency's roles and responsibilities: Arblaster, Conway, Foreman and Hawtin (1996) in their research into inter-agency working to meet the care and support needs of people in ordinary housing found *'widespread lack of understanding of the aims and priorities of other agencies'* and that this resulted in false expectations of what other agencies should and could be doing. This was described by Hudson (1987) as a *'lack of a domain consensus'*. The Department of Health (1998a) concluded that *'sometimes various agencies put more effort into arguing with one another than into looking after people in need'*. Means and Smith (1994) note that *'the demarcation line between health care and social care has always been disputed territory, both in terms of institutional provision and of domiciliary services'*. The difficulty in ensuring a co-terminosity between criteria for continuing care services, covered by the NHS and community care services funded by social services departments continues (Easterbrook, 2003). Lack of agreement about roles and responsibilities links to a history of resource rivalry. An important difference to the service user is that health services are free at the point of delivery whilst eligibility for local authority welfare services can be means-tested.

Social housing managers have also been increasingly concerned that they receive the 'fall out' from this demarcation dispute between health and social services as the numbers of vulnerable people living in ordinary housing have grown. Yet *'widespread confusion exists about the role of housing management and its responsibility for social care'* (Bochel, Bochel and Page, 1999). Although the 1989 white paper underpinning the 1990 community care reforms referred to housing provision as *'a vital component of community care'* (Department of Health, 1989a) little attention was given to the role of housing in guidance. It was 1997 before practical guidance for joint working, including with housing agencies was produced (Means *et al.*, 1997). Lund and Foord (1997) found a widespread view that the contribution was limited to 'bricks and mortar'.

There have also been conflicting messages about the role of housing agencies in community care. The 1996 Housing Act and the Homelessness Act 2002 placed increased pressure on local authorities to rehouse vulnerable people with support needs. Yet there are countervailing financial pressures. Local authorities' access to additional funding for future development and to improve the properties they manage is influenced by the performance rating awarded by the Audit Commission. Performance is judged against indicators that concentrate on core business tasks – rent collection, speed with which repairs are carried out and empty properties relet and which do not adequately recognise the impact working with vulnerable people and communities can have on the difficulty of the housing management task. Housing associations as independent not-for-profit organisations have greater financial, statutory and regulatory freedom, and were encouraged by the Housing Corporation and the National Housing Federation to adopt the concept 'housing plus' (Housing Corporation, 1997) which recognises that housing services can link up with other community services to provide wider social benefits. However, housing associations are also under increasing pressure to demonstrate greater operational cost efficiency which may not fully recognise the more qualitative aspects of service provision (Freeman, 2004). These pressures combined with the increasing emphasis on a zero tolerance approach to neighbour nuisance and anti-social behaviour with enhanced powers for housing agencies to evict and exclude perpetrators from housing can undermine the longer term preventative and rehabilitative social work approach (Foord, Young and Huntington, 2004).

Organisational restructuring

Difficulties in working together were increased by the organisational restructuring affecting the agencies involved in community care during the 1990s. It can be argued that the shift to a purchaser/provider split, markets and contracts undermined co-operative working and resulted in increased demarcation.

> *'There is a potential tension and conflict between market principles, characterised by competitive pricing, formal contracts and low trust relationships and the contrasting pressures towards joint planning and joint working alongside the needs of enabling effective inter professional work through shared values, beliefs and common goals, cohesion, collaboration and morale and high trust relationships'* (Leathard, 1994).

At the strategic level, the complicated interface, including different tiers in local government, geographical boundaries and planning cycles, between health, housing and social services can result in duplication and gaps in services. At operational level, organisational restructuring hindered the building up of inter-professional networks. Change in itself can create change overload and uncertainty inhibiting the establishment of relationships with other organisations and resulting in short term rather than long term planning (Hoyes and Means, 1993). Alongside organisational restructuring there has been increased fragmentation of service provision making co-ordination more difficult. For example, the requirement that 85 per cent of the special transitional grant be purchased from the independent sector, voluntary and private sectors, has stimulated the provision of such services by independent agencies. By 1997 44 per cent of homehelp/care contact hours were provided by the independent sector compared with two per cent in 1992 (Department of Health, 1998e). The political wish to reduce the dependence of public sector housing agencies on government funding to improve existing stock and provide new homes has resulted in increased diversity of housing providers with council housing stock being transferred to specially created housing associations or managed by arms length management organisations.

Professional ideologies and values

Differences in professional practice and status, lack of agreement on terminology and cultural perceptions about different professions also create inter-agency working tensions, particularly at operational level. There has been a long history of distrust between social workers and housing workers, and health workers have not traditionally liaised well with social services or housing agencies. Health workers have tended to have a very medical, 'I know best approach' in their work with service users, whilst social workers tend to have a more 'rights based' approach, seeking to empower service users to find the right solution for themselves. Housing workers in contrast are responsible for managing 'patches' of property and use administrative guidelines on eligibility for services to guide them

(Allen, 1998). Different systems of needs assessment, differing priorities and failure or unwillingness to share information have contributed to vulnerable people slipping between agencies (Leigh, 1994).

Joined up working to meet community care and housing support needs – improved prospects?

The government's drive to improve partnership working to meet community care and housing support needs has moved from exhortation to compulsion backed by incentives and sanctions. The King's Fund (King's Fund and Banks, 2002) carried out a review of progress in implementing partnership policies and found that progress has been made. There is an increasing trend for health and care staff to work together in combined teams, recognition of the value of a whole systems approach to meeting users' needs, growing willingness to pool budgets leading to jointly commissioned services and increased working together to produce strategies and plans. Glendinning (2002) in an evaluation of the use of the 1999 Health Act flexibilities came to a similar conclusion. With regard to housing support, Supporting People has provided for the first time a clear recognition of its role, a dedicated budget and an implementation framework requiring health, local authorities and probation service together to produce a joint strategy and to jointly commission provision. This approach to improving joined up working could be seen to stem from what has been described as the rational planning approach or an optimistic model of policy-making and implementation (Challis *et al.*, 1988). In contrast an analysis of policy-making and implementation using a 'pessimistic model' would suggest that the goal of collaboration and partnership needs to be tempered with realism and an awareness that organisational and financial restructuring may not be enough to achieve effective intera-gency working. The 'pessimistic model' suggests the notion of 'organisational altruism' is naïve. Policy implementation will be influenced by the impact of individual agencies, professional power and status, structural complexity and the short term perspective of politicians, each will distort the vision of 'rational' planning'. Instead it draws upon 'exchange theory' which holds the view that organisations are self interested and will bargain, negotiate and compete for resources with power and status differentials influencing the outcome (Loxley, 1997). As Hudson (1987) notes:

> *'From an agency's viewpoint, collaborative activity raises two main difficulties: First it loses some of its freedom to act independently, when it would prefer to maintain control over its domain and affairs. Second, it must invest scarce resources and energy in developing and maintaining relationships with other organisations when the potential returns on this investment are often unclear or intangible'.*

Health, social care and housing support providers are still working in a context of financial restraint and pressures for increased cost effectiveness of service delivery. The existence of a designated fund for housing support may result in an even tighter boundary around social services care budgets, undermining the scope of Supporting People to extend low level support to more marginal groups as was originally intended. There is already concern that in some cases, services previously paid for out of health and social care budgets, such as residential homes for people with learning disabilities, have been re-designated as housing support and transferred to the Supporting People budget (SITRA, 2004). Health and social services appear reluctant to supplement Supporting People funding where support services are meeting a range of needs in addition to housing-related support (Weaver, 2004). Some agencies and/or professions may have greater power to influence the way problems and issues are perceived. The dominance of the health agenda and the proposed merger of health and care services into care trusts raises the possibility of the medical approach having greater influence on the future development of community care and support services, than the user empowerment approach of social work and housing support. With regard to the funding of housing support, the differing perceived power and professional status of social services, health, probation and housing may influence the strategy and funding decisions of the Supporting People commissioning body.

The extent to which partnership is achievable in the current fragmented framework of service delivery agencies can be questioned. Foord and Simic (2001) argued that the desire of government to move to a *'system of integrated care based on partnership'* will be more complicated than just dismantling the 'Berlin Wall' between health and social care. This implies just one divide between two big power blocks whereas the inheritance of the neo-liberal reforms of the public sector is a multiplication of public, private and voluntary agencies involved in delivery of services, each with 'different funding streams, cycles, cultures and drivers'. For example, housing associations who are major providers of housing support services are not part of the main statutory framework and are classed as the independent sector. The growth in partnership working appears to be mainly restricted to statutory health and social care agencies without involving the independent sector and other local government functions, such as housing. There is still only limited recognition of the wider contribution housing authorities and agencies can make to developing innovative new services such as extra care (Padgham and Spencer, 2003). There are also perverse incentives in the system. Performance indicators for health and social care agencies emphasise success in preventing emergency admissions and reducing delayed discharge. Lower level preventative measures do not necessarily result in quick fixes and their impact may take longer to register against performance indicator targets. Housing support providers need to collect and publicise evidence which demonstrates how their services can help to meet health and social care outcomes. Professional and organisational pressures may also impede consideration of service users' views and result in a limited notion of partnership.

Although fragmentation of service delivery can result in vulnerable people having to deal with multiple agencies and assessment procedures there may be some disadvantages from closer partnership working. Biggs (1997) suggests that closer links between professions and agencies may result in less choice for service users. At strategic level the Supporting People framework has introduced centrally based commissioning of services and a central database, known as hub services, which record information on how vulnerable people use support services, is being developed (Hill, 2004). Although the benefits of a more systematic overview of needs and available provision are to be welcomed, there is a possibility that smaller housing projects developed in response to a particular demand will find it harder to become accredited support providers, thus resulting in a loss of service diversity. At operational level, standardised forms of assessment and single entry points may result in a one size fits all approach with those whose needs do not fit into a predetermined profile finding it harder to access services. Without careful safeguards, the sharing of information could lead to labelling and thus exclusion by all the professions involved.

Loxley (1997) suggests that it is unrealistic to expect total service integration, as the growth of knowledge makes specialism necessary. Differentiation becomes an issue when divisions become self serving rather than valuing their contribution to a holistic goal shared with other divisions. To tackle this, what is required is more attention to *'frontline professional worlds and interprofessional partnerships'* (King's Fund and Banks, 2002).This is particularly the case for what have been defined as 'wicked issues', *'where the problem is hard to define, causal chains are difficult to unravel and complex inter-dependencies are involved'* – which form much of the work of frontline health, care and housing practitioners. The government has gone some way towards addressing this by removing structural barriers, through measures such as pooled funding and commissioning. In addition there is potential for care trusts to be established, bringing different professions together in a single organisation. This will encourage collaboration between agencies and the professional groupings which work within them, but as the experience of bringing housing and social workers into one directorate demonstrate, this may not resolve inter-professional tensions. In addition to developing a 'whole systems' approach, there is a need to place greater emphasis on developing the skills, knowledge, trust and supportive structures necessary for increased inter-professional understanding (Hudson, 2002). Information about the roles of different professions and agencies and opportunities for bringing different professions together for joint 'problem solving' training should form part of professional training courses and continuing professional development. Arblaster, Conway, Foreman, and Hawtin (1996) identify the key elements of effective collaboration:

- Clarify roles and relationships of all partners at strategic and operational levels (joint protocols, jointly agreed procedures for needs assessment).
- Build mutual trust (share information, make formal commitments to partnerships, ensure confidentiality).
- Develop understanding of the roles and functions of other agencies.
- Recognise mutual compatibility (i.e. recognise wide goals).
- Develop resources (recognise that more may be achieved by resource sharing).

In 2005, prospects for effective partnership working to meet housing and support needs, appears to have been enhanced by the post 1997 policy framework, and is still being developed by the government, as indicated by the recent green paper *Independence, Well-being and Choice – Our vision for the future of social care for adults in England* (Department of Health, 2005). It is important however, that partnership working is not seen as an end, rather than a means. It has to be of value to frontline staff who deal with 'the wicked issues' on a daily basis and not another 'top down' requirement.

Inevitably differential agency and professional power, vested interests and human capacity to perceive the 'whole picture' will form a powerful undertow to the 'rose tinted' rhetoric of the optimistic approach. However, programmatic changes to service delivery structures must be combined with support for the development of horizontal networks which are motivated by, and judged by their success in meeting, holistic service outcomes developed in partnership with current and prospective service users.

CHAPTER 4:
Scoping the supported housing sector – the funding and regulatory framework

Deborah Bennett

Introduction

Publicly funded housing agencies play an essential role in the provision of care and support in the community. This provision extends from schemes that provide nursing and personal care, through a range of different types of accommodation with support (hostels, shared housing, sheltered housing), to the support and assistance needed to enable people to live independently in ordinary housing.

Box 4.1: What provision is needed to enable a person with care needs to live independently in the community?

Property related services	Housing-related support	Personal care	Health care
Making a home and its amenities suitable and accessible: • Adaptations • Equipment services • Home improvement services • Community alarm services	Support to maintain a home in the community: • Setting up/maintaining a home • Developing domestic/life skills • Managing finances/ claiming benefits • Advice, advocacy, access and liaison with other services • Emotional support and counselling • Establishing social contacts and activities • Supervision and monitoring of health and well-being • Advice on provision of home improvements and repairs • Provision of community alarms • Cleaning and low level shopping as defined under transitional housing benefit	Domiciliary and day care services: • Personal care • Help with getting up, going to bed and bathing • Domestic and home care • Provision of meals • Cleaning • Laundry • Shopping • Housework	Nursing: • Administering medication/ dressings • Specialist treatment, rehabilitation and therapeutic care

Changes to the regulation, inspection, funding, and the strategic framework for housing, health and social care are fundamentally challenging the nature, delivery and financing of housing, care and support services. These changes have created uncertainty and challenges for the sector, particularly for those providing accommodation based care and support. But they have also created new opportunities for housing agencies and for users of these services. Supporting People, for example, recognises and resources the role of housing agencies in meeting the support needs of vulnerable people living in the community and breaks the tie between service users and a particular tenure or scheme. The requirements of the white paper *Valuing People* outlined the shape of future services for people with a learning disability (see chapter by David Race in this book). This has continued the long process de-institutionalising support for people with learning difficulties. Increased funding for extra care schemes has the potential to increase quality and choice for older people. These opportunities go to the heart of the approach outlined in the white paper, *Caring for People*:

> *'Community care means providing the support and services which people ... need to be able to live as independently as possible in their own homes or in "homely settings" in the community'* (Department of Health, 1989a).

As Hawtin points out in this book, many of these changes are founded in learning the lessons of past policy failures, and listening to practitioners and users. But turning opportunities into success depends on the resolution of the challenges and problems that are also part of a rapidly changing agenda. These include problems that have dogged the implementation of community care from its inception:

- the way in which funding regimes distort consumer choices;
- the tension between budgetary and cost controls and quality and choice for users;
- the tension between local governance and top down financial controls and inspectorates;
- the difficulties of achieving effective joint working;
- and partnership between housing, health and social care and the failure to recognise the contribution that housing makes to the partnership.

A significant new challenge is the pace and scale of change itself, and the uncertainty this creates and the resources it absorbs.

Aims of this chapter

This scoping chapter aims to give an outline of the sector and of the changing funding and regulatory framework. It considers the interaction of new policies and initiatives and the consequent challenges and opportunities for the housing sector and for care and support services in particular. It has three main tasks:

- Firstly, it begins with an overview of the way in which funding and regulatory change is affecting the provision of accommodation with care and support.
- Secondly, it gives a brief overview of the property related services required to enable people to stay in their own homes or 'homely' settings.
- Thirdly, it considers the opportunities and challenges posed by Supporting People and the way in which these exemplify some of the tensions in the modernisation agenda for housing, health and social care.

Accommodation based care and support

Housing associations have an established role in providing specialist accommodation for vulnerable groups including, but not exclusively, community care groups (see Box 4.2 listings of community care groups and groups considered 'vulnerable' for the purposes of Supporting People). After the 1974 Housing Act, housing associations were expected to *'complement and supplement'* the general needs provision of local authorities (Cope, 1999). Until the changes brought in by the 1988 Housing Act, capital and revenue funnelled through the Housing Corporation provided a low risk environment for housing associations wishing to establish themselves as providers of specialist accommodation and support schemes for a wide range of vulnerable groups. The expectations of the 1988 Housing Act that housing associations would become the main providers of new social housing and bring in private finance to fund expansion, led to both higher risks and higher rents and was less conducive to the development of specialist schemes. However, supported housing management grant revenue funding

Box 4.2: Community care and Supporting People categories

Community care categories	ODPM Supporting People specified groups
NHS and Community Care Act 1990 Older people People with physical and sensory disabilities People with mental health problems People with learning disabilities **DOH/DOE Circular 10/92** Drug and alcohol misuse HIV and AIDS	Older people People with physical and sensory disabilities People with mental health problems People with learning disabilities People with alcohol problems People with drug problems People with HIV and AIDS Young people leaving care Women at risk of domestic violence Refugees Teenage parents Rough sleepers Single homeless with support needs Homeless families with support needs Offenders or people at risk of offending Mentally disordered offenders Travellers

continued to give a relatively high level of surety for associations that had Housing Corporation and local authority support for development, until its replacement by the Supporting People programme in 2003.

In 2002 the National Housing Federation reported that data from Housing Corporation Regulatory Returns and Supported Housing CORE suggests housing associations provided 12,926 units of very sheltered housing, and supported housing for over 19,000 people with mental health problems or drug and alcohol problems. Over 500 of these schemes registered as residential care and/or nursing homes (Ramsden, 2002).

The figure of 500 registered care homes in the social housing sector is small relative to the size of the care home market as a whole, and is likely to diminish. In May 2003 there were 29,890 registered care homes in the UK (Laing and Buisson, 2003). *Housing Today* reported that *'In the past five years between 700 and 1,000 homes run by independent providers – charities, housing associations and private owners – have closed'* (Stothart, 2003). In the same year *Community Care Market News* reported that care home provision for elderly and physically disabled people was 13 per cent lower than when at its peak in 1996 (Laing and Buisson, 2003). Two main issues reoccur as reasons for closure, the 'burden' of standards, regulation and inspection and, more fundamentally, the under-funding of the sector. The Care Standards Act 2002 set a new regulatory framework and standards to be enforced by the National Care Standards Commission. The setting of national minimum standards and inspection and regulation to ensure these standards and other legal requirements exist to protect service users and to raise levels of care. As such, care providers concerned for the welfare and quality of life of service users should welcome them. The minimum standards of good record keeping, proper procedures, risk assessment and assessment and review of care needs can also be seen as protection for service providers, enabling them to justify decisions and evidence good practice should there be a problem or a complaint against them (Wing, 2003). But more often, the standards and the regulatory framework have been seen by private providers as a bureaucratic burden and a factor in care home closure.

A key concern has been the number of different inspections to be accommodated, with some organisations experiencing health care, social care and Best Value inspections. Government agencies have acknowledged concern about the proliferation of inspection and the need for a lighter touch that recognises good performers. There has been some rationalisation of inspection with the Commission for Social Care Inspection taking over the duties of the Social Services Inspectorate, National Care Standards Commission and the joint review team from April 2004. The new Commissioner stated her intention to,

> *'... work with providers in the public, private and voluntary sectors to develop a system that recognises good performance – possibly similar to plans for lighter touch inspections for the best performing councils'* (*Community Care*, 2003).

Other criticisms are those that are applied more broadly to performance assessment procedures; that they are more concerned with process than outcome and that they assess procedural compliance not quality (Foord, Savory and Sodhi, 2004). An anniversary review of the National Care Standards Commission reported the following care provider's criticisms: inspections inconsistent; inspections too bureaucratic; inspectors not distinguishing between standards and regulations; some standards unfair; delays in receiving inspection reports; and the inspection scoring system not reflecting quality (Leason, 2003).

More fundamental than these concerns has been the fact that financially pressed homes have simply not been able to meet the extra costs involved in meeting the new minimum standards. Whilst the case for free nursing services for those receiving continuing care was won in Scotland, personal care in England, Wales and Northern Ireland remains chargeable. The 1999 Royal Commission on Long Term Care reassembled before the Labour party conference 2003 to challenge the government for refusing to accept its recommendations for free personal care. They praised Scotland but stated: *'the situation in England, Northern Ireland and Wales, where the state supports nursing but not personal care (except on a tightly means-tested basis) is unstable and, if not dealt within the near future, will implode'*. Charges are means-tested and fees are determined locally by individual councils. Care homes are closing, or private care homes are not accepting local authority funded residents, because the fees set by local authorities, managing community care budgets, simply do not enable care homes to provide services at expected standards. A study by William Laing for the Joseph Rowntree Foundation concluded that the fees councils were *'currently willing to pay were between £75 and £85 a week below the reasonable costs of running an efficient and good quality care home'* (Joseph Rowntree Foundation, 2002). The report recognised that local authorities would not be able to fund the increase in fees necessary to make care homes viable and proposed central government grants to fund phased increases linked to improving care home standards. So great was the government's concern about care home closures that it withdrew aspects of the new space standards a few months after they came into force in 2002.

The closure of residential homes adds to existing concerns about the provision of long term care in the community. Two key factors are driving an increasing need to address long term care in the community. Firstly, the ageing population, with older people being the largest community care group and the population as a whole is becoming older with a particular increase in frail older people. Secondly, chronic care and rehabilitation is increasingly moving from hospitals into the community. The government focus on intermediate care and the introduction of fines on local authorities for delayed discharges are indicative of this drive. A possible growth area for the social housing sector is residential care for specialist client groups, for example people with mental health problems or learning difficulties that attract money from health funds for health-related care, as well as local authority monies. Some housing associations who manage a small care home as part of a mixed package of housing provision may choose to transfer their homes to larger specialist associations such as Abbeyfield or Anchor, who, because of their specialism and scale of provision may have better unit costs and may be willing to cross subsidise schemes within their portfolios of provision (Chapter 10 by Mark Foord explores the housing role in supporting frail older people). But the general direction of provision for older people appears to suggest a polarisation between the corporate residential care home sector able to operate economies of scale, and care and support received in people's own homes, either ordinary housing or reconfigured sheltered services.

The new strategic framework which encourages joint planning and commissioning, pooled budgets and flexibility across budgets has provided opportunities for housing organisations to take the lead in developing innovative approaches to housing and care in the community. In 2003 the government ring-fenced £87 million of Department of Health *Access and Systems Capacity* money for the development of extra care housing for older people to be administered in partnership with the Housing Corporation. The allocation was competitive and proposals were expected to include the reconfiguring of existing residential and sheltered provision. Extra care therefore provides an opportunity to re-provision where, for example, older residential homes are unable to meet the requirements of new care standards or sheltered accommodation has become difficult to let due inadequate facilities or unpopular locations. Extra care provides a suitable environment for meeting care needs but differs from residential care in enabling people to maintain an independent tenancy or lease.

Care and support in general needs housing

Whilst specialist provision is an essential component of the provision framework for housing and community care, a high and increasing proportion of the recipients of care and support will receive these services in houses that were built to meet the general needs of the population. During the year 2001-2002, an estimated 1.64 million clients received care services that were provided, purchased or supported by local authorities with social services responsibilities (Department of Health, 2003b). Community based services were provided to 84 per cent of these clients (1.38 million). The Department of Health describes community based services as services provided to support people living in the community or their carers, including home care, day care, meals, equipment and adaptations, direct payment and professional support.

The ability of people with care and support needs to continue living in their own home as they become frailer, and the capacity of people to move from institutional environments into a more homely environment is dependent on strategies for the provision of suitable, accessible and affordable housing in the community. This raises serious questions about whether enough housing in the community is designed to meet these needs and whether the resources and the planning and standards frameworks are available to make housing suitable and accessible for people with care and support needs. Key aspects of this provision are listed below:

- Part M Building regulations: require downstairs toilet, doors wide enough for a wheelchair, and level access threshold – but only houses built since 1999 (see the chapter by Pam Thomas and Marcus Ormerod).
- Lifetime Homes: homes that are accessible and adaptable to meet changing care needs, very limited development (only social housing built in Northern Ireland and Wales must meet Lifetime Homes standards. In Scotland the nearest equivalent is barrier-free housing).
- The provision of services that enable people to stay in their home:
  - Disabled Facilities Grants.
  - Home improvement agencies.
  - Community equipment.
  - Community alarms.

The low income levels of many people with community care needs means they are over-represented in the general needs housing provided by housing associations and local authorities, which are allocated on the basis of need rather than ability to pay. The Housing Corporation's (2003a) National Investment strategy for 2004/05-2005/06 has *'meeting the needs of a wide range of vulnerable people by continuing to fund the provision of new supported housing'* as its third key objective for the spending of social housing grant. But as the figures above show the majority of people will receive care and/or support in housing that was built to meet people's general needs. So the Housing Corporation's two key objectives: to provide new, affordable and sustainable housing in areas of economic and demographic growth and contribute to regeneration, housing market renewal and neighbourhood renewal are equally important to people in need of housing with care and support. There is concern that the priorities of the Communities Plan and the Regional Housing Boards will mean that investment plans are geared towards quantities of housing and speed of delivery with less concern given to meeting disability needs. Habinteg Housing Association (a specialist developer of housing for disabled people) has raised concerns about the lack of acceptable accessibility standards in the standard house designs for the 2003 Housing Corporation bidding round. Some households will also require housing-related support to sustain independent living in the community,

> *'Those who are vulnerable should not be left "home alone" struggling to cope with everyday tasks and demands of household management as well as their own care needs'* (Audit Commission, 1998).

The Chartered Institute of Housing's good practice guidance on housing services for people with support needs identifies two ways in which support can enable vulnerable people to live in the community: additional support to complement an existing care package and secondly, support where there is no care package in place, and without which a person's circumstances may deteriorate enough to require a care package (Edwards, 2000b). In 2003, following the introduction of the Supporting People programme, the Office of the Deputy Prime Minister estimated that the provision of housing-related support (excluding sheltered and community alarms) had increased in three years from 100,000 to more than 250,000 and that there were 100,000 units of floating support.

Supporting People

The Supporting People programme is a central government initiative, co-ordinated and administered by local authorities, to provide housing-related support for vulnerable people (see Box 4.1 and 4.2 illustrating who is vulnerable for Supporting People purposes and what type of support is provided). It will be the central plank in the contribution of housing agencies to whole systems working (see Chapter 12 by Brown, Richardson and Thompson-Ercan). Supporting People brought together funding from a number of sources including transitional housing benefit, probation accommodation grant, and supported housing management grant into a single pot. The 'pot' is in the hands of a commissioning group, consisting of representatives of the housing authority, social services, health and probation services, which will commission and monitor support services. The administering authorities review services to ascertain quality, value for money and relevance to the authority area's Supporting People strategy.

In key aspects of its operation Supporting People reflects the modernisation agenda for housing, health and social care:

- Integrated planning and funding.
- Separation of the provider and commissioning roles.
- A quality framework of inspection, regulation and performance assessment.
- Cross cutting – links to national and local priorities and strategies across housing, health, social care, social inclusion, crime and disorder and homelessness.

As a significant and strategic investment in housing-related support it has the potential to give housing a stronger position in its relationship with social care and health and to address some of the housing-related 'weak links' for care in the community. Supporting People offered the following opportunities:

- Separation of housing costs from support giving users greater potential for choice about where they want to live and genuine independence.
- Addressing the gaps in support left by the community care system that have prevented some people making a success of independent living. It addresses the little bit of help that may be missing from the community care package for some people and provides support for those who are vulnerable but not in a community care group. So it could help to address the tenancy sustainment concerns of social housing managers who sometimes feel they are the last agency left working with some of the most vulnerable and/or challenging households in the community.
- Its strategic focus should enable local authorities to plan, regulate and co-ordinate provision of housing and support in their districts ensuring it reflects assessed needs and that gaps and overlaps in provision are addressed.

But even before the programme began in April 2003 it was clear there would be difficult challenges as well as opportunities:

- Uncertainty and instability for providers and users:
  - Concern from providers that there would not be enough money to continue funding all the current commitments and this would mean costs for new schemes being met at the expense of existing schemes. In particular that it would take money from accommodation based schemes making them unviable.
  - Uncertainty about funding streams with some organisations experiencing losses because of void deflators, and expected to make savings in response to budget cuts.
- More administration – substantial increase in administrative costs for both providers and local authorities.
- Another level of inspection.
- Services being reconfigured to access Supporting People funding, and make savings in other budgets, rather than to meet users' desires and needs.

The way in which the programme was introduced exacerbated many of these concerns and left a legacy of further problems to address. The Supporting People programme was introduced following an audit of needs and existing provision by district authorities. These audits formed the basis of the shadow Supporting People strategies. They aimed to provide a comprehensive mapping of supply and demand for services in districts and set the priorities for the future. They also identified gaps in knowledge about the needs of some groups that would have to be filled in future strategies. Supporting People teams have a responsibility to inspect and review services in their districts. Continuing needs and supply analysis and the outcomes of the reviews inform Supporting People strategies that are the basis of planning and commissioning of all housing-related support services.

Despite this focus on strategy the initial allocation of funding was not at all strategic. It was based on the pattern of service provision existing at the inception of the programme. This meant Supporting People monies for long standing provision that may or may not have had a strategic relevance. It also benefited districts that had acted premptively to maximise access to support costs through transitional housing benefit and build up the Supporting People pot. But it left potential clients in districts that were not proactive without services. It has locked money into existing patterns of provision that do not necessarily fit with strategic objectives and do not offer clients the flexibility and choice that Supporting People could provide. The 're-engineering' of services required to unlock this money is proving difficult, painful and slow. It has also created long term insecurity for clients in schemes that had been costed as high as possible to maximise the transitional housing benefit pot and which are likely to be subject to cost savings as the government reins in the programme.

In October 2003, Office of the Deputy Prime Minister (2003a) announced the Supporting People allocation for 2003/04 would be £1.8 billion (£0.4 billion more than originally allocated in April). This initial allocation broadly funded the existing services in the local authorities but was almost double the original estimate for the programme. The Office of the Deputy Prime Minister announced a review of how funds were being used before funds for further years would be determined. This was triggered by both the scale of the costs, and disparities in costings for support between districts. Future allocations will be made on the basis of a distribution formula, which may help to address some of the current inequities of provision.

Supporting People and the wider framework of housing, care and support

Supporting People exemplifies the way in which provision, funding and regulation of housing, support and care services are at the centre of a difficult and dynamic relationship between central government and local government. Figure 4.1 illustrates this relationship. The figure shows an outer ring of national control which determines legislation, and policy, and the money (amount and type i.e. direct grant, borrowing, private finance) that can be spent on provision.

Figure 4.1: The strategic framework for provision of housing, care and support

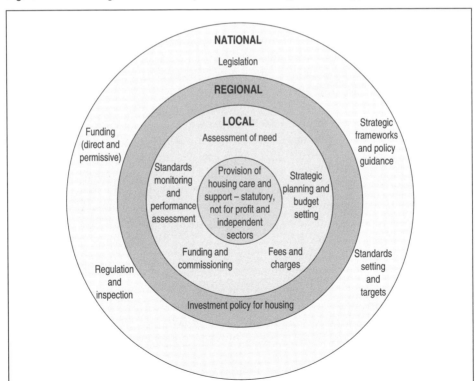

It also measures, regulates and monitors standards and performance in the implementation and delivery of services. At a local level, authorities must respond to legislative and policy requirements in a way that best addresses locally assessed need within the funding constraints set by central government. There are inevitable tensions in this framework. Those at the centre of the circles providing housing care and support must manage a complex, constantly changing set of relationships, whilst attempting to maintain continuity for their clients and financial viability for their organisation.

The devolution agenda has added a new dimension to the local/central government relationship. Most particularly it has enabled different approaches to provision, funding and regulation to be developed in Scotland, Wales, Northern Ireland and England. In Scotland, for example, the Scottish Executive followed the recommendation of the Royal Commission for free personal care, while in other parts of the UK personal care is means-tested. In England, the move towards Regional Assemblies and the development of Regional Housing Boards means that decisions for directing capital investment for housing in the localities will increasingly be made at the regional level. This has the potential for more effective management of housing markets and a move beyond the different district borders of local authorities. But there is concern that the regional agenda is primarily about meeting the needs of the Communities Plan for increasing the quantity of housing in the south and regeneration in the north. Also there is worry that the real and pressing affordable housing requirements of some districts will get lost in regional groupings that represent wide ranging investment needs. The Regional Board adds another dimension to an increasingly complex web of funding and regulation that housing providers must key into to enable them to meet housing and related needs.

Providers must make professional decisions for client services in the context of addressing national, regional and local strategic priorities, performance management expectations, structural change and uncertainty and resource constraints. In some cases these factors combine, as discussed earlier in relation to older people's housing, to make the provision that is needed impossible to achieve. This leaves those with a duty to meet the need in an untenable position. Supporting People has been subject to this effective paralysis, with housing agencies prevented from meeting identified needs for housing and support because it has not been possible to bring together the required revenue and capital funding streams from the Supporting People programme, health, the Office of the Deputy Prime Minster, the Housing Corporation and Regional Housing Boards. A recognised strategic need to reconfigure sheltered housing for older people, for example, requires the following commitments if it is to more effectively meet the needs of older people and of the strategic housing authority:

- Department of Health funding (and possible capital investment funding via Regional Housing Boards) to enable suitable sheltered schemes to be adapted to meet the needs of frail older people in an extra care environment.

- Supporting People funding for the extra care scheme.
- Increased social services funding for care packages to meet the higher care needs of residents in extra care schemes.
- Supporting People funds to expand the work of home improvement agencies, and provide community alarms and floating support for those older people remaining in or moving back into housing that no longer has a sheltered designation.
- Disabled Facilities Grants from the Office of the Deputy Prime Minster to enable older people to remain in general needs housing and additional supported capital expenditure from the Regional Hosuing Board to enable the local authority to make its 40 per cent contribution to the Disabled Facilities Grants.
- Recognition from the Regional Housing Boards and the Housing Corporation that registered social landlord approved development programme investment will need to be directed towards redevelopment of existing sheltered schemes not suitable or required for extra care provision, enabling other identified housing affordable housing need to be met.

The complexities of these changes, and the necessity of working across a range of agendas and agencies, could give housing agencies and the strategic role of the housing authority, the place they deserve in the community care agenda. But there is a serious risk that health and social services are so busy meeting the challenges of fundamental structural change themselves that housing will, again, be marginalised. The absorption of adult social care services into the Department of Health and the transfer of statutory responsibility for children's services, following the publication of *Every Child Matters*, to the Department for Education and Skills have challenged the very basis of social care as a separate service. The social care magazine – *Community Care* noted that at the 2003 Labour conference the health secretary, John Reid failed to mention social care once and the education secretary Charles Clarke made only a passing reference to *Every Child Matters*. In the same magazine the following week, Andrew Cozens the new president of the Association of Directors of Social Services stated social workers would need to *'make a pitch for social care as a mainstream service so that a future for social care in local government is assured, not absorbed by education or the NHS'*. As social care struggles to maintain its voice in the realignment of services coming out of the modernisation agenda, there is a real risk that the role of housing will be sidelined once more. If this is the case it will have serious consequences for communities and for those providing housing services and meeting housing duties, as more and more people with high care and support needs become dependent on housing in the community.

Conclusion

In this chapter I have sketched a picture of the housing and support sector in the UK; the increasing momentum towards forms of home based support; and some of the issues and challenges raised by the Supporting People programme and the modernisation agenda. Many issues I have touched upon will be revisited in greater detail in relation to specific needs and needs groups in later chapters.

CHAPTER 5:
Involving users and carers in housing and social care planning – the rhetoric of 'user empowerment'

Charlie Cooper

Introduction

Involving users in social care decision-making has been prioritised in several pieces of legislation, particularly since the NHS and Community Care Act 1990. However, it has also been suggested that *'users and carers have continued to occupy a disadvantaged position within a rhetoric of user empowerment'* (Means *et al.*, 2003, p.157), blamed in part on the absence of effective structures for involvement (Douglas, 2000). More significantly, there would appear to be a chronic tension at the heart of community care policy between two contradictory objectives – the containment of public spending and the stated aim of offering needs-led provision (Means *et al.*, 2003).

This chapter will evaluate user involvement in housing and community care in Britain. It will argue that despite the many fine statements on the need for user involvement from policy-makers and practitioners, the participation of users and carers in the planning and delivery of housing and social care has largely remained tokenistic. Moreover, despite further recent policy commitments on involving users and carers in care planning – contained in, for example, *Supporting People: Policy into Practice* (Department of Transport, Local Government and the Regions, 2001c) and the *Community Care Assessment Directions – Consultation on proposed draft Directions 2003* (Department of Health, 2003a) – it is argued here that New Labour's policy agenda will continue to fail community care service users and their carers. This is primarily because the basic societal preconditions necessary for effective participation in decision-making – that is, a social system that serves to create the circumstances whereby financially secure and informed individuals can engage equally in meaningful decision-making processes affecting their lives and well-being – have not been put in place. The chapter concludes by offering an alternative strategy for enhancing democratic decision-making in housing and community care based on the community development approach.

Background

While policy guidance subsequent to the NHS and Community Care Act 1990 states that the views of service users should be taken on board in needs assessments, the final say over what is to be offered rests with service providers who are, in turn, constrained by limited resources controlled from the centre. A pattern of, *'provider-led' policy and provision has dominated social policy, with a range of key interests including politicians, managers, academics, planners and practitioners shaping them, with service users and citizens more generally having little or no say in them'* (Beresford, 2001, p.496).

The thrust of the Conservative's community care reforms was a concern about the spiralling cost of social care provision to the public purse (Pascall, 1997). Consequently, decisions about priorities for social care would largely remain resource led:

> *'Care management systems were soon dominated by debates about which types of client should be a priority for a care package, as social services authorities sought to target scarce resources by bureaucratic means. Eligibility criteria and priority matrices abounded as devices for defining evermore narrowly the number of people likely to receive services'* (Means et al., 2003, p.55).

Moreover, as Doyal and Gough argue, all too often community care has acted as a metaphor for the unpaid care provided by women: plans based on the 'community' care of elderly infirm people, for example, even when backed up by generous local services, can condemn women carers to years of near-servitude and can inhibit the autonomy of the person being cared for (Doyal and Gough, 1991, p.308).

In reality, the community care reforms implemented under 'New Right' Conservative governments effectively individualised social care. Government policy since the NHS and Community Care Act 1990 has emphasised the targeting of those in greatest need through individualised care plans. There has been little or no emphasis on community involvement. On the contrary, the development of community care policy in the 1990s emphasised the comprehensive assessment of individuals against centrally-prescribed eligibility criteria and in competition with others for the scarce resources available – *'a process which individualises and separates people from their community context'* (Sharkey, 2000, p.11). It was a policy designed in the context of rising 'consumerism' in British society and which sought to furnish service users with 'customer care' in the form of better information about provision, rights to consultation in relation to care package needs and housing, and the right to complain, rather than seeking to empower users by redistributing power. In addition, while adequate housing provision has been recognised as a central prerequisite for independence, disabled people and social care users have largely been excluded from living in ordinary housing:

'Housing for people with health or social care needs is often distinctive (if not stigmatizing) in character and although placed geographically 'within' a community it may not necessarily be part of it. Normalization requires disabled people and community care users to have an 'ordinary' home while maximizing their ability to control decisions about their everyday life' (Hawtin and Kettle, 2000, pp.121-122).

An ordinary housing approach, however, required significant public investment in affordable social housing, domiciliary support services, aids and adaptations, Lifetime Homes, and home medical care – measures the Conservatives were hardly prepared to support. Little appears to have changed under New Labour who have continued with the Conservative's individualistic, market-led approach to welfare organising. As Baldwin suggests:

'New Labour has a philosophical ambivalence about individualism and community. Identifying the need for social justice within geographical communities or communities of need is part of New Labour rhetoric and commitment (Manifesto Commitment 137). This is the bridging that the Third Way is supposed to achieve. Targets for delivery of social care, however, are couched in individual terms' (Baldwin 2002, pp.184-185).

This ambivalence is explained by Sharkey:

'There is no mention of a community approach within the Department of Health's guidance for practitioners ... The most likely explanation of why this should be so is that community development work supports collective provision and the redistribution of power in communities and in society. This emphasis does not fit easily with the very individualised approach to users, and the competitive and consumerist objectives being advocated in official guidance' (Sharkey, 2000, p.10).

New Labour and community care

New Labour's approach to social care emphasises provision which *'supports ... independence and respects ... dignity'* (Department of Health, 1998b, section 1.8). One interpretation of this approach is a 'Third Way' in British social policy – beyond the politics established by the New Right Conservatives and 'Old' Labour, *'somewhere between the harshness and individualism of the market and the private sector on one side, and the restrictions of public ownership on the other'* (Popple and Redmond, 2000, pp.393-394). While New Labour's policies on social care include stated commitments to user involvement and equality issues (particularly through Best Value, the Supporting People programme and the *Community Care Assessment Directions – Consultation on proposed draft Directions 2003* (Department of Health, 2003a), in practice they appear to reflect greater continuity with the New Right's market philosophy. This is evidenced, for instance, in Whitehall's rejection of the Royal Commission on Long Term Care's recommendation on universal provision of free personal care (although this was accepted by the Scottish Executive), as well as the retention of internal markets and centrally-defined managerialist performance targets (with their emphasis on quantitative indicators such as number of assessments completed rather than qualitative indicators such as user satisfaction or equality issues):

> *'Government rhetoric is strong on user participation and there are outcome indicators that relate to this value. In general, however, the technicality of the Personal Social Services Performance Assessment Framework outcome regime reflects a managerialist ethos that is rationalist in its design and expectation, in much the same way as the Centre for Evidence Based Social Services at Exeter University adopts an evidence-based approach. The result is policy targets that are less SMART (specific, measurable, achievable, relevant, timed) than contradictory, reactive, unclear, disconnected and excessive'* (Baldwin, 2002, p.183).

Some commentators argue that New Labour's principles towards user involvement in social care come close to those underlying John Major's ideas on the Citizens' Charter. Charters define the standards users could expect from a service and how they could complain if these were not met. Despite doubts about the efficacy of charters, New Labour has continued to use them in the delivery of welfare provision. In respect of social care, local charters are guided by the government's *Better Care Higher Standards* document and these have subsequently been subjected to a study conducted by the Nuffield Institute for Health. The initial findings of this study found that *'charters varied widely in their content, style and approach'* (Hudson, 2001, p.1). In particular, despite the requirement to involve a wide range of interests in charter development, few managed to do this because of *'time limitations and "consultation fatigue"'* (Hudson, 2001, p.2). In short, as Baldwin suggests, firstly:

> *'... charters provide little more than 'soft' and easily manipulated targets and they have reduced local democratic accountability in favour of customer satisfaction. Second, given government failure to fund the Royal Commission's recommendations designed to improve services, local authorities are left with NHS colleagues to implement charters, but without the necessary resources'* (Baldwin, 2002, p.173).

The 2003 *Community Care Assessment Directions Consultation* – which simply states that local authorities should comply with the requirement to consult users and (if *it thinks* appropriate) any carer. This does nothing to address the issue of insufficient resources or the final decision resting ultimately with the authority. As a consequence, user involvement in social care has barely moved beyond the most basic level of influence and certainly has had no influence on resource distribution.

In his investigation of user and carer involvement in community care for older people in one local authority's social services department, Guy Daly distinguishes between participation at an individual level (for instance, over decisions about a person's own care package) and at a strategic level. He found that participation did occur at the individual user level and that older people do have some opportunities to participate at a strategic level through a service improvement group for elderly people's services, which includes lay representatives. The social services department had also set up a watchdog for community care (the Search Team) and a Carers' Unit to support carers – both with the involvement of older people. However, in general, the effectiveness of older people's involvement has been questioned. In particular, older people's involvement has been impeded by barriers erected by professionals. In his own study, Daly found a cross-section of opinion about the effectiveness of participation ranging from tokenism to a belief that participation had increased (Daly, 2001). In the case of the former, carers in particular expressed the view that professionals were reluctant to give up power. More positive views about participation were expressed by politicians, although even here the views were qualified. For instance:

'I think there has been some empowerment, though I am a bit wary about trying to quantify it … Certainly there is more consultation but … at the end of the day decisions are not taken by users and carers; they are taken by the [Social Services] Committee' (senior politician quoted in Daly, 2001, p.68)

Under the Local Government Act 2000 there is a requirement for local authorities to consult widely with service users when implementing Best Value reviews and planning for the future management of services. Local authorities are encouraged to work more corporately, in partnership with other agencies and community organisations, in identifying and meeting local needs.

'New Labour has highlighted participation, partnership and empowerment in social policy … There are now legal requirements, statutory guidance and detailed policy statements requiring and encouraging user involvement and partnership across policies. But the reality is complex and ambiguous' (Beresford, 2001, p.501).

In particular, there are fears that economy and efficiency will remain the main drivers of social policy initiatives rather than accountability or equality concerns (Baldwin, 2002). Additionally, as Douglas argues, effective user involvement in community care will not happen without *'a major change for the culture of organisations to become more user friendly, answerable, [and] independently audited'* (Douglas, 2000, p.1). This view is shared by Nolan and Caldock, who argue that assessment practice needs to involve users and carers as full partners, something that will require providers to *'shed their "professional" perspective'* and *'have an open mind and be prepared to learn'* (Nolan and Caldock, 1996, cited in Means *et al.*, 2003, p.53). Baldwin also shares this observation, arguing that the *'problem for New Labour is that it will take time to change organisations built on the power base of "technicist" professional expertise and managerial resource control'* (Baldwin, 2002, p.183).

New Labour's Supporting People programme does appear to offer prospects for changing the balance of power between users and professionals. This initiative includes specific aims to offer 'vulnerable people' the opportunity to enhance their well-being by having *'greater independence and control in making choices within their lives'* (Department of Transport, Local Government and the Regions, 2001c, p.7). The approach expected under Supporting People is 'needs-led provision' of key health, housing and community services, achieved through the establishment of prescribed 'structures' of provision. Notwithstanding the various concerns raised about the implementation of Supporting People – for instance, the likely mismatch between need and resources (Means *et al.*, 2003) – the initiative still opens up the possibility for new ways of thinking about how agencies might engage around user involvement and ways of widening equality of opportunity.

> *'The development of the [Supporting People] strategy starts with consultation with a wide range of consultative bodies and users, which should be done in a way which is inclusive of all members of the community, including Black and Minority Ethnic groups. The strategy needs to be informed by an understanding of the needs and opportunities from the user's perspective'* (Department of Transport, Local Government and the Regions, 2001c, p.14).

Ostensibly, this offers real prospects for ensuring that the support needs of culturally diverse groups are more appropriately met – a long-time concern of the Black and Minority Ethnic population for whom *'adequate and appropriate provision continues to be hampered by prejudices and stereotypes about minority ethnic communities'* (Department of Transport, Local Government and the Regions, 2002a, p.1). As Beresford argues, New Labour's approach to 'special needs' – in particular, mental health service users – is *'located within an overarching framework of "public safety", which prioritises the protection of "the public" from "service users"'* (Beresford, 2001, p.503). There has been a tendency within New Labour's welfare discourse to present service users as 'dangerous people' (see chapter by Paul Simic), with a disproportionate emphasis on:

> *'... their association with an increase in homicides following the move to 'care in the community', regardless of the contra-indications from existing evidence ... Research has highlighted the destructive effects which service users report such stigmatisation as having'* (Beresford, 2001, p.503).

Additionally, the extent to which agencies themselves have to change their stigmatising practices is illustrated by the recent inquiry into the death of David Bennett, a Jamaican diagnosed 'schizophrenic' who was killed at a 'secure' unit in Norwich after being held face down on the floor for 28 minutes by at least four mental health 'nurses'. Five years on from the McPherson report on institutional racism and almost a year on from the implementation of Supporting People, the inquiry into David's killing established that *'institutional racism is present throughout the NHS'* (cited in Carvel, 2004, p.1). This case is not an isolated incident:

'After taking evidence from leading practitioners including the government's mental health tsar, Louis Appleby, the inquiry concluded: 'The views of our witnesses were virtually unanimous. Institutional racism is present throughout the NHS' … The report quotes evidence from Kevin Gornay, professor of psychiatric nursing at King's College London, who said institutional racism in NHS mental health services was 'an element of institutional arrogance … They already saw black patients, for instance, as potential crack dealers and a source of violent incidents' (cited in Carvel, 2004, p.1).

African and Caribbean people living in Britain are ten times more likely to be diagnosed schizophrenic than white people, and more likely to be kept in locked wards (often with high doses of medication). Unsurprisingly, many black people fear contact with health services as well as other welfare organisations in Britain (Francis, 2004, p.9). This highlights the importance of user involvement in social policy to ensure that agencies transform themselves and offer genuine opportunity for enhancing equality and choice in service provision. However, such involvement has generally not been prioritised by service providers (Beresford, 2001), particularly in the case of black service users. At the time of writing, doubts about the role of Black and Minority Ethnic (BME) housing associations in British social policy have been raised again. Lupton *et al.* argue that:

'… the BME tag may not always be helpful in terms of long term strategic development and moves towards greater self-sufficiency. There is a danger of being pigeonholed and only considered in relation to work on BME issues or even in relation to a specific ethnicity, which may limit the ability to expand the business, and an attendant risk of being perceived not as successful housing associations in their own right, but as organisations requiring special assistance' (Lupton, *et al.*, 2004, p.21).

This emphasis on business-related indicators of 'success' ignores the significant contribution of BME housing associations in challenging both subjective and institutionalised racism evident throughout the social-housing movement (Harrison with Davis, 2001). As Soares argues:

'Ever since BME housing associations were set up, their reason for existence has been questioned … If it were not for these organisations, there would have been little challenge to racist and discriminatory policies and practices' (Soares, 2004, p.15).

At the same time, the Chartered Institute of Housing has conducted research examining the future viability of BME associations, which has led others to conclude that its recommendations could lead to the furtherance of a (white) business-ethic throughout the black housing association movement (see Lupton, *et al.*, 2004), diverting it away from crucial social objectives. As Francis argues, generally *'the only services that are universally popular with African-Caribbean people are those provided by black voluntary and community organisations'* because they also *'offer advocacy and social support'* for people experiencing difficulties with mainstream services. *'More systematic support for these groups is vital'* (Francis, 2004, p.9).

Specific concerns about the ability of housing agencies to respond effectively to the needs of community care users also need to be set in the wider context of housing policy reforms since the 1980s which have privileged the *'superiority of owner occupation over renting'* (Means *et al.*, 2003, p.141). The implications of such reforms for housing and community care are important in terms of, first, the increasing level of support likely to be required by disabled and elderly people owning their home (Means *et al.*, 2003) and, second, a reduction in the availability of affordable options for those reliant on non-market housing provision (Harrison with Davis, 2001), many of the latter being Black and Ethnic Minority households. These structural barriers to access raise serious doubts about the ability of Supporting People to respond effectively to needs. Indeed, as Means *et al.* put it, it would be interesting to speculate just how many people with support needs could manage in mainstream housing with the help of the Supporting People programme if only such housing *'was available, affordable and in reasonable repair'* (Means *et al.*, 2003, p.141). However, the huge decline in investment in affordable housing since 1980 has meant that, for many people, such housing is not available.

Local authority house building completions in the UK fell from 88,500 in 1980 to just 207 in 2003. Completions by housing associations (registered social landlords) have failed to match this decline – reaching a peak of just 38,500 in 1995/96 (around 8,000 more than in 1977) falling to 12,727 in 2003. In 2003, 70.8 per cent of households lived in owner occupied housing with only 10.2 per cent privately renting, 7.6 per cent living in a RSL scheme and 11.4 per cent renting from a local authority. The average property price in the UK rose from just over £20,000 in 1982, to around £160,000 outside London, and £262,000 in the capital, by 2005.

The decline in availability of affordable social housing, exacerbated by the right to buy and stock transfer, disproportionately impacts on groups who have traditionally been heavily reliant on such housing – the economically inactive (including those permanently sick or disabled, and people with caring responsibilities in the home), Bangladeshis, Black Caribbean, Black Africans, Black British, White and Black Caribbean, White and Black African, and women-headed households. Homeless households in priority need, accepted by local authorities have continued to rise over the past decade, with 9 per cent having a mental illness and 5 per cent with a physical disability (2003). There has also been a steady increase in the number of homeless acceptances living in temporary accommodation (Office for National Statistics, 2004). Alongside the decline in affordable housing has been a sustained attack on housing benefit – due largely to the significant increase in benefit being paid out (mainly due to the shift in emphasis away from capital subsidies to individual subsidies, but also in part due to the increased use of housing benefit to pay for support needs). The government's strategy for reducing the cost of benefits includes both the Supporting People initiative, which limits what support needs can be paid for from benefits, and restrictions on entitlement to benefit based on 'local reference' rents for an area and restricting the amount of space people can claim for. *'The end result has been that the concern for the public purse has far outweighed concern for low-income vulnerable people who rent'* (Means *et al.*, 2003, p.143).

From April 2004 a completely new organisation – the Commission for Social Care Inspection took charge of promoting improvement in social care in Britain, empowered under the 2003 Health and Social Care (Community Health and Standards) Act. This included responsibility for inspections, registering services, holding performance data on social care and publishing the 'star ratings' for social services. As a consequence, it continues to serve centrally prescribed performance criteria rather than allow service users and carers to *'guide [their] work'* and ensure *'genuine user involvement'* (Commission for Social Care Inspection, 2003, p.1) as the Commission for Social Care Inspection claim. Indeed, genuine involvement here entails little more than providing *'easy to understand information about the quality of social care services in their local area'* (Commission for Social Care Inspection, 2003, p.1).

All in all, therefore, it is, perhaps, not surprising that an early pathfinder inspection report by the Audit Commission highlighted *'the absence of meaningful service user involvement in the development and delivery of the [Supporting People] programme'* (Audit Commission, 2004a, p.3). In particular, refugees, Travellers and people with HIV were generally excluded from consultation on service provision.

The following sections set out how a community development based model of empowerment, might better integrate users and carers in planning housing and social care.

An alternative perspective

A major attempt to address the problem of needs-satisfaction is Doyal and Gough's thesis, *A Theory of Human Need*, in which they stress the centrality of social participation – defined in terms of the ability of individuals to engage fully in society without serious limitations being placed on what they attempt to accomplish. Citing Harris, they suggest:

> *'... an individual is 'in need' for the purposes of social policy to the extent that he [sic] lacks the resources to participate as a full member of society'* (cited in Doyal and Gough, 1991, p.52).

Clearly, there are things we need for physical survival – basic individual needs that we must realise if we are to survive and achieve other goals. However, we also need freedom and autonomy to choose the life we want, so long as this does not interfere with the choices of others. Doyal and Gough suggest this requires basic societal needs to be met whereby society ensures the social preconditions for people to achieve their individual needs. For example, in order that people can meet their basic human need for food, there is a societal need for an economic and social system that can produce and distribute sufficient food to the entire population. Furthermore, if people are to become autonomous beings, living their life to the full as they choose, there is a societal need to encourage self-development – requiring, for instance, support for child-rearing, or an education system which enables all people to learn and to develop their own capacities and capabilities to the full, or a health system that protects the physical and mental well-being of everyone. Doyal and Gough, therefore, conceptualise needs in terms of the inter-dependency between an individual's basic human needs and societal needs, thereby presenting an argument for a social system that serves to create an environment where people can compete equally together, and look after themselves and each other in ways that fairly maximise their creative potential. To achieve this environment requires opportunities for individuals to participate in key decision-making on substantive issues, including resource distribution. As Held argues:

> 'A constitution and bill of rights which enshrined the principle of autonomy would … involve not only equal rights to cast a vote, but also equal rights to enjoy the conditions for effective participation, enlightened understanding and the setting of the political agenda. Such broad 'state' rights would, in turn, entail a broad bundle of social rights linked to reproduction, childcare, health and education, as well as economic rights to ensure adequate economic and financial resources for democratic autonomy' (Cited in Doyal and Gough, 1991, pp.301-302).

Instead of trying to design a fixed formula for understanding human needs, Doyal and Gough offer an analytical framework that has scope to adapt and change in the light of evolving debate. This will require the establishment of civil and political rights to 'enable people to engage in open and rational debate and thus to improve decision-making about how to optimise need-satisfaction' (Doyal and Gough, 1991, p.225). This contrasts with classical state models of representing needs (e.g. absolute or relative definitions), which presume that all or most needs can be known and calculated by some central authority; or classic liberalism, which assumes that there is little possibility of any general knowledge of needs (other than through market allocations). Instead, Doyal and Gough's approach is analytic and educative, dynamic and open-ended, depending in part on the self-awareness of the individual. Thus, there is a societal need for a participatory, democratic system, requiring a type of institutional framework within which people can become educated and self-aware as to their needs, and be enabled to influence the policy agenda that determines how these should be met. Satisfying human needs, therefore, requires the enhancement of democracy within society and greater attention to the perspectives of service users:

'[An] appropriate and effective understanding of needs can only be obtained through informed communication between all those with relevant experience – communication which is carefully structured to optimise the rationality of its outcome. Experts constitute just one group of participants in such a debate. Here, we shall argue that central planning and democratic participation are both necessary components of social policy formation if it is to succeed in optimising need-satisfaction' (Doyal and Gough, 1991, p.297).

Doyal and Gough advocate a dual strategy on needs-satisfaction emerging from a 'rational' concept of need (founded on social research and 'expert' knowledge) and a 'consensual', open-ended notion of need (based on democratic participation). Ensuring effective user involvement in social care requires rights enshrined in law alongside effective support structures. Elsewhere, this author has argued the case for user involvement supported by community development and encouragement for active inclusion (Burden *et al.*, 2000; Cooper and Hawtin, 1998; Cooper and Hawtin, 1997). Sharkey presents a similar argument in suggesting that community care provision needs to draw on the values and practices of community work, with a (re)emphasis on encouraging *'independence, self-help, confidence-building and collective action'* rather than 'dependency' (Sharkey, 2000, p.16). An example of such a community development approach is the Normanton patch system, established in the West Yorkshire mining town in the 1980s. Social services were divided into three patches comprising around 5-6,000 people. The thrust of these patches' work was to conceptualise the needs of the local community and advocate on their behalf with other agencies – effectively, a community development model. Here, user participation was valued as a political activity rather than a passive administrative process. For instance, where statutory services were deemed inappropriate, patch workers referred back to the community on why this might have been the case and facilitated a discussion on what should be done about it. As a result of such an approach, services are often *'more immediate and comprehensive and people are maintained in the community who might otherwise be in residential care'* (Cooper, 1981, p.177). However, the patch approach was unsustainable due to resource constraints, making it too small-scale to provide a sufficient range of expertise to each community. Consequently, the local authority, Wakefield Metropolitan District Council, restructured its provision to form specialist teams.

The way practice in social policy has become cut off from radical ideas in community development is lamented by Jordan, particularly in relation to social work. He sees social work becoming increasingly focused on individualised problems and dysfunction rather than embracing communal issues and seeking to empower 'communities' (as citizens) to respond collectively:

'The management of individual care plans, purchased from commercial providers, has become the dominant model of social service. On the other hand, the problems of deprived communities have increasingly been seen in terms of the organizational management of risk, dangerousness and

correction – as issues of assessment, control and punishment. These changes privatize and familialize issues of care, and criminalize issues of poverty and insecurity. As British society has become more divided, social work practitioners have been drawn back into the administrative sphere, as assessors, managers and monitors of care, and enforcers of the law and standards of behaviour ... All these developments have pulled social workers away from the perception of themselves as brokers of the informal sphere, who humanize and particularize the public provision of welfare, and help strengthen community networks of social support, and towards the authoritative enforcement of legal rules and societal norms. The social control element in social work – as in other social services professions – becomes the dominant element in professional activity, and the enabling and preventive aspects of the work become neglected' (Jordan, 1998, pp.186-187).

In contrast, community development involves a 'bottom up', non-directive approach to solving community problems, including a critique of capitalism and representative democracy. The facilitator seeks to encourage 'communities' to understand the nature of power in society, and to unpack systems of domination (to appreciate how power works – its basis in forms of exploitation, violence, destructiveness, etc.) and, subsequently, to challenge these and transform them. Community development seeks to liberate through a style of community education which adopts an approach based on dialogue, allowing everyone to be included. The facilitator participates as an equal (a co-learner) and seeks to create 'social knowledge' and raise the consciousness of the group (or as Paulo Freire's describes it 'conscientization', see Burden *et al.*, 2000).

Given that one of the main obstacles to effective joint working in the design and delivery of housing, health and social care is inter-agency conflict *'over roles and responsibilities, and a lack of knowledge of each other's networks'* (Means *et al.*, 2003, p.152), a better conceptual understanding about the overall activities and priorities of each agency may come about through the adoption of a community development approach. Improving communication and awareness between agencies, and linking this with effective structures for the participation of users and their carers (including community development support), offers greater opportunity for achieving more appropriate needs-assessments, and housing and social care solutions.

The approach advocated here is not too dissimilar from a version of social work – *Sozialpedagoge* or social pedagogy – as practised in Europe. Social pedagogy:

'... draws on ideas of social reform, renewing society through the skill of developing a person's inherent potential ... [S]ocial pedagogy seldom targets individuals, but addresses groups of users ... [using] preventative, developmental, and educative forms of intervention with communities of users ... [S]ocial pedagogy is related to Freire's pedagogy of the oppressed' (Higham, 2001, pp.24-25).

Social pedagogy offers opportunities for developing a non-stigmatising, humanistic approach to meeting needs by placing circumstances in context and harnessing *'the creative social potential inherent in individuals'* (Lorenz cited in Higham, 2001, p.26) to transform social conditions. Applied in this way, a community development approach to Supporting People could help to mobilise collective resistance to the medical model of disability, promulgated in the interest of 'professionals', and allow the social model of disability – the disabling physical, social and cultural environment – to be exposed and confronted. A community development approach could also draw greater attention to the processes of subjective and institutional racism, discussed above, and mobilise resistance to these. Finally, a community development approach could also allow for New Labour's acceptance of 'global' economic neo-liberalism as inevitable – and the unquestionable basis upon which its social policies are to be based – to be placed under greater critical scrutiny.

Conclusions

Involving users and carers in housing and community care has, since the reforms of the 1990s, largely been tokenistic. The reason for this is because the ideology at the heart of the community care policy reforms was neo-liberal, with policy aims and objectives focused on cutting back public expenditure on social care – partly by exposing it to the discipline of the market. As a consequence, resource control has consistently been prioritised over need, and other possibilities for housing and community care, such as the empowerment of service users and their carers, have been frustrated.

Building on theories of human need and meeting these needs, this chapter has set out an alternative perspective on how users and their carers can become more genuinely empowered in the design and delivery of housing and community care provision. While this perspective only presents the broad outlines of a strategy for involvement rather than specific proposals for organisational structures and rules, this is consistent with the values of the community development approach advocated. That is, it is not intended to prescribe here a particular model of user participation but to suggest instead the necessary preconditions and values whereby more effective structures and rules for involvement can be more freely negotiated by all concerned. Only then – when the equal involvement of service users and their carers has become part of mainstream policy and practice – will we have the kind of social care policies and practices that people want.

CHAPTER 6:
Housing needs assessments: time to move on?

Bogusia Temple

Introduction

This chapter will look at the implications of lessons from recent advances in community development for traditional housing needs assessments. Whilst the focus is on minority ethnic communities the points made could equally apply to much work in housing research and in research generally.

Across legislation user need is a focus of policy. For example, the 1990 NHS and Community Care Act and the white paper it was based on, *Caring for People* (Department of Health, 1989a), identified a key component of community care to be services that responded to the needs of individuals and carers. Other policy documents include *Supporting People: Policy into Practice* (Department of Transport, Local Government and the Regions, 2001c); and *Bringing People Together: A National Strategy for Neighbourhood Renewal* (Social Exclusion Unit, 1998). The *National Strategy for Neighbourhood Renewal* committed the government to *'ensuring that communities' needs and priorities are to the fore in neighbourhood renewal and that residents of poor neighbourhoods have the tools to get involved in whatever way they want'* (Neighbourhood Renewal Unit (NRU), 2003). Indeed, one of the main reasons put forward for regeneration initiatives not having succeeded is the failure to put communities' needs and priorities to the forefront (NRU, 2003).

Looking specifically at minority ethnic communities, the Department of Transport, Local Government and the Regions guide *Reflecting the Needs and Concerns of Black and Minority Ethnic Communities in Supporting People* (DTLR, 2002a) is intended to ensure that issues of concern to such communities are included in local programmes. This document advocates needs-led service provision locally and nationally and a common approach to needs mapping. It states:

> *'In the light of national trends in population and other indicators of need, local information about the needs of Black and Minority Ethnic communities and existing services to meet those needs should be comprehensively mapped and measured'* (p.7).

It then goes on: *'Local authorities will want to involve and consult Black and Minority Ethnic users, community groups and providers in strategic planning, commissioning, and delivery of services'.*

This document is interesting in that it includes a review of lessons from existing 'needs' research and a small section on capacity building (p.45). Here the strengths of community groups are put forward and an argument made for funding such groups. Needs assessments are the order of the day and the cure for many ills.

How it's done

Practitioners wanting to carry out housing needs assessments have a number of sources to turn to for advice on how to carry them out, including Office of the Deputy Prime Minister (ODPM, 1999 and 2002a; London Research Centre and Lemos and Crane, 1998; Mathias, 2001; Harrison with Phillips, 2003; Bramley *et al.*, 1999; and Watson *et al.*, 2003). This is, of course, in addition to looking at the numerous examples of existing needs assessments. The number of needs assessments already carried out is huge and growing fast (see for example, Ahmed and Sodhi, 2000; Barrow, 1999; Bowes *et al.*, 2000; Goodby, 1998; Jones, 1994; Jones, 1998; Karn, 1999; Khan, 1997; Radia, 1996; Ratcliffe, 1996; Sodhi and Ahmed, 2001; Steele, 1999 and 2001, Tomlins, 1999 and 2002 for a small sample).

There are different ways to assess housing needs and most researchers use a combination of methods. For example, whilst recognising its drawbacks, Steele's (1999) research with older people from Black and Minority Ethnic communities in Derby used 1991 census data as contextual information. These drawbacks were seen to be: the narrow range of ethnic categories available that meant that it was impossible to identity some communities; the under-estimation of Black and Minority Ethnic populations; and the fact that the data was now old. Steele therefore also used a mixture of personal interview (survey) and focus group discussion. The study looked at a range of pre-determined topics, including satisfaction with current accommodation, knowledge and perception of sheltered housing, health, services used and needed. Such an approach is typical of many other housing needs assessments that have provided a wealth of information. Researchers are also looking within minority ethnic communities to map needs, for example, considering age, gender and generational needs (see Temple and Steele, 2004) for discussion of some of this work. For example, Ratcliffe *et al.* (2001) consider the views of young Bangladeshi men and women on social rented housing and indicate increasing interest in social housing amongst young people, unemployed people and people who are disabled/long term sick.

Many reports on the needs of different communities produce the same findings, e.g. the importance of religion, diet, and proximity to family. As discussed above, for example, the DTLR guide (2002) contains a useful overview of the needs of people from minority ethnic communities (see also Harrison with Phillips, 2003). The Chartered Institute of Housing (CIH) policy paper *Providing A Safe Haven – Housing Asylum Seekers and Refugees* (2003b) documents the range of needs that have been found as relevant for this population, including translation services for health and education, mental health issues and community care needs such as adapted housing and lack of local housing.

Given the vast amount of information now available, some researchers are beginning to question whether such assessments produce anything new. There is a concern that much of this kind of traditional needs assessment *'may sometimes soon be forgotten'* (Harrison with Phillips, 2003). Much of it is grey literature and in research terms akin to re-inventing the wheel. However, there is also a broader concern about what such assessments are in fact assessing and about the perspective being applied. Most are survey based or built on focus groups that have had the agenda set by the researchers and their funding bodies.

Whose needs are they looking at? It could be argued that they are more focused on assessing what housing service providers think is important to look at rather than what people from minority communities consider relevant. The question is therefore whose needs they are assessing and what the point of the exercise is. In this vein, the CIH has been accused of using minority ethnic communities as 'cannon fodder' and it has been claimed that relentless research on Black and Minority Ethnic communities is of 'no help to anyone' (*Property People*, 2003). It is charged with *'writing the script and calling us (Black and Minority Ethnic housing sector) to act it'* (*Property People*, 2003). The point here is that different people may have different perspectives on who should be included in needs assessments and who should do them.

Another example of the problematic nature of the way communities are assessed can be seen by looking at the CIH policy paper *Providing a Safe Haven – Housing Asylum Seekers and Refugees* (2003). The choice of the word 'assimilation' as a way of describing the way refugees and people seeking asylum should relate to others is unfortunate in a document that otherwise is a valuable addition to debate. 'Assimilation' has connotations of a one sided relationship and signals an approach that has long since been challenged in mainstream social sciences. It has been dropped as a term in work with minority ethnic communities generally, including refugee communities, as it is premised on a one directional process of influence: the minority community loses its identity within the 'host' society. Looking at needs within this framework raises the question of how we can allow in any perspective other than that of service providers/'host' society since it is built in from the outset that people from minority ethnic communities have no influence on the agenda as they are to be 'assimilated'. Although there is some debate about whether the word 'integration' is assimilation by another name, at least the premise that minority ethnic communities have some influence on other communities has been accepted in theory, if not in practice. The authors of

Mapping the Field (Castles *et al.*, 2002) have pointed out that there is no research with refugees that involves their active participation in the identification of the agenda even in relation to integration. This review relates to refugees and asylum seekers in the UK and the authors comment that: *'It is striking that we were not able to identify any UK-based research that focuses specifically on asylum seekers/refugees' attitudes towards integration and/or their vision about what constitutes 'successful' integration'* (p.158).

In relation to this they also stress lack of participatory/social action research (p.179) and a lack of research that focuses on the process of building bridges between refugees and the established communities (p.191). It seems that the agenda is not led by the needs of those involved. Since *Mapping the Field* there has been an explosion of interest in 'user views' across health, social care and housing research with refugee communities. Recent research with refugees has in many ways been at the forefront of attempts to meaningfully engage service users in service development. For example, The Housing Associations' Charitable Trust's (HACT) Community Toolkit project aims to foster understanding between new refugee groups and long term resident or 'host' communities and the HACT report entitled *Between NASS and a hard place* (Carter and El-Hassan, 2003) demonstrates the value of trying to reduce the barriers to involving refugees in research. In a similar vein, the website of the Information Centre About Asylum And Refugees (ICAR) collects details of projects using approaches designed to be inclusive.

Research by Temple *et al.* (2005) and again by HACT has also begun to address the lack of involvement of refugees in defining integration and community cohesion noted by Castles *et al.* (2002) above. However, much research on housing needs still follows the traditional route of 'using' skills that people bring to the research, such as interpretation skills, with the reins on the research still tightly held by the academics/service providers. This kind of research perpetuates the view that users can only be 'used' in certain aspects of research. Moreover, active participation in needs assessments is resource intensive. As Charlie Cooper (in this volume) points out, for effective participation in decision-making people have to be financially secure and informed. Many needs assessments 'involve' people for very short periods of time as 'community researchers' to carry out surveys or run focus groups. It is questionable whether this is real involvement or convenient cheap labour (see Temple and Steele, 2004) for a discussion of some of the issues of employing community researchers, including the thorny question of who they represent. It is rare to find a project where active participation has been funded from the outset, from putting a research proposal together through to writing the report.

The format of outcomes such as reports expected by funders and publishers also discourage active participation by users. There are, therefore, some concerns expressed within communities and by academics about the extent to which traditional housing needs assessments are provider driven with communities treated as research fodder. People within these communities are seen as lacking resources that have to be provided. Their strengths and capabilities are rarely acknowledged. There is now a move away from such a deficit model of service provider needs assessments towards more community driven community development/capacity building research (see below). In the meantime, good practice guidance on needs assessments continues to grow, often with no input from communities other than as 'subjects' of research. This is particularly prevalent in the field of community cohesion and integration research (Temple *et al.*, 2005). Part of the problem may be due to the fact that health, social care and housing research literature are still separate domains for many researchers. The lessons learnt in social care research about user participation are rarely, for example, acknowledged in housing needs assessments. Yet the value of the work of people like Croft and Beresford (1992) researching with users rather than on them is not limited to concerns with housing.

Moving on

There has therefore been a growing literature on methodological issues in current needs assessments with minority ethnic communities (see for example, Temple and Chahal, 2002; Harrison with Phillips, 2003). I do not want to rehearse those debates in this chapter but to focus on the general limitations of existing needs assessments in terms of community development. Other limitations include a focus on expressed need and on existing service users. Recent research, for example with people with learning disabilities, older people and refugees and people seeking asylum, has moved on from needs assessment snapshots to talk about active participation and empowerment in capacity development over time. This kind of approach is in part a reaction to researchers being 'parachuted in' (Jan-Khan, 2003) to communities with little knowledge of their histories, politics or issues.

A participatory model of community development, rather than a passive recipient model of needs assessment with limited user involvement, actively engages people in communities over time in service development. It helps to avoid portraying communities in negative terms that deny that they have skills that can be used to produce sustainable growth rather than constant injections of help (see Smith, 1994 on the way needs assessments make older people supplicant). At its best, it helps people build on their skills to become active within communities themselves (See Moran and Butler, 2001; Nichter, 1984; Barr *et al.*, 1997; Barnes and Walker, 1996).

One version of this participatory approach to community development is Kretzmann and McKnight's (1993) *Building Communities from the Inside Out*. They argue against a 'needs-driven dead end' which leads to a deepening cycle of dependence and is the result of a service provider led agenda (see also Subhra and Chauhan (1999) and Schwabenland (2002) on the passive recipient model perspective of needs assessments:

'Because the needs-based strategy can guarantee only survival, and can never lead to serious change or community development, this orientation must be regarded as one of the major causes of the sense of hopelessness that pervades discussions about the future of low income neighbourhoods. From the street corner to the White House, if maintenance and survival are the best we can provide, what sense can it make to invest in the future?' (1993, p.5).

Kretzmann and McKnight argue for a model of engaging communities that they call 'capacity-focused development'. The focus, they believe, must move from clients to citizens and from needs to capabilities, skills and assets of people. As McKnight (2003) points out, communities are built by focusing on capabilities not deficits of need and we should *'ignore individual needs'*. This position is very relevant to housing needs assessments, particularly with minority ethnic communities where the skills of people within communities are ignored. However, there are some issues about this kind of total rejection of the analysis of needs. There is some danger of throwing out the baby with the bath water and dismissing all evidence of discrimination and disadvantage. For example, it would be difficult to argue that we can build cohesive communities with refugees and people seeking asylum without addressing their physical, emotional and social requirements at both the individual and social levels. Ignoring these kinds of needs is akin to telling people to build on their capabilities without any resources to do so when many service providers and policy-makers have defined their capabilities as not relevant. For example, for people who speak more than one language these cross-language skills are rarely valued or rewarded even when they are employed as *'cultural brokers'* (Temple, 2002). For people who do not speak English, access to language support must be made available as simply defining their knowledge of their communities as an asset will not address the fact that lack of English proficiency may be a barrier to access to services and to employment. However, the point about moving from a totally needs-based involvement model towards a participation and capabilities based model of assessment is important. A participation model of community development should therefore value capability but also acknowledge power bases and exclusion.

All the alternatives to the parachute model of needs assessments have a common strand in that they make community development a central feature. Tandon (2002) puts it well when he states that empowerment means *'simultaneously learning and organising'* (p.37). The examples given in Boxes 6.1 and 6.2 of community development as part of needs assessment illustrate the different ways in which the approach has been developed. The Wakefield Project (Box 6.2) involves the employment of a development worker supported by an advisory group. The RAPAR Project (Box 6.1) goes much further along the route towards participation in that it has a team of development workers, six of whom are either asylum seekers with work permission, people with exceptional leave to remain or foreign nationals with the right to work. Both projects involve longer term commitments to communities and funding that identifies community development as central to the projects.

Box 6.1: Salford Refugee and Asylum Seekers Participatory Action Research Project (RAPAR)

RAPAR was set up in the spring of 2002, in response to the forced dispersal over the last 18 months of upwards of 12,000 asylum seeking people from 63 countries into Salford. The project is funded by Single Regeneration Budget Five. With the core aim of developing evidence about needs and action in services with asylum seekers, refugees, the indigenous communities and service providers, Salford RAPAR has a community development team of 4.5 whole time equivalents. Six of the workers are either asylum seekers with work permission, people with exceptional leave to remain or foreign nationals with the right to work.

The project focuses on refugees' and asylum seekers' perspectives. Methods used include documentary evidence, focus groups, interviews, questionnaires, observation and consultation events. The issues that it is prioritising within its research programme are those that refugees and asylum seekers bring to it. Examples of good practice include the production of a video as part of a training package developed with asylum seekers and a summer play scheme and a Saturday school. Parents are gradually taking the lead in organising and delivering the Saturday school. An example of good practice particularly relevant to this chapter is the process used to evolve a response to eviction into destitution. This included developing and delivering a learning event where representatives from over 20 agencies came together with people from different communities seeking asylum and a family directly threatened by eviction into destitution. The aim was to identify communication gaps and to develop pathways that would enable agencies to better serve the needs of families directly affected. The impact of this opportunity is continually being evaluated with all the parties involved.

Contact details: Salford RAPAR Project, Pendleton House, Broughton Road, Pendleton, Salford, M6 6AP. Tel: 0161-743-0861 Fax: 0161-743-0863

Box 6.2: Wakefield Refugee Interaction Project

The underlying principles of the project set up by Wakefield Metropolitan District Council are:
- To provide support tailored to individual needs.
- To encourage independence and self-help.
- To encourage integration into the community.
- To encourage the development of refugee communities.

The Project has five main elements:
1. Community development.
2. Access to employment.
3. Health.
4. Housing.
5. Education.

These elements feed into each other. For example, some of the key tasks in the housing element are to provide basic life skills support where necessary including help with budgeting and paying bills and to make introductions to community and tenants' and residents' groups. Refugees are encouraged to be independent and support is gradually withdrawn as skills develop.

→

The community development element involves a refugee community development worker funded by the European Refugee Fund who:
- Encourages the development of refugee community organisations.
- Works with existing community and voluntary groups to encourage the development of services for refugees.
- Develops opportunities for refugees to participate with other local people in social and cultural events and activities.

The development worker is helping to set up the district's first independent refugee community organisation: Rasa Advocacy Project. Rasa is supported by an advisory group of local organisations including the Citizens Advice Bureau, the Wakefield District Asylum Team, Refugee Action, Wakefield Asian Community Forum and St. Georges Community Centre. The main aim is to make sure refugees' and asylum seekers' voices are heard. This is done through peer support, and everyone involved develops skills and confidence. The support varies from helping someone to talk to a housing officer or a doctor, to getting involved in the district's Racial Harassment Partnership, for example. With Positive Action Training in Housing Yorkshire Ltd (PATH) the project is providing training placements that improve refugees' employment prospects.

Contact Details: Community development worker: 01924-304268
Rasa Advocacy Project: 01924-368855

In comparison, the housing needs literature is still very much focused on a service led needs assessment model with limited 'involvement' of users and little recognition of capabilities (for example, Karn *et al.*, 1999; Goodby, 1998; and Radia, 1996). Many housing needs assessments have not included the perspectives of service users, or non-service users, at all in the process of assessing needs, let alone helped them to use the research process for community development. The development of participatory methods of research and work with community researchers in capacity building comes with its own set of issues, not least of which is the question of representation already discussed above (see Forrest and Kearns 1999; Temple, 2003 in relation to community researchers). If a service provider wants to move from a totally needs based model of service provision to one that acknowledges a more positive view of communities, the kind of information collected may have to change and there is also the question of who within the communities they are going to work with.

Other issues include: Whom does the community researcher represent within their community? What is their position in the organisation they are employed in and do they represent the organisation or the community? There is a danger in arguing that only particular researchers can carry out research with people from minority ethnic communities. Twine (2000) argues persuasively that race (or ethnicity) is not the only significant marker of difference or similarity. For service providers the issue becomes the thorny question of who can work with minority ethnic communities to either assess needs or build capacity in the long term. Following the 'only people from minority ethnic communities can do research with people from minority ethnic communities' line to its logical conclusion would mean that other characteristics such as gender, age, sexuality, generation, political orientation, class would also have to be matched. As Twine points out, insider status also produces 'different' information from outsider status rather than better information. Being different may stimulate discussion and it would be a shame if we could only do research with people like us. None of this should, however, be taken to mean that researchers should carry out research 'on' minority ethnic communities. I am instead arguing for dialogue across difference on a more equal footing, something that traditional needs assessments do not allow with their emphasis on deficiency.

Concerns have also begun to surface about how people from minority communities can work with service providers on a more equal footing given their lack of training in either needs assessments or capacity building. The level of training that is given to community researchers is often extremely brief, underestimates the skills involved in research, and may leave the researcher ill equipped to do anything other than the specific task at hand. It would almost certainly not give them the tools to challenge the process. This is not what community development aims to achieve (see Campbell, 2002 for a discussion of issues of validity). However, there is no doubt that it can help communities to 'own' the findings and has much to offer housing needs assessments.

Discussion

Much useful work has been done on the housing needs of minority ethnic communities. For example, it is increasingly being accepted that existing service provision is inappropriate for some communities and that there are ways of making services more culturally appropriate. However, it is now time to move on and to build upon what has been done to date by recognising that constantly carrying out needs assessments is unlikely to break the cycle of dependency and to position people from minority ethnic communities as anything other than a drain on resources. There is an issue also about the result of the constant drive to 'BME' housing needs assessments policies that assumes that ethnicity is the sole or main determinant of need (see Maginn, 2004 and Baumann, 1996 on the pitfalls of reducing everything to the influence of ethnicity and Temple and Steele, 2004 on the effects of dividing populations into 'white' and 'BME'). Moreover, policies such as those aimed at community cohesion may work against the provision of services according to ethnicity. What do housing service providers do with needs assessments that indicate that people want separate housing with people who speak their language in areas where there are facilities for their cultural needs at a time when government policy is urging integration and cohesion of communities? Forrest and Kearns (1999) point out that:

> 'There is also a tension between those who seek diversity and difference as the essential ingredients of a vibrant community, and a view of cohesion and community which emphasises similarities of life stage, attitudes and circumstances' (p.13).

Perhaps one of the most important advantages of a wider community development based model of service provision is that it is intended to allow a more open debate about what it is feasible or desirable to provide than a standard one way collection of information 'from' communities. Ultimately acknowledging that final decisions take on board community views but are not totally determined by the needs of any one community is more productive in terms of relationships between service providers and communities since it allows, in theory, for the process of decision-making to be made more transparent. It also acknowledges that there are questions about who represents communities, as communities are not undifferentiated wholes. Carrying out endless surveys of need according to ethnicity or race does not move us on to even begin to tackle how services are provided across communities.

There is one important issue that has not been discussed so far and that is the resources that a capacity building model of service provision takes. It is far cheaper to carry out a quick needs assessment by buying in a consultant to do a survey. Training a community development worker or a few workers and resourcing the posts long term is much more expensive in the short term. Assessing the skills in communities and training community members to become active requires resourcing. Relying solely on volunteers for such long term and demanding work sends out the wrong message – we think it is worth doing only if we don't have to pay for it. Funders of these kinds of capacity building programmes would also have to broaden their definitions of what counts as evidence of need and potential for development. The sort of information now used to develop services would have to be expanded to include qualitative data on experiences of service use, for example, and a mapping of what communities regard as important for building up community skills. The examples of good practice given in Boxes 6.1 and 6.2 show the potential for housing providers of taking on board some of the developments in approaches to community development spelt out in this chapter.

PART TWO

Housing, care and support – key user groups

CHAPTER 7:
Learning disability, housing and community care

David Race

Introduction – far from ordinary housing

In what was then described as the first *'group home for the mentally handicapped'*, a purpose built establishment with twelve 'beds', new carpeting was laid down, ready for the opening in 1973. The carpet was made of a material whose only other current use was in the transit lounge at Heathrow airport, walked on by thousands of people daily, (Race and Race, 1979). The mindset that made this unremarkable is symbolic of the relationship between learning disability and housing that has existed for well over a hundred and fifty years, and illustrates in miniature the issues raised by this chapter. These issues hinge on assumptions about 'learning disability' and the 'ordinary things of life. A roof over one's head, some say in how others are invited to live under that roof, and the expression of a view about the design and location of that building, is regarded by many people as at least a basic human need, by some a basic human right (Turning Point, 2003). Yet how people come to be viewed as 'needing' something significantly different to the rest of the population, and therefore as being themselves significantly (and usually negatively) different to their fellow human beings is no better exemplified than in the story of housing and learning disability. Our opening illustration, from 30 years ago, is also relevant, in that it will be argued that the historical legacy from three-quarters of a century before even that so-called 'breakthrough' still has a major bearing on what goes on in housing and learning disability today.

The themes to be interwoven in the chapter start with that historical legacy, in particular the period since the Industrial Revolution, especially the development of large institutions and the assumptions behind the perceived need for them. Second, the growth and power of a critical analysis of that legacy via what was known as the principle of *normalization*, Wolfensberger (1972), Flynn and Lemay (1999), which then had a number of developments and/or offshoots, most notably the theory of *Social Role Valorization*, Wolfensberger (1998), Race (1999a), and the work of O'Brien, especially around so-called 'person-centred' approaches, O'Brien and Lyle (1986). The third theme examines the origins and effects of 'community care,' and the relation of ideas from learning disability to the policy. Fourth, a similar question as to whether the slightly later development of advocacy, empowerment, and the 'voice of the service user' drew on ideas from the notion of 'citizen advocacy' in the learning disability field, Wolfensberger (1973), Race (2003), or were merely part of the developing consumerism in the world of services that followed its wider manifestation in the Thatcher years (Hutton, 1996). The emphasis on 'advocacy' and 'rights' in the government white paper *Valuing People: A strategy for Learning Disability for the 21st Century*, (Department of Health, 2001c) and the objectives of that white paper concerning housing will be highlighted here. Concluding remarks will then draw these themes together, with reference to the possible effects of the *Care Standards Act 2000* and *Supporting People* as contemporary examples of the thesis of the chapter.

The historical legacy – still 'special people with special needs'

In two separate presentations, as yet unpublished, Wolfensberger powerfully puts the view that, as revealed both by the number of words in all the world language groups to describe 'stupidity,' (Wolfensberger, 2000) and the way human services have developed (Wolfensberger, 1996), pre-industrial societies had a clear understanding of the reality of intellectual impairment, and a clear response to it. This was, crudely, that such people lacked judgement, were slow to learn, and thus needed to be 'looked out for,' but did not need to be 'put away'. Societal views on the two points mentioned above, namely a clear understanding of who were the 'idiots' and what was an appropriate response of society to them, were then changed dramatically in the second half of the nineteenth century. The legacy of such changes is still with us, and goes some way to explain why even as recent a document as *Valuing People*, with its claims to be a *'strategy for the twenty-first century'* will not commit itself unequivocally to the position that people's housing needs are best met in houses. Williams (2002), quoting Wolfensberger (1975), notes the irony of the fact that:

> *'... recent concepts have come full circle from those held in the mid-nineteenth century. Samuel Howe, an American pioneer of services for disabled people, was invited to open a new residence for blind people in 1866. He used the opportunity to criticise the establishment of large institutions. He said that the only buildings that should be specially built are "school rooms, recreation rooms, recitation rooms, music rooms and workshops; and these should be in or near the centre of a dense population. For other purposes, ordinary houses would suffice"'* (Williams, 2002, p.55).

In contrast, the next 50 years saw the 'eugenic alarm' period. Its influence was so massive that it really requires more detail than can be given here. Three recent news stories reveal the reach of eugenic ideas. In the first, (*The Guardian*, 2003b) the National Institute for Clinical Excellence has given its seal of approval for automatic screening of all pregnant women for Down's syndrome, whilst at the same time reducing other antenatal checks. In the second, (*The Guardian*, 2003d) a curate is bringing a case against the police for not prosecuting doctors who aborted a child, at 24 weeks and therefore only allowed to be aborted on the ground of 'severe disability.' The child had a cleft palate. Third, (*The Guardian*, 2003c) a debate has just taken place in the media over claims by a respected academic that the reason African nations are poorer than western ones is their 'inherited lower IQ,' reportedly averaging 70. I have described the 'eugenic' period elsewhere as follows:

> *'As well as being marked out by the developing school system as of limited academic ability, the group of people at the bottom of the fully developed and powerful class system of the late Victorian era were also subject to increasingly moral approbation from society ... Prior to the last decade of the nineteenth century, the group who became known as the 'feebleminded' had scarcely been thought of as a distinct category of people. Those who now fell into that category had previously been described in various ways as "lazy," "feckless," "idle," "wicked," "sturdy beggars," and so on, Thane (1982). Now, the growing impact of Darwinism on the study of human beings ... increasingly saw the behaviour of such people as evidence of an inherent defect of mind, or "feeblemindedness," that could be put alongside the centuries old common understanding of the identity of "natural fools"'*
> (Race 2002a, p.27).

Such was the force of the eugenicists that a Royal Commission, set up in 1904 to make recommendations as to the 'care of the feebleminded' soon requested that its remit be extended to cover all forms of mental disorder, including 'idiots' and 'lunatics.' Their report, in 1908, was essentially the start of the process that would end with the 1913 Mental Deficiency Act, and embody in law the classification, that was to last nearly 50 years, of people into groups labelled 'Idiots,' 'imbeciles,' 'feebleminded persons' and, most controversially, 'moral defectives'. The last group, the 'moral defectives' were defined by the act as persons who *'from an early age display some permanent mental defect coupled with strong vicious or criminal propensities on which punishment has had little or no effect,'* and such a definition was to lead to the institutionalisation of many people whose only 'defect' was getting pregnant, if female, or getting drunk and fighting in a pub, if male.

The act then went on to set up the policy of segregation, quickly building or converting what one of its chief proponents described as *'suitable industrial and farm colonies'* (Tredgold, 1909, p.7). Once Binet, in Paris, added the prospect of a standardised instrument to measure something called 'intelligence' the building blocks of the legacy were in place. To quote again from my own account, and remembering the three recent manifestations of the issue, we see the picture that is still with us:

'... the idea of an inherited intellectual ability, which is unaltered by training or education, and in fact determines one's response to education or training, was not new at the turn of the century, but was somewhat in a minority. The combination, however, of genetic 'findings' on the inheritability of many characteristics, beyond physiological ones such as eye colour, and the arrival of a supposedly 'scientific measure' of intelligence persuaded many in academic circles of the invariance of this "inherent ability"' (Race, 2002a, p28).

Acceptance of these two key assumptions, therefore, namely the idea of a degeneracy of society caused by inherited defect, and the idea of an intellectual hierarchy measured 'scientifically' by IQ, were powerfully reinforced in practice for the next 30 years by the development and extension of the institutions known as 'colonies.' Their effects were then compounded by the legal and administrative processes of the post war welfare state regarding education and health. In education, the 1944 Education Act deemed those with an IQ below 70 as 'uneducable.' In health, the 'colonies' that had burgeoned in the 1920s and 1930s as local authority concerns were handed over to the new National Health Service, with the corresponding credibility for staff of now being called 'nurses' 'consultants' 'clinical psychologists' etc., and the training, qualification (and salaries) that went with this new professional status. The historical legacy was thus complete, no better exemplified than in the categorisations of the 1959 Mental Health Act, ironically deemed by some to be the beginnings of 'community care.' In that act, the definitions that replaced 'mental deficiency,' namely two levels of 'subnormality', refer in both cases to people as 'patients', and talk about the degree of 'medical or other treatment' to which they might respond as being the determinant of a person's classification as 'mentally subnormal'.

What has this to do with housing? The answer is that the deeply embedded assumptions of this historical legacy ensured that, even by the time a critique of them (our next theme) had combined with various 'hospital scandals' to produce a relatively radical white paper, *Better Services for the Mentally Handicapped* (Department of Health and Social Security, 1971), the contemporary picture of residential *services* for people with learning difficulties was effectively 'hospital or own home.' In addition, because in reality who was, or was not, admitted to hospital, was extremely arbitrary, the make-up of the populations of those two places of residence were far from distinct. So of two people, say with Down's syndrome, with pretty similar backgrounds and, as far as could be measured, pretty similar intellectual abilities, one could be living in an ordinary house (though almost always with parents); with their own room, possibly interacting with neighbours and possibly being trained for some sort of basic employment. The other, by contrast, could be living in a ward of 30 to 40 people, with a person-sized space between their bed and the next, in a hospital many miles from neighbours, and subject to a highly variable range of 'treatment' (for example Morris, 1969; Barron, 1996; Ryan and Thomas, 1987).

Reaction to the historical legacy – a small voice getting louder

The previous section has deliberately dwelt at some length on the historical legacy, to emphasise that its effects still permeate learning disability services, in particular housing provision, despite what are claimed to be great advances in the years since the 1971 white paper. That there have been some advances is undeniable, and the final two themes will attempt a critical examination of them. Before that, however, it is important to look at the critical analysis that formed the basis of reaction to the historical legacy, both to explain the impetus for the other themes, but also to use that analysis as an arbiter of those changes, and thus support the critical stance of this chapter.

There is always a temptation to talk as if major social and intellectual change was settled by (intellectual) 'mortal combat'. Reading personal accounts of what actually happened, by people who were there, for example Wolfensberger (1999), what strikes one as amazing is the relative size and fragility of the 'force' for change. The acknowledged fact of the great influence of a small group of people, who began to formulate ideas around what became known as 'normalization' in the 1960s and 1970s, could be interpreted as revealing the power of the ideas themselves. Certainly the controversies over their interpretation suggest a core of truth that people can wrestle with at length, see for example, Flynn and Lemay (1999), Race (1999b). Others, however, for example Emerson (1992) put the 'success' of the normalization movement down to its timing, and cites the radicalism of the 1960s as being fertile ground for challenges to many institutions, both physical and social. Certainly, significant differences between countries in their application of normalization (and its successor, *Social Role Valorization* (SRV)) lend themselves more to a politically nuanced interpretation of cause and effect than the somewhat simplistic assertions of the dominance of any particular set of ideas, or any particular person, Flynn and Lemay (1999).

Space does not permit a full exposition of the ideas of either normalization or SRV, for which Wolfensberger (1972, 1998) and Race (1999a, 2002b, 2003) are suitable sources. This is unfortunate, because accounts of the ideas, especially as they relate to housing and learning disability, have often been superficial, sometimes misleadingly so. 'Normalization' received its first published definition in a document that was to become immensely important in the small circle of academics and policy-makers involved in learning disability in the late 1960s. This was *Changing Patterns in Residential Services for the Mentally Retarded* (Kugel and Wolfensberger, 1969), from an original report for the President's Commission on Mental Retardation in the USA. Initially set up as a relatively esoteric and academic account of 'leading edge' services in the 'Western world' the report produced a substantive critique of the institutions, and a radical alternative in terms of comprehensive services based around ordinary houses within communities. This was the meaning specific to housing within the broader definition given by Nirje in that document (p.181), namely *'making available to the mentally retarded patterns and conditions of everyday life which are as close as possible to the norms and patterns of the mainstream of society'*. By that time Wolfensberger (in conjunction with a parents' organisation in Eastern Nebraska) had set up what was to become a world model of service in a project known as ENCOR, Wolfensberger and Menolascino (1970a, 1970b) whose residential element was based on ordinary houses, even for the most severely impaired.

As one of the authors of the *New Patterns* document, Jack Tizard, an English psychologist, had himself been doing influential research on residential care for children with learning difficulties (see Tizard, 1964), and was used by the government as one of their few non-medical policy advisors. The fact that the 1971 white paper recommended a 50 per cent reduction in hospital places suggests some degree of acceptance of the critical analysis by the Department of Health and Social Security. The fact that no clear suggestions appear in the white paper as to the type of accommodation to be provided as an *alternative* to the hospitals, however, also suggests that the extension of the analysis to propose ordinary housing had not been as well received. Indeed, advice from the Department of Health and Social Security on the building of 'hostels' (Dalgleish, 1983), taken up with alacrity by the new social services departments in the capital rich days of the early 1970s, suggests that the detailed lessons of the normalization analysis had not been learnt, despite a fuller exposition of the ideas of Wolfensberger.

Put crudely, normalization analysed the devastating and dehumanising effect of groups of people being put into a series of 'historic deviancy roles' such as 'eternal child', 'menace', or 'sub-human.' When such roles are reinforced by the symbolic messages of the physical settings (segregated and isolated institutions reinforcing the 'menace' role); the groupings of people (children and adults in the same setting reinforcing the 'child' role); the activities provided for or demanded of people (herding together of people for mass 'washing down' reinforcing the 'sub-human' or 'animal' role); the personal presentation of people (child-like clothes and hairdressing for adults reinforcing the 'child' role); and language and other general imagery surrounding people (derivations of clinical labels as being 'identity defining', such as 'retards', reinforcing both the 'sick' and the 'sub-human' roles) then the roles become powerfully and negatively life-defining.

Living in an ordinary house in an ordinary street, again somewhat crudely, can be one of a number of key strategies to address these negative effects. This is partly in terms of the perceptions of others, in that many of the negative roles come from ignorance of the group concerned, and negative images generated by the physical settings in which they have been placed, which can be challenged by people being seen in ordinary physical settings and being part of communities. It is also important in terms of the development of the individuals themselves however, since exposure to the normative competences demanded of a domestic setting increases the chances of learning to cope in that setting. Put even more crudely, if you are not in a community you cannot learn how to live in one.

The theme of 'integration', however, which was present from the beginning in normalization and has carried through to current versions of SRV, never confined itself simply to physical integration, to just 'being there.' 'Social Integration', expressed more fully later as 'valued social participation' has also always been a key element. John O'Brien, a key figure in the UK interpretation of these ideas, was later to develop his own formulation of what the 'five accomplishments' of services should be (O'Brien and Lyle, 1986). Two of these, 'community presence' and 'community participation,' are obviously indicative of ordinary living arrangements, but the others also point in that direction. 'Growing in competence' parallels the SRV emphasis on the developmental potential inherent in ordinary living, whilst 'growing in respect' addresses the perceptions of others being affected by proximity and participation. Both perceptions and competence are also involved in the fifth of O'Brien's accomplishments, 'growing in relationships.' In fact, the overall structure of his picture of quality services being about the three way interaction of people and their families, services, and communities points to an ordinary housing solution as offering the greatest prospects for success in this process.

Despite these obvious implications of normalization and SRV as far as housing is concerned, performance has been less consistent. In exploring the next theme, the development of 'community care', it is argued that the combination of the historical legacy and professional and national politics resulted in a housing situation in learning disability that can still be powerfully criticised from the perspective both of normalization and SRV and of O'Brien's 'accomplishments.'

Community care and learning disability – ideological chicken or political egg?

Other chapters have addressed the phenomenon of community care from the perspective of other service user groups, and there is considerable overlap in terms of policy and legislation to the situation of learning disability. This next section therefore tries to tease out the specifics of community care in practice, as it relates to housing, in particular the lasting impact of the historical legacy, and the slow infusion of ideas based on the critique.

We noted above that the *use* of ordinary housing seemed to develop more quickly in the 1970s in other countries influenced by normalization. Nevertheless the *language* of community care had already taken hold in the UK by the time Bayley (1973) made the important distinction between care *in* the community and care *by* the community, a key difference argued by all exponents of the institutional critique. As people slowly began to come out of hospital in the 1970s, or, more usually, be admitted directly to 'community care' from their parental homes, they did not generally go to ordinary houses. The capital building boom of the early 1970s, supported as we have seen by 'building notes' from the Department of Health and Social Security, resulted instead in many purpose built 'hostels,' normally of 24 'beds.'

Even by the early 1980s, the number of 'ordinary housing' projects were very few, despite the influence of normalization on public documents such as the 1980 King's Fund Report *An Ordinary Life*, a number of Regional Health Authority policies such as *A Model District Service* (North West Regional Health Authority, 1982) and the 'service principles' of a major government committee set up to investigate 'mental handicap nursing and care,' (Jay Committee, 1979). All these documents supported the idea of ordinary housing as the obvious choice for residential services for people with learning difficulties but, with certain well publicised exceptions (see Blunden, 1975), projects on the ground were few.

At this point there is contention as to cause and effect, in analyses of the observable phenomenon of a growth, over the ensuing 20 years, of ordinary housing as the basis of residential learning disability services. The scale of that growth is also contentious, making it possible for a major government survey in 1999 to conclude:

> *'All of these authorities can demonstrate examples of significant improvements in practice. However, the overall conclusion reached from the detailed analysis of current services must be that the realisation of the 'better life' principles was a long way off for most service users. The process of transforming the more congregate forms of accommodation and care into more individualised support in one's home or other homely surroundings appears to have faltered during the last decade'* (Department of Health, 1999a, p.31).

What is incontrovertible is the inexorable movement towards a social care market in the Thatcher years (Le Grand, 1990; Hadley and Clough, 1996). This sought, first, 'value for money' via the Audit Commission, and then, as spending on social security soared despite a reduction in spending on services, the Griffiths Report (Griffiths, 1988), a white paper (Department of Health, 1989a) and the NHS and Community Care Act of 1990. By the time of the act there were many examples of residential projects based on ordinary housing, and, such was their accord with the normalization/SRV movement, they received wide coverage. There were, however, no real surveys, until somewhat later (see Hatton and Emerson, 1996; Department of Health, 1999a), of either the *precise* models of residential care that were being put into effect, or, more importantly, the *proportion* of these different models that were actually implemented. As long as they were in 'ordinary houses' that seemed to be enough, and many staff of the hospitals, either on a private basis or as part of the new 'hospital trusts' set up 'community services' which often carried the traditions of the institutions out into the community (Hadley and Clough, 1996). Within service organisations, the new split into 'purchasers and providers' gave immense power to the former group, both within health authorities and social services departments (Lewis and Glennerster, 1996), and more and more 'horse-trading' took place as people were returned to their 'authorities of origin.' Horror stories began to emerge of people effectively being dumped on doorsteps along with a rapidly changing and untrained staff presence.

Other residential services, especially hostels, were not under as much financial pressure to close as were the hospitals, and the arguments of the normalization/SRV movement, that they too had all the features of the larger institutions, did not seem to have as much effect as the naked financial motivation that the NHS and Community Care Act had brought to the competing NHS trusts. Many hostels therefore stayed open, and there was some new building of hostel sized residential projects, often to house the remaining 'patients' of a closing hospital whose relatives mounted powerful resistance to their final closure. A document, entitled *Made to Care* (Cox and Pearson, 1995) was the most public representation of these groups' views, arguing for 'village style' communities.

The response of the Department of Health was to commission a series of surveys into the research on people coming out of hospital and the relative costs of different forms of care. The researchers, Emerson *et al.* (1999), were meticulously empirical, mindful of the academic opprobrium in some quarters that had attached itself to the 'idealistic' notions of 'normalization' (Race 1999a, 1999b). They found, not surprisingly, examples of low quality in all forms of residential provision since, as Cocks (2002, p121) notes, *'being small and community based are not sufficient conditions for quality'*. Emerson and his colleagues did, however, go so far as to recommend the closure of the remaining hospital based schemes, and re-provisioning these within *'small, community based dispersed housing schemes'* something the 2001 white paper was to take up. Again, however, the fact that such a survey reviewed nearly 20 years of research into 'models of community care housing,' and still left the door open for those proposing villages to have an obvious influence on the white paper, shows how both the historical legacy and the academic denigration of its critique in normalization/SRV had combined to keep alive major assumptions about 'special housing.' At the same time, other ideas, said by some to have 'replaced normalization' (Walmsley, 2001), shifted the focus from the *model* of housing to the part played by service users in the *process*. These ideas form the starting point of our final theme, the development of advocacy, empowerment and self-determination.

Empowerment or abandonment to choice – 'Valuing People' and beyond

'Citizen Advocacy' the idea that ordinary people can be recruited on a voluntary long term basis to 'represent the interests' of a vulnerable person 'as if they were their own', was first developed by Wolfensberger in the late sixties (Race, 2003). As with normalization, however, the import of advocacy into the UK had many peculiarities. Despite the steady growth and success of citizen advocacy schemes (Williams, 1998), ideological clashes between a growing movement around 'self-advocacy' and the perceived 'imposition of views' of citizen advocacy, led to many different schemes being called 'advocacy.' When this was set alongside the growing consumerism in society at large, and the service world in particular, that the years of Thatcherism had set in train, as well as notions of empowerment and self-determination coming from social work (Dominelli, 1997) and the disabled person's movement (Oliver, 1990) a new dynamic emerged. This judged services, including housing, primarily in terms of who had power in the process, with measures of the outcomes in quality terms being secondary.

In housing, the notion from normalization/SRV had been that supporters of disabled people, *together with* the people themselves, would seek to influence the settings in which they lived so as to reduce their devaluing characteristics. In the new thinking, greater weight appeared to be given to whether that person or persons had *chosen* the setting, and their power in the process, almost regardless of the outcome. In many cases, of course, the two philosophies (or their developments such as O'Brien's work in the UK on person-centred approaches) were able to work together, in that the person would be the focus of the efforts of the supporters. In other situations, however, and in the balance given in the white paper to participation in *planning* processes beyond the individual, it could be argued that 'empowerment and choice' have sometimes been at the expense of quality outcomes. Certainly when one looks at the Key Action Points on housing from *Valuing People* (Box 7.1), the emphasis is much more on the process and involvement of people in the 'Partnership Boards' than any specific targets for particular sorts of housing, apart from 'supported living' approaches for people living with older carers.

Box 7.1: Key Housing Action Points

- Housing and social services to work together to expand housing, care and support options.
- Department of Health and the Department of the Environment, Transport and the Regions to issue new joint guidance in 2001.
- Legislation to introduce a new duty on local housing authorities to provide advice and information.
- Learning Disability Partnership Boards to develop local housing strategies for people with learning disabilities.
- Learning Disability Development Fund will prioritise 'supported living' approaches for people living with older carers.
- Enabling people living in the remaining long stay hospitals to move to more appropriate accommodation by 2004 will be a priority for the Learning Disability Development Fund.

(Department of Health, 2001 p.72)

The 'Key Action Points' follow from the objectives for housing in the white paper, and again the emphasis on choice and involvement in the process is clear, as Box 7.2 reveals

Box 7.2: White paper objective 6 – Housing

To enable people with learning disabilities and their families to have greater choice and control over where, and how, they live by:

Sub-objective 6.1
Increasing the range and choice of housing open to people with learning disabilities in order to enable them to live as independently as possible.

Sub-objective 6.2
Ensuring people with learning disabilities and their families obtain advice and information about housing from the appropriate authorities.

Sub-objective 6.3
Enabling all people currently in NHS long stay hospitals to move into more appropriate accommodation and reviewing the quality of outcomes for people living in NHS residential campuses.

(Department of Health, 2001, p.126)

The 'target' attached to sub-objective 6.3 of closing all the remaining long stay hospital provision by 2004, one of the few prescriptive statements in the white paper, might come as a surprise to readers of some of the literature on learning disability, where the impression is often given that they were long gone. Readers of this chapter will, of course not be so surprised, nor will they at a document from a large provider organisation suggesting that the target is unlikely to be met, (Turning Point, 2003). The 'options for housing' given in the white paper also suggest that the historical legacy is still alive and well. It is interesting that in this part of the white paper there is a much greater emphasis on 'people with learning disabilities *and* their families' (my italics). Box 7.3 lists what the 2001 white paper thinks of as 'housing options'

Box 7.3: 'Valuing people' housing options

The government expects local councils to give people with learning disabilities a genuine opportunity to choose between housing, care and support options that include:
- **Supported living:** this approach is concerned with designing services round the particular needs and wishes of individuals and is less likely to result in housing and support that is designed around congregate living. Department of Health research has shown that supported living is associated with people having greater overall choice and a wider range of community activities.
- **Small-scale ordinary housing:** Department of Health research has shown that small-scale ordinary housing is likely to lead to better outcomes across a range of factors than is large housing or hostel provision.
- **Village and intentional communities:** These comprise houses and some shared facilities on one or more sites. Department of Health research shows such communities were associated with better activity planning, more routine day activities and better access to health checks. A study commissioned as part of the white paper's development found 3,000 people living in 73 village and intentional communities. This study and *Facing the Facts* also indicated that some local authorities are reluctant to support people with learning disabilities who wish to live, or whose families make arrangements for them to live, in a village or intentional community.

(Department of Health, 2002, p.73)

As well as the Department of Health nailing their colours firmly to the fence in terms of stating preferences, the dead hand of the pressure groups is still clearly evident in these options, both in the noted emphasis on families in this section and in the inclusion of the third category, 'village and intentional communities.' Thus despite the supposed 'dominance' of the normalization/SRV movement in the learning disability field, segregated and congregated settings are still sanctioned. In the meantime, as we shall see in the conclusion below, the government initiative that has figured widely in the rest of this book, *Supporting People*, could be said to have come up against the radical edges of housing and learning disability, for precisely the same reasons that have formed the thrust of this chapter.

Conclusion – 'supported living', 'Supporting People' and a real home – hopes and fears

One of the earliest promoters of the notion of 'supported living', Kinsella (1993), talked of it as a 'new paradigm' – i.e. something that was not just another 'model of residential care'. Yet 'supported living' schemes, within the white paper definition, are still the exception rather than the rule. Despite many notable individual achievements in this area, e.g. Harker and King (1999), the overwhelming impression remains that the congregate form of living, whether in 'ordinary houses' or larger institutions, is still the norm. Further, in activities during the run up to *Supporting People*, government agencies seem to be pressing for even the more radical forms of housing to be brought under the heading of 'residential care'. Anecdotal evidence abounded of pressure being put on housing providers of 'supported living' schemes to register as 'care homes' and thus be subject to the regulations of the Care Standards Act 2000. This was brought fully to public view in an unsuccessful appeal, by a supported living provider, *Alternative Futures*, against a refusal by the National Care Standards Commission to deregister a number of its care homes that it said were now operating as 'independent living schemes,' Care Standards Tribunal, 2003). Ironically, it was the exercise of 'informed choice' that became the major grounds for this refusal, in that the Tribunal insisted that service users not only had to be deemed 'able' to choose to move to an independent living arrangement, but also to choose who was to provide them with the personal care that they need. All the other trappings of an 'ordinary life' that were represented by these leading edge schemes – tenancies for residents, care and accommodation provided by separate agencies, choice over décor, furnishings etc., did not, in the Tribunal's view, constitute sufficient grounds for the residential arrangements being regarded as people's home. The implications of this in terms of people being able to make use of the *Supporting People* initiative should be apparent, and will not be dwelt on here; the point of the example is to pull together the threads of this chapter by suggesting that the decision sums up where we are with housing, community care and learning disability.

In physical terms, a lot further on, though far from the goal of normalization/SRV and its successors for housing that does not adversely stigmatise the residents (and still not as close as we might be to the views of Samuel Howe quoted in the introduction). Most people now live in domestic dwellings. In terms of social integration, however, the picture is far less rosy, and neither *Supporting People* nor *Valuing People* have really provided support *in practice* to achieve it in housing terms, despite the fine sounding words on inclusion and independence. The historical legacy is still with us, acting as a drag chain on the hopes and demands of a new generation of people with learning difficulties and their families, and as a reminder to the older generation, especially those now elderly parents who have provided an 'ordinary home' for fifty years or more, that 'better is the enemy of the best'. Until we confront the tensions in attitudes between the fine sounding principles of *Valuing People* and the view of learning disability illustrated by the three contemporary stories with which this chapter began, then the results for people with learning difficulties will still be to live where other people want them to, in a building not of their choosing, and with those whom other people dictate they will live.

CHAPTER 8:
Adapting to life – are adaptations a remedy for disability?

Pam Thomas and Marcus Ormerod

Introduction

This chapter has a particular focus on disabled people with physical impairments, and the impact of housing, adaptations, and assistive technology on their lives. It argues that inaccessible housing is an inevitable consequence of a society that does not take account of people with impairments, and considers the capacity of adaptations and assistive technology to compensate for this.

The chapter is based upon research carried out by the authors with disabled people who are economically active, yet have found barriers to finding a suitable home to buy. It provides evidence of the experience of disabled people who are taking responsibility for their own housing and adaptation requirements. Examples included show the resourcefulness of disabled people in attempting to avoid the barriers to independent living. There is also an indication that the availability of adaptations is problematic and does not solve the fundamental problem of dwellings that are designed for a perceived 'normal' human.

Adapting to life

Very few homes in the UK are accessible to disabled people with mobility impairments, particularly wheelchair users. Housing is designed with a perceived bodily norm in mind; those falling outside this perceived norm are deemed to have 'special needs' or in the current parlance – 'support needs'. Mainstream housing developers do not consider this to be an issue with which they need concern themselves (Imrie, 2003). The societal assumption that mainstream housing does not need to take account of people with impairments (of any age) has a major impact on individuals, their families, communities, and society. Whilst owner occupation is the preferred and by far the largest tenure in the United Kingdom at 70 per cent of households (Office of the Deputy Prime Minister, 2002b), there has been little concern by government or housing developers for making suitable properties available for disabled potential purchasers to buy. Part M of the building regulations provides minimal standards of 'visitability' but fail to provide 'liveability' standards (Imrie, 2003). It has fallen to the social sector to build accessible housing, whilst the much larger private sector ignores this as a market issue. Even within the social sector few properties are wheelchair accessible (Stewart *et al.*, 1999) and those that are tend to assume isolation, inactivity and dependency (MacFarlane and Laurie, 1997). Whilst social housing is needed and welcomed by some disabled people it is not a universal solution to the problem of disability in housing. There is little if any recognition of children, families, economic or social activity within mobility standard housing. Also there is a mistaken assumption that the requirements of people with other impairments can be met with mobility standard or wheelchair accessible housing (Allen *et al.*, 2002; Hanson, 2001).

Many disabled people want and could achieve independence but an assumption that to be disabled automatically means vulnerability creates barriers and limitations and is a disincentive to becoming economically and socially active. The immediate consequences are that people who could lead active and independent lives as part of the community may be forced into dependency (Zarb, 1991). Indeed, they may feel they have to emphasise dependency and a need for 'care' in order to obtain the support or facilities they require to increase their activity. The exclusion of people with impairments due to inaccessible housing has far reaching consequences such as additional demands on the community care budget that might not be required if dwellings were accessible in the first place (Cobbold, 1997). However, welfare systems themselves may also contribute to an emphasis on vulnerability, dependency and care (Finkelstein, 1991) rather than economic activity and supporting independent living.

The route to exclusion

The history of British society cannot be ignored if we are to understand how this situation has come about. Since the Industrial Revolution, homes have been built for workers (Sim, 1993). To this day, the house building industry is focused on the need to design and build homes for people who are in employment (for example, note the shift to considering the needs of 'key workers') and they are aware that higher status higher paid employment brings an expectation of better quality housing. Historically, towns and cities have grown to accommodate factories but also the infrastructure (e.g. transport for workers, schools for future workers) including housing for workers. Speculative builders realised they could build and sell properties to skilled workers (Crabtree and Hemmings, 2001). Areas of high employment generate more housing; areas of low employment have a surplus of housing. The first phase of growth of homes for owner occupation happened following the depression in the 1920s when workers began to find that they had some disposable income. The shift from renting to ownership has accelerated rapidly since the Second World War.

For the majority of the population, the key to good housing is having adequate funds. Half of those considered to be living in poverty are owner occupiers

(Burrows, 2003). The difficulties encountered by those on average wages in attempting to become owner occupiers have become a matter of concern for the government of today and proposals for affordable homes are becoming a priority (Cowan, 1999). Recent government intervention in promoting the construction of homes for key workers emphasises the link between work and housing. For disabled people the links between paid employment and the sort of homes that people have is significant, since historically disabled people have been excluded from the workplace (Barnes, 1991; Oliver, 1990; Roulstone, 1998) with Finkelstein (2001) claiming that to be disabled has meant to be unemployable.

Traditionally, disability has been viewed as a feature of certain individuals whose minds, bodies or senses work or appear to be different from a perceived norm. People with disabilities are viewed as being the source of the problem; their exclusion is therefore essentially reducible to their inherent inadequacies or disabilities (Wood, 1981). So in order to find a solution to disability attention must be focused on the individuals concerned. An analysis of the way their bodies, minds or senses malfunction is required to understand this phenomenon. Emphasis is on correcting this malfunctioning to bring the individual closer to a perceived normality, a normalization or rehabilitation process is required. The adoption of this *individual model* of disability has implications for all parts of society.

As the result of discussion and debate people whose minds, bodies and senses do not match up to a perceived norm have identified barriers in society as the cause of disability (Union of Physically Impaired Against Segregation, 1976). This perspective describes a society that does not take account of those who do not match the perceived norm and so excludes and thereby disables them. This interpretation of disability has been termed the social model of disability (Oliver, 1983) and the term 'disabled people' means those who are disabled by society.

Health, social and community care

Legislation, policies and practice in health and social care have been based on the individual model of disability and the requirements of those that cannot work. The premise is that disability is to be found in individuals and that independence is achieved through correction, rehabilitation and self-sufficiency. The emphasis is on providing care for the vulnerable rather than ensuring that disabling barriers are removed or not created. Traditionally in health and social policy living independently means doing things for oneself. This could mean spending hours attempting to carry our basic tasks leaving little or no time or energy left to get on with leading a full life. Analysis by disabled people has produced a different definition of independent living that is about having choice and control over one's life (Morris, 1993). Using a social model of disability changes the definition of independent living to mean having choice and control and having access to necessary facilities, such as equipment and housing (Davies, 1999).

Independent living

In order to be active citizens in the modern world non-disabled people need several things to be in place (Davies, 1999; Finkelstein, 1980; Oliver, 1990): transport systems, usable walk ways, means of getting into the workplace, information and communication in usable formats, and equipment are all factors in keeping with the modern age both in, and outside the workplace, a social network of people with shared experiences, and finally of course, a usable home. Disabled people need and benefit from the same things but the way in which these facilities are made available may need to be different. Yet people with impairments are deemed to have 'special needs'.

Assistive technology, fixtures and fittings

Recent rapid developments in new technology have changed the way in which people use their homes. Facilities that were not included in new properties a few years ago are now commonplace. Technological advances over the last half century have introduced much automation which is available to the general public and has benefited very many people in western society. The benefits of technology, the alleviation of the drudgery of many household tasks is taken for granted and allows some families the opportunity to participate in areas of social and economic life previously denied.

Many of these developments have enhanced leisure and for some it has enhanced autonomy. Automatic controls on central heating and microwaves for example are the sorts of equipment that are now taken for granted in most households and have had the effect of assisting disabled people to live independently.

Smart technology

Smart or intelligent technology is relatively new and the benefits have only tentatively been explored. A similar situation was the potential of having electricity supplied to our homes 70 years ago; it was first introduced at the upper end of the market and considered something of a luxury. Smart technology today is being introduced into new homes at the upper end of the market usually to assist with security or enhance entertainment systems. It is also used, to ensure optimum use of energy by being sensitive to the usage of the property and controlling energy usage. Apart from those appliances which have become commonplace such as washing machines, dishwashers, microwaves, TVs, remote controls, telephones, the technology now exists to link these appliances through computers and mobile phones. Technology is available to pre-set the functioning of appliances and this extends to doors, windows, cupboards and sinks, water, lighting, heating, detection, alarms and security, and in order to link up with existing appliances (Gann *et al.*, 1999; Venables and Taylor, 2001). These recent developments in technology allow for the reconceptualisation of what is standard in housing provision. It is possible to facilitate the removal of many barriers to independent living for disabled people, it is feasible to construct and run Lifetime Homes, it is possible to move away from the notion of 'special needs' (Dewsbury, 2001).

Yet the equipment that disabled people require is still deemed to be different and 'special'. Access to equipment remains problematic for disabled people, it is costly and often 'gatekeepers' determine who can have what and when. Complaints range from waiting months for equipment to being assessed for and issued with inappropriate equipment whilst the most useful equipment may not on the issue list (Morris, 1989, 1993; Roulstone, 1998). Disabled people have been critical of these systems that often result in their being issued with equipment that is neither wanted nor used whilst actually getting what is required can prove to be impossible. A government funded report entitled *Fully Equipped* showed the importance and positive benefits of equipment for many disabled people (Audit Commission, 2000).

Technology could assist disabled people to become socially included, live independently and become active citizens. But none of these things are of any use if people cannot get them and there is some recognition of this with the advent of the Department of Health's Integrating Community Equipment Services (see their useful website: www.icesdoh.org) which intends to make the whole process smoother. Nevertheless, fixtures, fittings and assistive technology are of limited use in a home that is profoundly inaccessible and unadaptable.

Housing in a disabling society

House builders argue that there is little need for them to ensure homes meet the requirements of people with physical impairments because so few people require such facilities (Imrie, 2003). They resist attempts to set standards arguing that they are too restrictive. There seems to be an assumption that dwellings can be 'adapted' to the requirements of individuals. Indeed 'adapted housing' has become the acceptable term for housing that is intended to meet the requirements of disabled people. Yet there is an unacknowledged inference in the term 'adapted' that there is no real problem with standard housing adaptation is required because certain individuals have 'special needs'. There is no question that perhaps if standard housing took account of the range of human physical form in the first place then any requirement for 'adaptation' would be radically reduced making it minimal and required by fewer than now.

Statistics relating to the housing requirements of disabled people are not easy to find. Those that exist emphasise the shortcomings of the individual rather than shortcomings in *housing design*. The Housing in England Survey (Office of the Deputy Prime Minister, 2001b) found that there were 130,000 people aged over 65 living in 110,000 unsuitable properties. The way the survey was designed located the reason for inaccessibility with the individual's *'serious medical condition or handicap'* rather than poor design.

In the social housing sector it was recognised in the 1970s that there was a shortfall in uptake of wheelchair accessible accommodation (Stewart *et al*, 1999). There is little information on the numbers of people whose homes are inaccessible and apparently missing are those disabled people who are trapped because of the lack of an accessible home, perhaps still living at home with parents well past the age when non-disabled offspring usually leave, or remain trapped in residential or nursing institutions.

Disabled people's experience of trying to access the inaccessible

The research we undertook showed the importance of having an accessible home in order to make use of necessary equipment or adaptations. Although in conducting this study we did not seek disabled people with any particular type of impairment it was only individuals with mobility impairments, particularly wheelchair users, who came forward saying it is almost impossible to find a suitable home to live in. When searching for a house to buy disabled people with a mobility impairment do not expect to find a property that is ready to move straight into, but rather they look for a property that is *adaptable*. Even this is largely a fruitless search. For example Liz (who is a wheelchair user) and Steve decided to look for an older property and went to local estate agents:

> *'This became a very frustrating exercise, we excluded most properties immediately, because it was obvious that they were not accessible nor could they be made accessible. We did try to visit some properties but were not able to find any that were even suitable for adaptation'* (Liz).

Similarly Eve (who is a wheelchair user) and her partner Ray started looking for a house together but it quickly became apparent that Eve could not even get to view properties because everywhere was inaccessible:

> *'So Ray searched on his own and then would let me know me if any might be a possibility. Inevitably Ray looked at more developments than me but he looked at probably every new development in Liverpool, Knowsley and Sefton'* (Eve).

They looked at properties developed by some of the big companies but they did not have anything that could be adapted. They had hoped to find a bungalow but they were quickly sold:

> *'We did manage to look at some on the Croxteth Park Estate but they were tiny providing no circulation space'* (Eve).

Carole (who has a mobility impairment) and Bob also found their searches to be fruitless. They were looking for a property they could adapt to suit Carole's requirements:

'We looked at new properties a few years ago, we looked at a new bungalow but it was far too small. The houses whether old or new did not have a downstairs toilet and showers, or if the toilet was downstairs the bedroom was upstairs, also the stairs were too narrow to take a stair lift with the leg room I need.

The problems we found, regardless of the age of the property, was that within our price range the properties were not accessible and could not be extended to provide the facilities needed. I would prefer to have a bedroom and shower room extension on a house than have a lift, but we have not found a property that we can afford with the space to add an extension' (Carole).

When looking for a property to buy disabled people keep money aside to cover the cost of adaptations. Helen (who is a wheelchair user) and John had wanted to move from the home they currently own because of career development:

'I have a new job so we want to live in between our two places of work. We are looking at properties between Blackburn and North Manchester. We have a large semi-detached house in a very popular area to sell and have a good double income. We are looking at properties in the region of £100,000 (early 2002) which will leave some money for adaptations' (John).

Graham spent months looking for a property he could buy with his partner who is a wheelchair user. When they found a property with potential his partner could not actually move in until the work was complete, he kept £20,000 aside for this. Liz and Steve spent £20,000 on adapting the bungalow even though it was not complete when they told the builder what changes were needed.

Adaptability of properties bought

The benefits of building homes which take account of mobility impairment and are flexible enough to be adapted for a wheelchair user include savings to community care budgets (Cobbolt, 1997). Homes built to Lifetime Homes standards (see Joseph Rowntree Foundation website: www.jrf.org.uk) are not fully wheelchair accessible but they are adaptable, which is vital to disabled people with physical impairments. Most people with impairments have acquired them in adulthood and this increases as people become older. Despite the considerable commitment of the Joseph Rowntree Foundation and those working with them to develop Lifetime Homes standards these are not taken into account by mainstream housing developers and policy-makers. If homes do not meet the life long requirements of the occupants then they are not sustainable homes. It would seem to be uneconomic and therefore unsustainable to ignore a large section of the community and then have separate 'special' provision (Cobbold, 1997; Hanson, 2001).

As Hanson (2001) points out there is a danger that if only registered social landlords adopt Lifetime Homes standards they could be tainted with the 'special needs' label which will reduce private developers interest. But Lifetime Homes standards are gaining recognition and have been required in all new social housing in Wales since April 2001 (Welsh Assembly, 2002). However, in England there is no such requirement. However, the Housing Corporation (Housing Corporation, 2003b) will support a Lifetime Homes standard where the local authority housing strategy shows a need for it, but does not seem to make it a requirement otherwise.

However, few homes are built to this standard and those that there are, remain in the social sector. There is no evidence that people with a mobility impairment (including wheelchair users) are any less likely than the rest of the population to want to own their own home. In this study, none of the disabled people found a property on the open market that was ready to move straight into. The properties were selected because of potential to be adapted rather than it already being suitable. The sorts of adaptations required included equipment and technology such as a through floor lift or a ceiling track hoist, but often it was simply about ensuring ample circulation space. Those disabled people with the most satisfactory outcome were those who negotiated with a builder to alter plans before construction started but recognised that it is not easy to get this:

> '*I doubt whether or not I would have been so lucky in finding a co-operative and helpful builder of comparative size and competence in England. It is largely because he was interested in my proposal that it worked well*'.
> (The builder is a large family company in seven large residential building developments in this region of Northern Ireland) (Charles).

The second most satisfactory arrangements were for those that went into a shared ownership arrangement with a registered social landlord. Terry's property was not available on the open market and the registered social landlord has control over who may be the shared owner, however, it was built to wheelchair standard. The property is fully accessible to him; although he is having the bathroom wall knocked down to allow use of a ceiling hoist from the bedroom this has been a relatively easy job because the original design took account of this being required at some time:

> '*Having access to the whole of my house makes life so much easier and I can do more and have a wider range of activities that I could if my home was not accessible to me. Also it feels more like home because I can use it properly, I feel relaxed and confident here*' (Terry).

Kevin and Anne have also entered a shared ownership arrangement with a housing association:

> '*Because the house is built to a good mobility standard and clearly adaptable we decided to go for it, but it was not suitable for me to live in until the work was carried out*' (Anne).

They have had a lift installed and there were no problems about the ceiling strength to do that. The downstairs WC is too small for Anne to get in and there is no room to make it any bigger. They also had the kitchen refitted by a large DIY store to their own specifications. They applied for a Disabled Facilities Grant to help with the cost of this, a process which was complicated and drawn out. A less satisfactory solution has been to ask a builder to make adaptations to a property late in its construction. Eve and Ray had an extension built onto a partly constructed property. They compromised on location after an extensive yet fruitless search:

> *'When we found this property it was in an area we would not usually consider. It is a small development by a local developer and he was extremely helpful, we know this was the best deal we would get so we compromised on location'* (Eve).

However, there are other issues which led to a less satisfactory outcome than buying a property where wheelchair access is taken into account from the design stage:

> *'The bedroom extension is not big enough since it cannot accommodate a double bed or storage. The extension is fifteen feet long including the shower room'* (Eve).

Liz and Steve also arranged changes to a partially constructed bungalow; this was to arrange level access, a wider front door and a level access shower (instead of a bath). Problems have developed with drainage and the ramp from the back door:

> *'We have got a structural engineer to have a look at the ramps and stuff – he found major problems with the roof, windows and internal walls as well – we've sent his report to the HSBC, but haven't heard anything yet. I've got a horrible feeling its going to cost us a lot of money to put things right as most of it isn't covered by the warranty'* (Steve).

Some disabled people buy a property which is already constructed with the intention of making adaptations at a later stage. Graham had intended to convert the double garage into a bedroom with en-suite for his partner. Also, a ramp to the front and back door would have been required. Unfortunately, the relationship broke up before the work started so this was not done in the end. Gill had an extra handrail put next to the stairs and grab rails in the bathroom. There were problems because the house is new and the walls are quite flimsy and it was difficult to find points strong enough to take the fittings. She intended to have ramps put in at the front and back doors, but was unable to get this done before selling the house (as she is going to be married and will be moving elsewhere). David was living in a flat that was not accessible to him:

> *'There is a step into the building and I have put a temporary wooden ramp there, the hall way within the apartment is too narrow for me to use my wheelchair so that has to stay in the lobby'* (David).

The design of the flat is such that only knocking down interior walls and putting up new ones would make a difference. David realised that it would be better to find a more accessible property – even though this seems hopeless after attempting to view so many inaccessible properties.

All the participants had considered new properties. The most common reason why these properties were rejected was because of lack of space – no room to live, no circulation space. The lack of space in new properties is a criticism that comes not just from disabled people (Leishman *et al.*, 2003). Two respondents had considered and attempted to view loft type conversions believing they had potential to be accessible because of the open plan style. However, they found developers do not show any interest in taking this into account and design them with changes of level, narrow passageways, tiny bathrooms and narrow kitchens.

David had attempted to have changes made to a loft apartment, but the developer did not meet his agreed requirements and refused to return his deposit of £1,000. Eventually David went to the small claims court and the developers returned his deposit before it went to court. Part M does not provide a property which a wheelchair user could live in, nor does it ensure that the property would lend itself to being adapted at a later date. These regulations do little more than allow access into the property and the main living room. The downstairs toilet is helpful to ambulant disabled people who cannot climb stairs but is not necessarily wheelchair accessible.

Graham bought a property that was five years old in preference to the Part M properties; this property is not that old but was more spacious than brand new properties that met Part M of the building regulations.

Disabled Facilities Grants

In recognition that people with physical impairments require major alterations to standard housing the government requires local authorities to administer Disabled Facilities Grants which are intended to assist with this. Some of the participants in this study considered Disabled Facilities Grants as a way of funding the required adaptations, but some found they were not eligible. Eve was surprised and disappointed to find that she would not be eligible for help to adapt the home she is buying with her partner. Eve thought social services might give some help toward the changes that needed to be made since she would then be freeing up an accessible property for someone else, but she said she was told *'well you are in an accessible property – it is your choice to move'*. She and Ray are paying at least £8,000 on top of the basic purchase price to pay for adaptations.

Liz and Steve were not eligible for a Disabled Facilities Grants because of their joint incomes; they had to find £20,000 for adaptations on top of the basic purchase price. Graham had intended to apply for a Disabled Facilities Grants but did not need it in the end as his partner did not come to live with him. But he had allowed £25,000 toward the cost of adaptations. Anne and Kevin had many problems getting a Disabled Facilities Grants for their present home. Even though the house had the potential for adaptation Anne could not live in it until the adaptations were done. They applied for a Disabled Facilities Grant in January 1998 when they agreed to buy the house:

'This was a new house and there was no chain. The problems we encountered were with the Disabled Facilities Grant system which meant we could not actually move in until December 1998. The vendor gave me a deadline for completion because they had been kept waiting for so long to sell the property and probably could have let it go to someone else months earlier. We were aware that had the vendor not been a registered social landlord it is unlikely that they would have waited for the work to be done' (Anne).

Kevin added:

'We were told there was a waiting list of about two years for the DFG and this was mainly down to the wait for a council officer to oversee the work. We said this was no use to us and we would oversee the work ourselves, although the council were not happy about this they did agree. Even so the bureaucracy still delayed matters' (Kevin).

They preferred the control this gave them as well as the time saved because it meant they could check quality against price. However, the social services department lost the tenders after Kevin and Anne had submitted them. Because they undertook the tendering process themselves they chose better quality, which is better value for money. Even though it took 11 months to get everything sorted out the council were surprised that Anne and Kevin got the work done as quickly, which they did once they were allowed to have control over the tendering process. Most of the work was done on the same day that they moved in with 23 people in the house at some points during the day.

Anne and Kevin believe that the council are not used to disabled people who are assertive, active, in employment and have a political understanding of disability. The council seemed to be irritated by their persistence, and they seemed complacent about the situation not recognising any urgency. The council also seemed to think all Kevin and Anne were doing was to try to queue jump and that they were asking for something special.

Helen and John assume they would not be eligible because of their joint income, whilst Terry is having some work done to make the bathroom more accessible as an en-suite. The property was designed so this could be done quite easily. The council is paying for the work but Terry is not sure which pot of money it is from other than it is not a Disabled Facilities Grant.

Solutions

Disabled people in this study have identified the barriers and have specified the design solutions which are required to allow adaptability. The features identified as being essential are:

- space for circulation and for living (not just existing);
- turning space into doorways;
- storage space;
- level access throughout the ground floor;
- level access or potential to create level access to the front and back door;
- spacious kitchens and bathrooms or potential to increase the size and layout;
- making sure that electrical controls are easily accessible;
- if there are stairs then there needs to be space and structural strength for the future installation of a lift;
- walls and ceilings need to be strong enough to take a lift, a hoist and grab rails if required;
- car parking is important for those that have their own transport.

These requirements are very similar to the requirements expressed by non-disabled people who are searching for newly built homes for owner occupation (Leishman *et al.*, 2003). However, they are not as prescriptive as standards, and so designers could use them with the flexibility they enjoy.

Conclusions

Appropriate adaptations and assistive technology can be an advantage to many disabled people, however, without a home that is accessible in the first place adaptations may not be possible and assistive technology may not be enough to create an accessible environment, or there may not be enough space to store or use equipment. All the case studies in this study provide evidence that most homes for owner occupation are impossible to live in without adaptations and in most cases adaptations are not feasible. So it is practically impossible for wheelchair users and others with substantial mobility impairments to find a home to buy in the open mainstream market. In order to find an accessible home to buy disabled people with mobility impairments especially, wheelchair users do not look for a property that is fully wheelchair accessible, but rather a property that *has the potential to be adapted*. Individualised fixtures and fittings are not required at this stage but good flexible design is.

Compared to people who do not have a physical impairment and are in a similar financial position those with a physical impairment have many additional issues to deal with. When searching for a home to buy they will:

- spend a great deal more time searching for a property;
- have far less choice;
- seriously consider adapting any property that has potential;
- be more likely to compromise on location;
- will lose employment and career opportunities because of this;
- take the pragmatic (rather than passive) decision to give up the idea of moving house;
- have to deal with the additional stress on top of that which is usual for anyone who is house hunting;
- have less chance of finding a suitable home;
- make temporary arrangements whilst adaptations are done since it is usually impossible to live in the property until the work is carried out.

Exclusion from buildings is a key factor in creating the dependency of disabled people. This has an impact on society particularly in terms of the cost of the welfare systems. Disabled people want to be self-sufficient and in control of their own lives (Morris, 1989; Zarb, 1991). Yet a community care system based on 'care' for the 'vulnerable' creates barriers for those disabled people who, given the right circumstances, can take control of these issues themselves. Disabled people's lack of economic power as well as the shortage of accessible property in the choices available to disabled people in obtaining accessible housing (Morris, 1993) contribute to the exclusionary factors which inhibit social inclusion and citizenship. Disabled people are systematically omitted from consultation and discussion around design issues. Housing is only one of many key issues that must be tackled if disabled people are to be allowed to take an active part in society.

This situation arises not because people with impairments cause a problem, but because they are not taken into account. Disabled people's exclusion from housing and the lack of access to suitable equipment is a symptom of the profound social and economic exclusion of disabled people. In such a situation whilst equipment and adaptations are vital they are but a small part of the remedy to the experience of disability. Since disabled people are excluded by poor design and forced into dependency then that is a social rather than medical issue and needs to be dealt with as such.

CHAPTER 9:
'He went berserk and stabbed his mother 43 times ...'
Thinking in headlines:
mental health and housing

Paul Simic

The discourse on mental health is, more than any other policy area, dominated by a dramatic narrative and defined by how that narrative is persistently carried forward to form the views of the 'moral centre' (Cohen and Young, 1973). The chapter title is taken from a local newspaper's headline of the actions of a 'madman' (quoted in Symonds and Kelly, 1998). A news clipping (below) taken at random shows the type of language used and indicates the level of thinking on the subject. The main thrust of the chapter is that the level of discourse is held down by the weight of this narrative and that the crude stereotyping of mental health that runs as the perpetual sub-text operates to limit opportunities for mental health, as an issue, to become part of mainstream society. Housing has a particularly important role to play in this, if I can borrow Wolfensberger's term, 'normalization' process.

'Knife that cut through to a country's heart'

As Sweden mourns Anna Lindh, it has to confront a dark side the people have always denied.
Andrew Osborn in Stockholm and Ed Vulliamy, *The Observer*, September 14 2003

Extracts:
The first punch to her face dazed her, the second floored her and then came the knife slicing into her liver, slashing her arms and puncturing her abdomen. Within 56 frenzied seconds, Sweden's beloved Foreign Minister and mother of two young boys had been brutally, and fatally, attacked.

Anna Lindh had taken a break from campaigning for today's referendum on the euro, planning to buy herself a new outfit for a TV debate that same evening. Like most of Sweden's leaders, she was going about her daily business without bodyguards.

One shopper, Hanna Sundberg, ran to the wounded Minister, who cried out: *'God, he's stabbed me in the stomach!'* Another screamed for help, imploring the store's absent security guards to stop the fleeing attacker. But it was too late. The assassin, a tall, powerfully built man, had calmly walked down the escalator. He tossed the bloody knife aside, passing beneath Nordiska Kompaniet's shimmering art deco crystal chandelier, and broke into a run.

→

Lindh would stop breathing some 13 hours later. Although her condition was initially thought not to be life threatening the craftsman's knife used in the attack had gone deeper than first thought. Her liver, her aorta and her abdomen had all been badly damaged and the 46-year-old had lost far too much blood – the surgeons at Stockholm's Karolinska hospital pumped tens of litres of blood into her body. [...]

'I just can't understand it,' said Veronika Sundi, a sobbing pensioner who came to pay tribute to Lindh. *'Sweden has become a harsher place to live in. I'm very angry.'* Violent crime had, she added, become a terrible problem. *'This is very special for me because I lost my husband in the same way. He was robbed and stabbed to death and they never caught anyone.'* [...]

So where did Anna Lindh's killer come from? *'I only hope it's a case of a madman,'* said Ola Baechstroem, preparing a children's orchestra to play in tribute to Lindh and *'against all forms of senseless violence'.* [...]

'It's almost certainly the work of someone insane,' Matti Molin, a businessman, said. In the 1990s the then Conservative government closed down many of Sweden's mental homes , privatising the sector and turning many disturbed people out onto the street, he said, adding that the country had seen a wave of appalling crimes committed by the mentally ill. *'The same day as Lindh was murdered a mentally ill man stabbed a five-year-old girl to death. In May a mentally ill guy went berserk with an iron bar and killed an old woman. He thought he was fighting trolls. Another crazy guy chopped someone's ear off with a samurai sword recently and a couple of years ago we had "laser man" who shot at anyone who looked foreign.'*

'We never used to have this but there are more homeless people and mentally disturbed people on the streets than ever before. At the beginning of the nineteenth century we had space for 2,000 [mentally ill patients]. Now we have room for just 600 and many have been released onto the streets.' [...]

Introduction

I picked a dramatic mental health story I saw in *The Observer* to trail this chapter. The country of origin is irrelevant, it is the style and content that caught my eye. The lurid coverage (reflecting the equally lurid mindset exemplified by the quotes), the juxtaposition of mental illness with threat and danger and the odd distinction made with the emphasis on 'senseless' violence being, presumably, more repellant than other forms, its association with mental illness as something senseless and 'irrational', the nostalgic lament for a better way (the segregated model of care) without any knowledge as to whether it was any better – it just wasn't 'here', even the ultimately, ironic subtext of extremist political activists whose psychotically distorted thinking allows them to kill for principles (but who are nonetheless 'sane') being OK, taken together all represent the restricted, 'headline', thinking that seems to characterise the debate.

I have three 'headline' (sic) points to make in reviewing the whither and whence of mental health policy.

The first is rather mundane but important nonetheless: *closer joint working between housing support and care services is essential* because housing services represent the mainstream link which mental health services need to forge to come in from the cold. But, as I write (December 2004), it has been announced that the government will go ahead with cuts in the 'Supporting People' budget. Supporting People is important, pitched as it is to cross the divide between social care and housing on the one hand and between primary prevention ('upstream') and secondary and tertiary care ('downstream'), on the other. However, despite the recent *Benefits Realisation* report (ODPM, 2004a) showing its value, budgets are already to be reined in from the off. So my first point is made for me: while 'evidence-based practice', and similar perspectives on the efficacy of interventions, apply in other areas they do not apply to politics and policy-making.

The second headline point is that services will remain underdeveloped without a *stronger articulation of the 'social model' in mental health services and without, as part of that model, effective user participation* in planning and in providing services. This is particularly weak in the area of mental health (see Carr, 2004). It is to act to weaken the position further that mental health provision is increasingly seen as something that is not a part of 'social care', exemplified in the many social services departments losing mental health services back to health bodies and the suggested reframing of the role formerly occupied by the approved social worker (ASW) in mental health legislation. A parallel weakness is that 'health policy' is seen as identical with policy on health services (Harrison *et al.*, 1991). The consequence of the latter point is *'its ability to divert the attention of policy-makers from a broader view of health ...'* (ibid).

The third point is that should the many headline stories like the one shown above (you could as easily pick stories about Michael Stone or Christopher Clunis) that portray mental health sufferers as without capacity for reasoned thought on the one hand and liable to unpredictable and dangerous behaviour on the other, represent our level of understanding, as I assert it does, *there is still a 'way to go' even to get to the first level of a proper debate about mental illness*. 'Education, education, education' should be the government's role but they do not occupy a neutral position, may have no less stereotyped a view of mental health issues than others, and do not start with a 'tabula rasa'. A sociological perspective might highlight how the government itself seeks to recruit 'extremists' (those who engage in extreme behaviours) as a way of shoring up the government's role as protector, and none help in that task more than dangerous 'madmen' amongst us who could strike at any time. Modern government, now in 'continuous campaign' mode, will always view mental health from the perspective of political payback and, while mental illness remains characterised as a threat, the response will always be to control and contain that threat, or be sure to maintain the perception that that is the case. Hence the persistence and dominance of the 'medico-legal' model. This is not to argue that there isn't a need for safe and competent control within a social and legal framework of support and care for people with enduring and serious mental health conditions but that, as a policy area, mental health remains dominated by one relatively narrow perspective and this has consequences for how we frame policy.

I have some other points to make, too.

1. 'Mental illness' remains an area where there is much ignorance and fear and much stereotyping, not least at the level of policy-makers, who have one eye on the problem and one eye on the monster called public opinion itself fed on a diet of scare stories about mental health issues (as above).

2. It is an area where we struggle from the outset because of the very language we use to discuss the issues at hand: if I do not use the 'health' or 'illness' label what do I use to describe what we are talking about? A while ago people tried 'problems in living' but it doesn't exactly roll off the tongue.

3. We have an additional factor in the area of mental health, one that we don't have, certainly not to the same degree, elsewhere in the arena of adult care and support: this is the perception of danger or threat and the need for 'society' to be protected. The law on mental health has no real equivalent anywhere else. Child care law shows a comparable tension between potential opposites – 'care' and 'control' – but the juxtaposition of 'care' and 'control' is nowhere else so evident as a 'double-bind' (appropriately enough) as in the area of mental health policy and practice.

4. It is not surprising that as housing policy, community care policy, and health policy approach the issue from different directions they find on arrival, rather like the blind men of the parable investigating the apocryphal elephant, no agreement on the nature of the beast.

5. Getting the balance right between using scarce resources to deal with those in greatest need with specialist services while also, as a wider society, taking the collective responsibility to deal with the much broader range of anxiety and depressive disorders in the general population (and their correlates, such as the low rate of employment in the population of people with mental health problems) remains the biggest pragmatic challenge.

6. Enablement, empowerment and choice are concepts at the heart of policy (at least at a rhetorical level) elsewhere but are rather absent in the mental health arena (Carr, 2004).

7. Housing has an important role to play and Supporting People may be a way forward for integrating the housing and care sectors (or may not).

Language, paradigms and models

Nowhere is it more evident than here, when talking of mental illness, how much a prisoner of language we are and I'd like to unpick a few things before going on. The term 'paradigm' originates, at least in its more common usage, with Kuhn (Kuhn, 1962). It combines two important concepts: perspective and, implicitly, power. The notion of a perspective takes into the conceptual realm the metaphor of position and recognises that to look out on the world is to be somewhere in it. But it also, by definition, means that there are other perspectives and they may present very different views. Indeed, a famous mantra goes: '... *a way of seeing is also a way of not seeing*' (Poggi, 1965). How you see 'mental health' as a long term sufferer of chronic schizophrenia (and you may see it very differently still according to whether you are well or ill) may be very different from how you see it as a psychiatrist, or how you see it as a psychiatric nurse, or the sufferer's parent or spouse, or Mental Health Trust Chief Executive, or as a..., well, you get the point. If you bring in class, gender and ethnicity issues into the melting pot there are already, you can see, a large number of potential perspectives each of which may afford a very different view.

I'll quickly throw in a few terms, for those who don't have a social science background, that are crucial to understanding the 'social construction' of knowledge (Symonds and Kelly, 1998). The truth isn't 'out there' it's in here – or, more accurately, it is the product of a dynamic between mental processes and discourse in and related to the external 'world'. It is constructed rather than discovered and the process of construction is important and is related to power: meaning is imposed on something rather than derived from it and we do not all have equal power to define something for ourselves and others; some are more powerful.

'Paradigm' and 'discourse' are two terms that any sociologist would want to bring in at this point. The importance of paradigms (ways of seeing) is not just that there are competing perspectives but also that at some point one of these becomes predominant (Kuhn, 1962). Foucault's notion of 'discourse', the idea of 'gaze' (again, a way of seeing), and the process through which something comes to be in the wider public domain for discussion, first of all, and then how it is defined and by whom, are crucial for present purposes (Foucault, 1967):

> *'Foucault's notion of "discursive formation" ... emphasizes that sets of ideas cannot be divorced from language. In line with structuralism, Foucault regards thought and language as two sides of a coin'* (Cuff *et al.*, 1998).

So, in the present discussion, to refer to the social phenomenon under consideration as mental illness is to describe it as a 'health' issue (implicit in the terms 'mental health' or 'mental illness') and is already to have 'bought' into a particular perspective which defines the phenomena: it defines sufferers in a certain way, prescribes what responses are appropriate (medical interventions), ascribes roles to the various actors involved ('doctor', 'patient'), and places those roles within some social structure and dynamic which affords a differential in power and status to those roles which are acted out within some narrative on this thing called 'mental illness'. The power element in this is the power to define the phenomenon.

The 'anti-psychiatry movement' (most famously represented in the work of Laing and of Szasz) which was an attempt, inter alia, to re-define psychiatric illness, using terms such as 'problems in living' rather that 'illnesses'. 'Illness' was described as merely a metaphor (Illich, 1975) and that what was happening in psychiatry was that drug interventions mechanisms of social control were being used to manage human behaviour within a restricted definition of the norm under the guise of treatment. The boundaries between use and abuse were seen as narrow or non-existent.

Szasz (1970) used a metaphor of earlier ages' views of devilish possession and magic for the same behaviour we now call 'illness' to stress the culture-bound nature of our ways of seeing mental illness. Sociology has tried to use the language of 'deviance' and 'deviancy theory' but while this refocusing on social processes and labelling carries important insights it has little currency in the wider world.

The predominant model we live with has been termed by some the 'medical model' and by others, more convolutedly the 'biopsychosocial model' (Jenkins *et al.*, 2002). Whatever its label, 'we' see the issue as primarily a health one. The predominant view is that illness is not a metaphor, people are, indeed, ill. Ill people therefore need treatment and furthermore they need treatment from a particular licensed professional group. The power to define matters here does not rest with the sufferer. Their reality, and the response to how they experience 'illness' within that reality, is defined elsewhere.

It is a matter for the health services and for the courts when the behaviour associated with that illness crosses socially defined boundaries and, from the 1983 Mental Health Act on we can more clearly see the importance of the legal perspective on behaviours regarded as evidential of mental illness. The impact of the 'medico-legal' model can be seen clearly in latter-day social policy including the Mental Health Bill currently under consideration, and of which I'll have more to say shortly.

The 'social model' is a term that comes out of the disability lobby (e.g., Morris, 1991) who have challenged the medical model's individualisation of, and pathologisation of, disability. If there is one key concept here it is the repositioning of disability, placing it outside the individual and into the social world beyond the self. Thus the focus is on social structures, dynamics and meanings rather than individual disability or pathology. The sequelae to this repositioning are these: the analysis of problem and its remedy lie in the adaptation of that outside world rather than change in or to the individual.

In terms of a new narrative, this simple 'externalising' of fault brings a powerful challenge to society and its agents. The model has had more impact with younger people with physical disabilities than in the area of mental health (Symonds and Kelly, 1998).

The Seebohm Report (Seebohm, 1968) wasn't an expression of the 'social model' of care in the terms set by the later disability lobby but it was indeed a social model. It set a territory – personal social services and family care – and it pulled together diverse services including mental health social work services into a 'social services department' in 1970. The experiment continued for three decades until the 'modernising' agenda saw the unravelling of that social experiment with an increasing number of local authorities dismantling social service departments, the role of Director of Social Services sidelined or redefined, and mental health returning to health bodies, child care to education, and older care to the independent sector and the creation of new social care trusts (for example, the Manchester Mental Health and Social Care Trust or the Northumberland Care Trust, which has devolved all its adult care services, formerly run by the county council, to the Trust).

Medico-legal model

On the 15th September 2004 the government published a new draft mental health bill. While the focus of the *Modernising Mental Health Services* (MMHS) white paper was the structure of services, the mental health bill has great symbolic and practical importance as to how the law addresses mental health. The criticism of the 1983 act was that it focused on the legalistic side of mental health rather than the care aspects. The most straightforward example is how much of the act dealt with compulsory admissions, which affect the minority of people with mental health problems while bigger issues, certainly in utilitarian terms, of rights to treatment or rights to standards of care were ignored.

This is being written at the end of 2004 and, as I write, the new bill has been received with a less than enthusiastic response from the Mental Health Alliance (a coalition of more than 60 organisations including MIND, and the RCP). Indeed, its impact in uniting the many disparate bodies forming the alliance is remarkable. The headlining parts of the act relate to revising the definition of mental disorder and the new compulsory treatment in the community order. It has thus far been held as sacrosanct that compulsory treatment against one's will required the application of the Mental Health Act in the context of hospital admission. The Sainsbury Centre for Mental Health (SCMH) say the bill is incompatible with the express policy aims of tackling social exclusion, promoting patient choice and tackling issues of ethnicity and race in relation to mental health services. *Breaking the Cycles of Fear* (SCMH, 2002) reiterates earlier research showing that African and Caribbean people avoid seeking help because of the perception of coercive mental health services.

The Mental Health Alliance's Press release, 8th September 2004, lamented powerfully:

> 'We are living in the 21st century and need legislation that reflects society's deeper understanding of mental ill health and the vastly improved opportunities for inclusion and recovery. We need a law that respects patients' human rights and avoids stigmatising them. Instead, we have a Bill that is rooted in an out-dated, false stereotype that people with mental health problems are a danger to society and are unable to make their own decisions about care and treatment. The revised Bill remains objectionable in principle and unworkable in practice' (Mental Health Alliance, 2004).

The main point is the excessive focus on a relatively small number rather than the majority who may have difficulty accessing appropriate services. Mental health services will not shake off the view of them as punitive and threatening, in fact, anything other than the therapeutic agent they should be seen as, while the flagship mental health bill focuses so much on compulsion.

How did we get here? Mental health: A history and all that

> 'Rufus: a ruddy king – This monarch was always very angry and red in the face and was therefore unpopular, so that his death was a Good Thing ... Henry 1 was famous for his handwriting and was therefore called Henry Beau-Geste. He was extremely fond of his son, William, who was, however, drowned at the White City. Henry tried to console himself by eating a surfeit of palfreys. This was a Bad Thing since he died of it and never smiled again' (Sellar and Yeatman, 1066 and all that).

'History', in 1066 and all that, began with the Roman invasion of Britain in 56AD and is divided into 'good' things and 'bad' things. Modern mental health history is similarly divided into good and bad and can traced back to the 1959 Mental Health Act. The potted history of mental health is often discussed under the rubric of 'community care', and the two terms are often used interchangeably, ignoring the fact that 'community care' is a portmanteau term covering a number of social groups and circumstances rather than an unequivocal label for an unambiguous social policy.

The potted history goes that there were 'bad things' called asylums (with over 150,000 patients at their peak in the 50s) and it was a 'good thing' that we stopped them. People know they were a bad thing because we've all seen *One flew over the cuckoo's nest* and we know Jack Nicholson wasn't mad and some of us have heard of Goffman's *Asylums* (Goffman, 1961), and anyway places of incarceration are by definition 'bad things' (Houston, 1955). We started stopping them in the

50s because of the development of new drugs which facilitated 'community care' (which is a 'good thing' because 'community' is a good thing and so is 'care' so 'community care' is doubly good) and we stopped stopping them at the very end of the 20th century when there weren't any more of them.

'Community care' is not only a good thing, it is also cheaper, which is doubleplus good (sorry, slipped from 1066 to 1984) – except it isn't, but we don't mention this. Some old 'bins' were knocked down and turned into shopping centres (a bad thing) but it was also possible to turn them into new communities (a good thing), such as happened at Friern Barnet when the hospital and grounds were converted into a gated middle class 'community' (a 'good thing', because neighbours and neighbourliness are good things; even though no one in the new community knew who their neighbours were or whether they were alive or dead).

But we eventually learned from the Secretary of State (*Modernising Mental Health Services*, 1998a), that 'community care' was, after all, a 'bad thing' because we weren't safe and needed protecting. We agreed because we saw pictures of Michael Stone and Christopher Clunis who were clearly 'mad' – you could see that from the pictures in the newspapers. So, we needed a new mental health act to make people have 'treatment' in the community so they wouldn't be dangerous and for people with personality disorders to face the possibility of preventive detention for things that hadn't happened yet (aka, 'pre-crime', and thus weren't, technically, a part of history) and this made us feel even safer, sounder and more supported.

My faux history, done after *1066 and all that*, is scarcely more simplistic than the real faux history it caricatures. But as our potted history ends a new potted history begins with New Labour's 'modernising' agenda for new mental health services, the MMHS white paper, and the oft-repeated statement from Frank Dobson, Secretary of State for Health at the time, that *'community care has failed'*. The implicit suggestion is the need for a 'new institutionalism' following the logic that if containment outside community (which is what characterised 'total institutions') is redundant as a model then the need is for new containment, a new segregation, within the community.

What is important is that we have a very different set of services, under a new set of pressures, dealing with a long-established problem: how to deal, with limited resources, both with those 'upstream' (the one in four of us who will experience annually some episode of a mild to moderate mental health problem) with those 'downstream' (the one per cent who have more serious problems and the one per cent of those who experience the most severe and enduring mental health problems). This is bound up in the challenges facing 'primary', 'secondary', and 'tertiary' services on the one hand but also the challenges facing society more broadly when considering how to integrate people with mental health conditions with mainstream society rather than see them as in the province of services.

Marshall (Marshall, 1999) raised a central issue: the balance between primary, preventive, services (which also involve a whole range of social inputs other than health services, or indeed 'services' as such). He said in a British Medical Journal editorial:

> *'Since the reforms of the early 1990s psychiatric teams have been caught between the demands of a primary care led NHS (instant access to psychiatric care for all neurotic patients) and those of the Department of Health (concentration on the severely mentally ill). By trying to please everyone psychiatric services have succeeded in pleasing no one and have failed to develop the tightly defined, highly staffed, and narrowly targeted approaches that are known to be effective. Rather than relieve the competing pressures,* Modernising Mental Health Services *has increased them by guaranteeing 24 hour open access while insisting that resources should be concentrated on those with greatest need. Moreover, it has added a new pressure – responsibility for those with untreatable personality disorders'* (ibid).

This article raises the issue I raise again later in the book: the importance of the shifting balance between the prevention end of the care spectrum, and at its far edge, the wider society beyond 'services', and the so-called 'heavy' end, dealing with those in greatest need 'downstream'. The Sainsbury Centre in its 'futures' document recognised the importance of this area (SCMH, 2004b).

The implicit view of 'failure' and 'threat' – the failure of services and the threat from the problems tackled by those services – is bound up in the *Modernising Mental Health Services* white paper and carried forward into the review of the Mental Health Act, which the Mental Health Foundation referred to as a 'shameful' regressive step and concluded:

> *'We consider that [the] draft Bill will do little to improve the experience of those who use mental health services. The proposed compulsory powers are likely to exacerbate, not alleviate, the stigma attached to mental ill-health and increase the social exclusion of people with mental health problems'* (MHF, 2004).

Some basic facts

The earlier discussion about language can't stand in the way of trying to get some basic facts over. So read the following with the appropriate caveat:

> *'Classification of mental disorders has always been more contentious than classification of physical illness. This is partly because, with a few exceptions, psychiatric diagnoses tend to be based entirely on the clinical features of the illness rather than on a pathological, test … Inevitably, therefore, terminology of mental disorders is controversial* (Jenkins *et al.*, 2002).

It is common to distinguish 'psychotic' conditions from 'neurotic'. Thus, psychotic illnesses affect four per 1,000 while 'neurotic' conditions affect 156 per 1,000. Indeed, the oft-quoted Mental Health Foundation statistic suggests one in four (250 per 1,000) of us experience a mental health problem of some sort each year (the most common disorders being anxiety and depression). The Royal College of Psychiatrists suggest one per cent of the adult population (400,000) have a disabling condition as a result of whatever illness or condition they suffer from. About one per cent of that one per cent (4,000) need high levels of support. Often the term 'SMI' (severely mentally ill) is used to describe this population. There is some evidence that the nature of the 'SMI' population is changing as the newer younger generations, often with a dual diagnosis presentation, who have never experienced long term care, replace the older, and more quiescent, generations who've graduated into old age services through a more patriarchal, and now redundant, asylum care model (Inman, 2003).

Beyond diagnosis, the Mental Health Foundation estimate the total cost of mental health problems in England at £32 billion, more than a third of which is attributed to lost employment and productivity related to schizophrenia, depression, stress and anxiety (Mental Health Foundation, 2004). Over 91 million working days are lost to mental ill health every year. Half of the days lost through mental illness are due to anxiety and stress conditions.

The main diagnostic labels are:

- Schizophrenia.
- Depression and anxiety.
- Manic depression/bipolar affective disorder.
- Eating disorders.
- Personality Disorder.

Those of you who work in mental health know it's more complicated than I've presented but for the sake of argument, and for other readers, these are the main categories of illnesses/conditions that make up 'mental illness' and some measure of the broad impact of mental illness. The other concept used is to distinguish 'organic' conditions which aren't seen as formal mental illness as such (e.g., dementias; toxic states from, say, kidney failure) from the 'functional' disorders (those listed above). Some include learning disability and dementia in the range of medical classifications, as given above (Jenkins *et al.*, 2002). Whilst others also include alcohol and substance abuse and 'dual diagnosis' while others seek to exclude these from the ambit of 'mental illness'.

The picture is more complicated at all levels. There are those that challenge the very diagnostic process and language used to present these 'facts'; most famously the 'anti-psychiatry movement' (see earlier) while even if the principles of diagnosis are accepted each of the boxes above can be opened to reveal mixed contents. Schizophrenia, for instance, is really 'the schizophrenias', a group of disorders which have something in common but actually evidence a wide variety of symptoms most, if not all of which, are not unique to 'schizophrenia' and some so dissimilar as to be unrecognisable as indicative of the same category of illness. 'Personality disorder' is not accepted by many as mental illness at all and by some of those who accept it as an illness as an untreatable one.

Psychiatric services were once almost exclusively hospital based. This has changed dramatically over the last 20 years. Mental health beds declined from a height of approx 150,000 in the mid-50s to 34,000 (HPSSS, 2004). NHS spending is still hospital dominated: more than two-thirds of hospital funding goes on in-patient care) while Local Authorities still spend just five per cent or less of their budget on mental health services (HPSSS, 2000-2001).

Stranger danger: mental illness and stigma

The stranger is, thus, now in our midst and 'stranger danger' plays an important role in latter-day policy-making. Policy-making involves a narrative, it is a form of story-telling, and the mental health/illness storyline continues to involve danger and threat. The white paper, *Modernising Mental Health Services: safe, sound, supportive* began *'Mental health problems are common … suicide is now the 2nd most common cause of death in the under 35s … there is a relationship between active mental illness and violence.'* A dramatic opening strikes the tonic note of mental health policy.

However, basic statistics do not support the horror headlines in newspapers or the general tone of policy.

> *'There was little fluctuation in numbers of people with a mental illness committing criminal homicide over the 38 years studied, and a 3 per cent annual decline in their contribution to the official statistics. There are many reasons for improving the resources and quality of care for people with a mental disorder, but there is no evidence that it is anything but stigmatising to claim that their living in the community is a dangerous experiment that should be reversed. There appears to be some case for specially focused improvement of services for people with a personality disorder and/or substance misuse'* (Taylor and Gunn, 1999).

In April 1996-97 there were 479 suicides by people 'under mental health service care'. Over same period, of 238 homicides, just 17 per cent were found to have had symptoms of mental illness as a feature in the perpetration of the act; thus the mute, non-headline, fact is that 83 per cent of perpetrators did not have symptoms of mental illness. Four-fifths of victims were family members (Department of Health, 2002c).

Be scared of people who are not mentally ill particularly if they are members of your family could be a more correct interpretation of the facts but would not produce a headline soundbite useful to policy-makers and government.

Current initiatives:

- *Modernising Mental Health Services.*
- Review of the Mental Health Act.
- *National Service Frameworks.*
- User participation.

The modernisation agenda in health and social care (performance targets, national standards, regulatory framework, budgetary constraint, outcomes focus, inclusive approaches, service standards, central control) and the review of mental health legislation (rights and compulsions, care and control) represent the two key areas of mental health policy. The high level drivers are the same in the mental health arena as elsewhere (cost containment, re-defining the role of the state, new 24/7 politics and the open society, mixed economy of care, human rights, shift towards primary care/prevention) but unique to mental health is the perception of threat and danger and the undercurrent of stigma that dominates the medico-legal model characterised by *'controlling legislation [and] negative perceptions'* of users (Beresford, 2004).

This conflicts directly with the driver of 'user involvement' and user control. It is a notable comparison that the perspective of the older persons' green paper emphasises 'user' ownership and control in a way absent from mental health. A recent review of user participation noted:

> *'Challenges to traditional professional modes of thinking and operating are emerging as a result of participation. Organisational cultures and structures need to respond and change in order to accommodate new partnerships and new ways of working with people who have often been oppressed and marginalised. The service user movement seems to be exposing the limitations of traditional, fragmented, service categories for organising participation designed to promote strategic change. Participation provides a unique opportunity for organisations to develop through user led critical enquiry using the social model of disability, ideas about control, oppression, rights poverty and citizenship'* (Carr, 2004, p.7). The same review also noted that in the mental health arena: *'there is a relatively weak evidence base for the impact of user involvement on organisational change'* (ibid, p.17).

Housing and community care

'... the identification of housing conditions as social problems is the outcome of social processes involving ideologies, 'discourses' (ways of thinking about issues developed by professional elites), the media and the use of political and economic power' (Lund, 1999).

What is most apparent in policy terms is the disconnectedness of the 'drivers', as they're called, of the individual policy areas of health, housing and social care. This remains the fundamental flaw in any holistic approach to social problems and no amount of 'joined up' rhetoric will render the join invisible.

Why is this the case? Mental health has been dominated by the perspective of those providing the care (from professional elites in health and social care but particularly in health) and the discourse dominated by the major piece of social policy of the 1980s onwards, the 'deinstitutionalisation' of people in long term asylums (or what some have called, in fact, 'reinstitutionalisation', i.e., institutionalisation in a different form). The housing voice has been rather weak in the policy context of the run down of the asylum system. In this major social experiment, so-called 'total institutions' (Goffman, 1961), physically segregated from the community as well as socially, were replaced by new institutions that were, in effect, segregated within the community (see range of work from TAPS: e.g., Leff, 1998; Leff, 2000). Housing was peripheral to this experiment.

The Seebohm committee report (Seebohm, 1968) recommended that housing departments should take on some responsibility for adults with disabilities including people with mental health problems. Lund described that housing departments became rather detached from community care policy as they had to face a different set of drivers: family homelessness duties, reforms of the housing management system, 'difficult to let' properties in 'sink' estates, and the retraction in building homes imposed by central government (Lund, 1999, p.165). Lund also noted that the Barclay report (Barclay, 1982) recognised the chasm between housing workers and social workers which continued forward to present times (Means *et al.*, 2003). Means and colleagues commented on another wall (not the Berlin Wall), between social services and housing, citing conflicts over roles and responsibilities, lack of knowledge of each others' networks and a tendency for professionals to hold stereotypical images of each other (ibid, p.152).

The potential benefit of Supporting People, in this context, is that it can at the same time bring closer together two distinct sectors, housing and social care, and can also help span the functional divide between low level support (as a prophylactic to care) and higher level continuing care needs – the upstream-downstream debate discussed elsewhere here (see Simic in Chapter 14).

What evidence there is supports the proposition behind the Supporting People programme, namely that low level preventative interventions will increase or maintain independence with a resulting benefit to the individual and the exchequer over the longer term. The Benefits Realisation report (ODPM, 2004) said:

> '... the evidence supports the proposition behind the programme, namely that low-level preventative interventions will increase or maintain independence with a resulting benefit to the individual and the exchequer over the longer term ... This is in line with wider government policy, including recommendations around the preventative health agenda raised by the Wanless report.'

The 2005 budgets of all 150 councils administering the £1.7 billion scheme were cut in December 2004, in most cases by more than five per cent. A new formula for distributing the money is likely to mean a lower allocation in future. So the fact that low level prevention can maintain or increase independence, that this can benefit not only individuals and their kith and kin and the wider community, and additionally this may benefit the exchequer and is in line with the agenda on prevention raised by Wanless – *'the first ever evidence based assessment of long term resource requirements for the NHS'* (Wanless, 2002) seems to carry little weight when balanced with the exchequer's view of the spending.

The future: balancing act

Whatever the yield from the managerialist approach implicit in the UK service frameworks, and whatever the impact of forthcoming legislation on individual rights and on public safety, there are some fundamental questions for the future of mental health care. How they are answered will shape that care.

The questions all relate to some aspect of balance in the care system:

- Is 'mental health' a health AND social care issue, or just health? In terms of providers of health and social care, organisational change in NHS and social services departments seems to be saying this is exclusively a health issue.
- Can prevention and specialist care come into some balance? Will policy meet both the downstream needs (of those who have fallen in and need help getting out and staying out) and broaden the scope to include the majority of sufferers upstream (those with mild to moderate conditions who may, with the right type of support, maintain their independence within the mainstream – no pun intended). Or, will it keep the focus on the minority who have the greatest needs? There remains little evidence that the mental health focus has moved from margins to mainstream.
- Can the proper balance be reached between professional and user perspectives? User participation is crucial to renewing the enterprise that is mental health care but so is the discovery of a positive discourse around the role of the social care professional.

- Can the proper balance be achieved in legislation between a concern for rights and protection on the one hand and for quality of care and enhancement of life chances/empowerment on the other?

Supporting People is meant to address the broad range of low level preventive support that and fill the gap left by the shift of community care towards targeting resources to those most in need, those most seriously ill or disabled. Getting the balance right between the 'upstream' and 'downstream' services is the major challenge. One of the fault lines could be repaired at the preventive end by Supporting People. The fundamental separation of housing and community care policies may be repaired by this social experiment; the debate has always been limited by a crude '4 legs good, 2 legs bad' debate around 'institutions' versus 'community' or around an equally crude 'bricks and mortar' versus 'care' debate.

It was possible to be optimistic, then, on hearing Stephen Ladyman (then Parliamentary under Secretary of State at the Department of Health) in his 17th June 2003 speech to the Local Government Chronicle Conference say that mental health was a high priority, and noted that: *'mental health issues are all too often an important barrier to successfully reintegrating socially excluded groups back into society'* and that there was to be *'an increasing focus on a whole systems approach'*. But if implementation of policy is to be brought to heel at the first hint of the budgetary consequences of identifying unmet need and managing change then there is little reason for continued optimism about the reality of that change.

The persistence of stigma (both in the general public and in government), and its disabling impact (Corrigan and Penn, 1999), together add up to a major educational challenge. That challenge is to move the narrative on from the level of newspaper 'shock-horror' headlines and two dimensional characterisation. A more sophisticated story would recognise the important role of housing, and the Supporting People initiative, in helping move the focus of the mental health system 'upstream'.

CHAPTER 10:
Supported housing and frail older people – towards whole systems approaches?

Mark Foord

Introduction – the new challenges in context

Living in the slipstream of the government agenda for modernising health and social care provision, supported housing for older people is undergoing unprecedented change. 'Old style', 'traditional' models of sheltered housing, which have dominated debates about housing and old age, are giving way to more person centred responses to the housing and support needs of older people. Sheltered housing aimed to provide support in a 'homely environment' whilst reducing risk and postponing entry into residential care. It was part of an integrated community care system only in that it provided lower steps on an escalator leading to more institutionalised forms of care; as sheltered housing provided more recruits to residential care than other tenures (McCafferty, 1994).

The government is beginning to integrate housing into social care and health provision through its espousal of *'whole systems working'*. There are important implications for housing providers; housing authorities are urged to work in partnership to develop the *National Service Framework for Older People*, *Supporting People* and local housing strategies. The Department of Health (2004a) urges that joint commissioning for older people's services be accompanied with data on the housing needs of local populations, service provision, quality and its outcomes. Strong messages are emerging from government that the community based care and support offered by housing providers will be at the centre of future provision for frail older people. Stephen Ladyman (Minister for Community Care) setting out the government's 'vision' for adult social care services, compared residential care with extra care sheltered housing and noted:

> *'I have visited many care homes. Some of them are fabulous and some aren't. But, when I visit extra care housing schemes I enter a completely different environment where it is clear that the names on the doors are tenants or home owners who really are in their own homes and still in control of their own lives. And the experience of those tenants or home owners is so*

overwhelmingly positive that I am drawn, irresistibly to the conclusion that this will be the dominant model of supported living for the ageing generation' (Ladyman, 2004).

Housing agencies providing *'homes for life'* that is, the provision of support in existing accommodation, rather than referring tenants onto institutional care as their needs change, are pushing at an opening door.

New thinking about the role of housing has also been in response to *'fundamental changes in the make up, aspirations and living patterns within the older population'* (Sumner, 2001). The Audit Commission programme looking at the needs of older people in the 21st century suggested if we are to manage the transition to an 'older society' we need to *'provide an environment in which older people can thrive and live life to the full for as long as possible – contributing to society, rather than being dependent on it. We therefore need approaches that help older people to live independent lives – keeping people healthy, active and able to participate for as long as possible'* (Audit Commission *et al.*, 2004). The dual impact of the demographics of an ageing society and the aspirations of the 'baby boomer' generation will *'drive policy change in radical new directions'* (Huber and Skidmore, 2003).

However, not all is rosy consensus, and as Alan Walker has noted there has been a vacuum in debates around ageing, filled *'by a demography of despair, which portrays population ageing not as a triumph for civilisation but as something closer to an apocalypse'* (quoted in Dean, 2003). 'Apocalyptic' language has been used to outline a demographic *'age quake'* which will transform the west as services are overwhelmed by the needs of an ageing society (McKie, 2004). It is predicted that the numbers of 'dependent' older people living alone by 2031 will increase by 45 per cent whilst the over 85s needing long term care will grow by 88 per cent (Pickard *et al.*, 2000). The King's Fund suggest that care homes are in short supply in London and that older people struggle to access care services (Gilbert, 2004). How far people should fund their own care and far they should be publicly funded continue to be key issues. Scotland have introduced free personal care, whilst England, Wales and Northern Ireland have introduced free nursing care in care homes but not free personal care. How health, care and housing providers can meet the demands of a potentially frail and needy older population, whilst reconciling aspirations for independence with increasing frailty, will provide a growing challenge.

The aims of this chapter

In his 2001 Reith Lecture series, Kirkwood articulated the importance of choice as old age leads to greater frailty:

> *'... over protection can create or reinforce anxiety and self doubt. If we treat old people as weak spirited because they are frail, we do them serious*

injustice. Inevitably, ageing involves loss. But prejudice and lack of appropriate provision frequently force a premature closing down of options, sometimes through neglect, sometimes through benign but misguided over protection' (Kirkwood, 2001).

The purpose of this chapter is to sketch out how housing providers can contribute to meeting the housing and care choices of frail older people, through integration with whole systems approaches to housing, care and support. Particularly for those older people described in the *National Service Framework for Older People*, as in a *'transitional phase'* between healthy active life and the onset of increasing levels of frailty. The chapter will do three things:

1. Explore three key 'drivers' to housing involvement in providing innovative services for older people: demographic change; changing aspirations, and 'whole systems' approaches to health, housing and social care.
2. Set out what the 'whole systems' agenda means for housing providers. In particular, how it is leading to the development of the housing role in intermediate care and extra care sheltered housing.
3. The chapter concludes by asking whether these new developments bring us closer to the development of an integrated approach to addressing the aspirations of older people for choice, independence and voice.

Background issues

My starting point is an affirmation of research showing that the majority of older people prefer to live in ordinary, mainstream housing for as long as possible (Tinker, 1997), and 'defend' their independence for as long as possible (Peace and Holland, 2001). However, independence and autonomy may come under threat with advancing age. Jarvis *et al.* (1996) explored the abilities of older people and found that whilst the majority had few difficulties with personal care, a wider range of competencies were required for home maintenance tasks (for example, cleaning windows), and with mobility related tasks such as going upstairs. In all cases competency declined with advancing age. Today, a range of interventions and services can promote independence, and prevent/delay entry into institutional care, for example preventative services (such as Home Improvement Agencies) or assistive technology (Audit Commission *et al.*, 2004).

With increasing frailty some people reach a point at which they can no longer cope in their own homes. Traditionally, the accepted solution has been specialised housing with elements of support and care, ranging from sheltered housing to nursing homes. Robson *et al.* (1997) suggest there are seven levels in the 'housing and care' ladder:

- Staying put – non-specialised, mainstream housing.
- Retirement housing – independent housing which has been purpose built/ adapted for fit, active people.

- Category 1 sheltered housing – purpose built, self contained housing dwellings for the fit and active older person, built to mobility standards with a scheme manager in attendance and minimal communal facilities.
- Category 2 sheltered housing – purpose built, self contained housing dwellings for physically frail older people, built to full mobility and wheelchair standards with a scheme manager and access to a range of communal facilities and activities.
- Category 2.5 or extra care sheltered housing – similar to category 2 but with a extra personal care available and an option to take meals with other tenants.
- Category 3 homes – residential care homes for older people who may be mentally or physically frail and in need of constant personal care.
- Nursing homes or geriatric units – for older people who are very sick or frail and need qualified nursing care.

The tension between rejecting institutional care, and an acceptance that they continue to play a necessary role *for some people* has become clearer. Oldman argues that *'it cannot always be assumed that older people do not want to move on'* (Oldman, 2000). Jack (1998) argues that for the *'anti-residential care school of thought'*, the quality of life of older people is always *'unquestionably assumed to be higher in the community'*. Boyle (2004) in a study of choice and control in long term care argues that this is not always so. Her findings suggest that levels of perceived autonomy and choice were *'significantly higher among residents in institutions than the clients'* (of care providers) *'in private households'*. This research has great relevance for housing providers exploring the provision of extra care sheltered housing. The negative associations of communal forms of living have become more muted.

As housing providers have become junior partners in *whole systems* approaches to care and support, the *'rungs on the ladder'* have become less visible. There is still a long way to go, as the Audit Commission suggests *'services for older people must work together if they are to meet people's needs and aspirations more effectively ... All too often older people receive a disjointed, confused response when they need help or advice. Frequently the responses that they receive meet their needs only in part'* (Audit Commission, 2002).

Drivers to change

Demands for housing, support and social care for older people are being reshaped by a range of demographic and social trends. In this section we concentrate upon three: *demographic change*, *changing aspirations* and *policy change*.

Demographic change, older people and changing housing needs

The term 'demographic timebomb' is today less frequently used, as the positive aspects of an ageing society begin to be recognised (for example lower crime).

None the less, statistics show that the increasing age profile of the population challenges housing policy. The latest population projections from the government show higher growth than previously expected in the numbers of older people. The numbers of people aged 65 and over are predicted to rise by 81 per cent over the next five decades, from 9.3 million in 2000 to 16.8 million in 2051. The numbers of people aged 85 and over are projected to grow at an even faster rate – from 1.1 million in 2000 to 4 million in 2051, an increase of 255 per cent (Wittenberg, Comas-Herrera and Pickard, 2004). Older people tend to have a much greater need for health and social services. Two-thirds of acute and general hospital beds are used by people aged over 65 years (Department of Health, 2001a). The inclusion of sheltered housing support in the Supporting People programme has guaranteed that older people will take the lion's share of the pot. Total expenditure on long term care for people in the UK has been estimated at £12.9 billion in 2000, of which around £9.8 billion relates to care costs and around £3.2 billion to hotel costs (accommodation costs) (Wittenberg, Comas-Herrera and Pickard, 2004).

Old age will be increasingly gendered, as women will outnumber men. At the age of 75 and over women outnumber men by 2:1; at 85 4:1 and at the age of 100 by 7:1 (Bernard, 2000). Women already constitute a majority of sheltered tenants, and will provide a key future market for social landlords. A recent survey by Hanover Housing Association found that women were more likely to consider sheltered housing as an option in old age than men, who expressed more willingness to live in retirement or residential homes (*Community Care*, 2004b). There will also be steep rises in the numbers of people from Black and Minority Ethnic groups with particular social and cultural needs (Social Services Inspectorate, 1998). These trends are especially salient in social housing, where older people are more heavily represented. More than 40 per cent of households in social housing are headed by a person aged over 60 years old. A third of over 70 years olds are social housing tenants, compared to 15 per cent of people in their 40s (Department of Transport, Local Government and the Regions, 2002b). Social housing tenants are more likely to suffer from the impact of employment related ill health and higher rates of disability and chronic ill health. They are also more likely to live in poverty, have a lower pension provision and live in residualised areas of high crime and anti-social behaviour, than other sectors of the population. There are nearly four million pensioners living in the 88 most deprived local authorities in England. Nearly half (44 per cent) of all pensioners live in homes that are not in decent repair or thermally efficient – this being a contributor to the extra 23,000-50,000 deaths from cold in the previous five winters (Dean, 2003).

The Wanless Report (commissioned by the Treasury to review long term trends affecting the NHS), highlighted the so called *'compression of morbidity'* theory – that people make the most intense use of services in the year leading up to death, irrespective of age. Wanless concluded that while illness and frailty among older people is likely to decline, the number of minor health problems may increase as older people live longer (Wanless, 2002). Evidence to the Audit Commission *et al.* (2004) suggests that at any one time only about 15 per cent of older people are in touch with care services, many of whom will be in the final years of their life. Older and frailer tenants who may have experienced a lifetime of systemic disadvantage will place high demands for supported housing services on landlords.

Aspirations and housing choices

The concept of *'grey power'* has become a powerful reminder to government that people over the age of 60 will constitute a significant interest block. The 'baby boomers' (those born 1945-1965) arrived at adulthood in a strong consumer society. Their existence has led to calls for a radical rethink of residential care and supported housing, with more emphasis on making them 'elder enabled' (*The Guardian*, 2003a). In housing the aspirations of older people are at the heart of debates taking place about the quality and type of housing providers can expect older people to accept.

The Housing green paper of 2000 *Quality and Choice – a decent home for all* (Department of the Environment, Transport and the Regions, 2000), set out a holistic vision, but failed to explore the housing needs of older people. The government has published a series of reports which have stressed the importance of housing in delivering on the broader health and social care agenda. *Quality and Choice for older people's housing – a strategic framework* (Department of Transport, Local Government and the Regions/Department of Health, 2001a) put forward five key themes that should be developed in housing services for older people: *diversity and choice*; *information and advice*; *flexible service provision*; *service quality*, and *joint working*. The Housing Corporation strategy for housing and older people (Housing Corporation, 2003b) spelt out how housing associations could 'fine tune' their services to the needs of an increasingly aged and vulnerable clientele.

Yet until recently, we had little evidence about the housing choices and decisions of older people. Using a mixed method research design that placed users at the centre of the research (through the use of older people panels and users as interviewers), Bright *et al.* (2003) mapped the housing decisions of older people and their consequences. The key findings were that older people did not believe they were listened to, nor was action taken as a result of consultation. In terms of housing provision, they recognised an implicit ageism in the assumption that older people will accept lower quality housing:

> *'... just because people get older doesn't mean that they don't have visitors, for meals or to stay ... people need a private garden space ... council or housing association flats are more security minded but are too small. One person is expected to be grateful to be given a bed sit to live in'* (Bright, 2003).

Secondly they point out housing decisions are complex, and people struggle to accommodate this in their housing decisions – *'my home has replaced work – which formerly took all my time and energy – as the way that I present myself to the world'*. Thirdly, housing decisions cannot be viewed as *rational and objective*.

People are working through and with powerful emotional elements when they make housing decisions. Fourthly, people use housing to manage and structure their lives; hence design, quality and standards are critical factors in the way people live. Finally, people want housing that is designed to help manage reduced mobility and potential disability; provides safety and security, comfort and pleasure, and has sufficient space to allow them to construct their lives (for example, a second bedroom for visitors or hobbies). They conclude by addressing the factors that lead people rethink their housing situations – activities that become more difficult (driving, shopping etc.); changes to the locality (anti-social behaviour, changes to shops etc.); changes in the level of support (families move away, neighbours change), and finally changed priorities – such as *'wanting to go back to your roots'*, fear of dying alone, *all of which may lead to the acceptance of the need for help.* Whilst the majority of older people wish to remain in mainstream housing for as long as possible, many reach a point where they want to make the transition into housing which might include a range of communal settings.

The aspirations of older people are rising. Hence they are more likely to refuse offers of supported housing that do not meet their needs. In recent years there has been a flowering of innovation in housing and care for older people, driven by a desire for what Pastalan (1997) calls 'ageing in place', thereby enabling older people to remain in their homes for longer, delaying the need for residential care. Care services, technology, preventative services and innovative forms of independent living, have hastened the view that traditional forms of residential care are anachronistic and outmoded. A housing provider suggested: *'a generation of sheltered housing tenants were council tenants. But people want better facilities with a spare room for family or visitors. We need to ask if we are developing homes we would like to live in 30-40 years'* (Knutt, 2003). Housing which meets older people's desire for autonomy and independence can be provided in supported settings. A recent project exploring what older people meant by *'independence'* found that independence did not mean doing everything by yourself but was defined in terms of *choice* and *control*. A respondent noted that that moving into a sheltered housing scheme could at first feel like losing independence, however the security and support it offered – particularly for frail older people enhanced independence (Audit Commission *et al.*, 2004).

At April 2002 there were 511,300 residential care beds (Laing and Buisson, 2002). The numbers of older people going into residential care has fallen and are projected to fall further over the next five years by between 30,000-50,000 people. However, research suggests that occupied places in residential care homes will need to rise to around 1,230,000, whilst the number of care home hours will need to increase from around 2.0 million per week to over 4.8 million a week in 2051 (Wittenberg, Comas-Herrera and Pickard, 2004). These arresting figures assume we retain our current dependence on models of residential care. Influential voices call for new and innovative alternatives to residential care. The Association of Directors of Social Services submission to the Royal Commission on Long Term Care argued:

'Residential care for elderly people is arguably an outdated model if not an anachronism. It is unlikely in our view that such a model of communal living can survive long into the next century. Even older people without assets can acquire in certain parts of the country a very sheltered housing tenancy that will offer substantial levels of care, a better quality of life and dignity and greater security than can be offered in residential care'.

Providers should critically reflect on whether the services they offer meet the aspirations of older people for quality, user satisfaction and independence. Stephen Ladyman recently suggested:

'Older people want to stay in their own homes for as long as possible. If increasing frailty prevents this then they want to move somewhere that is more manageable, where they can still control over their lives. Communities must offer them real rights, where they are supported in their own homes and enjoy dignity and privacy, and have equal access services' (Gatward, 2004).

Disillusionment with the residential care sector offers opportunities to housing providers to develop new and innovative forms of extra care housing. This in turn will *'emphasise differences in standards between care homes and other forms of accommodation with care, and is likely to increase pressures on care homes to improve physical standards'* (Darton, 2004).

Policy change: community care to whole systems working

A central theme of the modernisation agenda for health and social care has been the promotion of the concept of *independence* (Secker *et al.*, 2003), returning to a key theme of the 1990 NHS and Community Care Act. The 1990 Act was predicated on the belief that nearly everyone prefers to live in ordinary housing rather than institutions, as institutions lack the capacity to be a 'home' (Means, Richards and Smith, 2003). It attached importance to social services and health working closely at strategic, operational and individual levels. Although the NHS and Community Care Act raised the profile of work with older people, and may have had a positive effect on service delivery (Lewis and Glennerster, 1996), the uncertainties caused by budget reductions after the first generous financial settlements resulted in a tightening of eligibility criteria and the rationing of care for those with high care needs (Walker, 1993). It led to a process which speeded up the shift from *universal* towards *targeted services*, and service users losing care services or facing long waits for assessments and funding packages. Far from facilitating closer partnerships, a 'joint working deficit' developed between health and providers. Hospitals under pressure to increase patient throughput and free up NHS beds were accused of inappropriately discharging older people back into the community. Social services and housing authorities were also working under different time constraints from health providers (particularly around the provision of aids and adaptations). Consequently patients could be discharged before domiciliary care and personal care support (social services) or adaptations (housing) were available. The lack of adequate home support led many to take the life changing decision to move into residential or nursing care.

The Coming of Age (Audit Commission, 1997) explored the provision of care services for older people, and concluded that many older people were locked into a 'vicious cycle' of care. A reduction in the number of hospital beds, shorter stays in hospital and the lack of convalescence and rehabilitation facilities meant that older people needed increasingly more expensive and intensive long term care. A later report *Home Alone* (Audit Commission, 1998) concentrated on the contribution of housing to community care, noting the increasing flow of resources towards older people with high care needs. Concluding, the report stated that, *'too many people fall through the net'* because of *'poor collaboration between housing, social services and health authorities'* and that *'a picture emerges of inadequate identification of needs, inflexible use of stock and insufficient early intervention to prevent vulnerable people reaching crisis point'.*

Labour's manifesto commitments to community care were limited (Means, Morbey and Smith, 2002), and these were seen as part of a wider set of policies (for example, addressing social exclusion). A key feature of Labour's community care reforms has been their intention to break down the 'Berlin Wall' existing between health and social care provision. The government appeared to believe that the community care reforms were unsuccessful in establishing a clear demarcation between health and social care and a willingness to work jointly (Means, Richards and Smith, 2003), and in consequence developed the concept of *'whole systems working'* (for a full discussion of the concept of whole systems working, see the chapter by Julie Savory in this volume).

Whole systems working and older people

The housing role in providing support to frail older people should be contextualised against wider changes taking place in the NHS and social care. Labour set out its ideas for the NHS in *The New NHS: Modern, Dependable*, (1997) which emphasised the need to switch resources away from acute hospital care towards primary care through a new system of primary care trusts. *Partnership in Action* (Department of Health, 1998c) recommended the removal of legal boundaries around budget pooling. The 1999/2001 Health Acts encouraged social services and health to pool budgets, develop joint teams and promote integration in service planning and provision. Partnership working and whole system working was conterminously emphasised in the white paper *Modernising Social Services* (Department of Health, 1998b). The NHS Plan (Department of Health, 2000) proposed that primary care trusts would become *'single multi-purpose legal bodies'*, able to commission health and social care, and indicated the government's determination to develop a primary care led NHS focusing on community services. Three 'pillars' of the health and social care are explored below.

The *National Service Framework for Older People*

In 2001 the *National Service Framework for Older People* established a broad framework for service development based on four themes: respecting the individual; joining up care; providing timely access to the best specialist care, and promoting healthy and active living. The government claimed the *National Service Framework* offered *'a 10 year programme of action linking services to support independence and promote good health, specialised services for key conditions, and culture change so that all older people and their carers are always treated with respect, dignity and fairness'*. The result, it claimed would be the first 'comprehensive strategy to ensure fair, high quality, integrated health and social care services for older people'. A crucial part of the *National Service Framework* was its ambition to promote whole systems working, to *'deliver person centred care across organisational boundaries by joined up processes for commissioning and delivering older people's services'* (Department of Health, 2001a). The *National Service Framework* set targets for the period 2003-2006:

- Improve the quality of life and independence of older people so that they can live independently wherever possible.
- Increase the numbers of those supported intensively to live at home to 30 per cent of the total supported by social services.
- Growth of under one percent in emergency hospital admissions.
- No growth in re-admissions to hospital.

To support these goals, the Delayed Discharge Act (2002) was passed which instigated a series of fines for local authorities unable to facilitate hospital discharge on a day to day basis. There is evidence that local authorities have been developing innovative schemes designed to avoid fines. Inspections of 23 local authorities found a wide range of services promoting independence particularly in the area of intermediate care as a planned response to delayed discharge (Department of Health, 2002a).

Intermediate care

The development of intermediate care formed a significant part of the NHS Plan. The Department of Health defines intermediate care as follows:

- Targeted at people who would face unnecessary prolonged hospital stays or inappropriate hospital admission, long term residential care or NHS in patient care.
- Provided on the basis of a comprehensive assessment resulting in a structured individual care plan.
- A planned outcome of maximising independence, enabling patients to resume living at home.

- Time limited to no longer than six weeks and frequently as little as two weeks.
- Cross professional working with a single assessment framework. (Department of Health, 2002b)

£900 million was set aside for the creation of 5,000 extra care intermediate care beds to promote independence. Including – rapid response teams, intensive rehabilitation services, integrated home care – each with a focus on reducing the need for older people to enter hospital and speed up hospital discharge. Housing providers have taken advantage of this funding to develop provision linked into health provision.

Good practice example:
Severn Vale Housing Society and Cheltenham and Tewkesbury Primary Care Trust

Joint funding was provided to re-model four flats in a sheltered housing scheme. This has enabled 17 people to move from hospital back into their own homes. An occupational therapist from the Primary Care Trust project managed the scheme and provided a link between the housing society and the Primary Care Trust. The cost saving to the NHS was £85,000.

Good practice example: North Yorkshire County Council

The county has developed a multi-agency older people strategy to replace all their own care homes with a combination of resource centres, which will offer short term care, and extra care housing. Together these will replace 26 residential homes that were in existence in 1999. This has been developed after full consultation.

The Single Assessment Process for health and social care

The *Single Assessment Process* (SAP) provides a key plank of the *National Service Framework for Older People*. First signalled in the 2000 NHS Plan, the SAP sought to address longstanding deficiencies in the health and social care assessment processes, as first identified in the 1990 NHS and Community Act. Agencies began using SAP in 2002, but had until April 2004 to be compliant with each aspect of guidance. The guidance on the SAP (Department of Health, 2002b) does not recommend the use of a single assessment tool, but seeks to provide a framework that will lead to a convergence of assessment methods and results over time (McNally, Cornes and Clough, 2003).

SAP represented an aspiration that local agencies would share assessment tools and approaches, and force them to review local procedures for unified working. As such, SAP underpins 'Standard 2 of the *National Service Framework*' which urged that:

'NHS and social services treat older people as individuals and enable them to make choices about their own care. This is achieved through the SAP, integrated commissioning arrangements and integrated provision of services including community equipment and continence service's'.

SAP focuses upon:

- Ensuring the scale and depth of assessment is in proportion to the older person's needs.
- Ensuring agencies do not duplicate each other's assessments.
- Ensuring professionals contribute to assessments in the most effective way.

SAP has four assessment levels: *contact assessment*; *overview*; *specialist*; and *comprehensive*. Its importance is that the approach remains the same regardless who asks the questions, their professional training or where they work. The SAP domain area *'immediate environment and resources'* is suited to the involvement of housing agencies.

Housing agencies and the challenge of whole systems working

In a previous section, we explored the impact of demographic change, changing aspirations and policy change on the development of services for older people. In this section we identify what the new agenda means for housing providers, and in particular how housing providers are playing a critical role in the development of extra care sheltered housing and intermediate care. Easterbrook (2003) argues that the changes implemented since 1997 have been *'rapid, complex, multi-layered, constant and ongoing'*. Organisations have been encouraged to look critically at their provision and think in fresh ways about choice, involvement, quality and participation for older people. She sets out the key themes as: standards of service and the quality of staff; evidence based practice; promoting independence; working in partnership; new plans and initiatives; involving users and carers, and finally, tackling age discrimination.

Our understanding of older people's housing needs has shifted decisively, the perspective that 'home' is central to lifestyle choice and maintaining/regaining independence is now widely shared. Housing based models of care are increasingly recognised as central to delivering the *National Service Framework*. The Social Services Inspectorate suggest a cultural shift has taken place from an *'era when users were offered what was available and were looked after, by services that cared for the individual and minimised risk'* to *'person centred needs led planning that is starting to offer choice and empowerment'* (Social Services Inspectorate, 2003). The Office of the Deputy Prime Minister/Department of

Health (2003) has published guidance on how housing issues should be addressed in local older people's strategies, which should contain:

- A 'whole system' view of services.
- Links with intermediate care and support services.
- Evidence of need.
- The inclusion of diverse views (for example Black and Minority Ethnic groups).
- Evidence of accommodation and support needs in other strategies.
- Targets for future improvement and action plans.
- Plans for getting people to work together.

In 2002 the Health Secretary announced a growth in the number of extra care housing by 2006; and the creation of a *Change Agent Team* which has focused on the development of housing based models of care such extra care sheltered housing; housing based intermediate care, and the role of home improvement agencies – to facilitate the discharge of older people from hospital. We can now begin to see what the shape of a whole systems working approach to supported housing might take. Fletcher (1999) suggests a programme for developing more person centred housing for older people would provide:

- Housing linked to health focusing on health improvement.
- Greater budget flexibility and integration.
- Shared information across disciplines.
- Collaborative models of joint working and staff.
- Inclusive approaches between sectors to service planning and delivery.
- Increased locality planning and budgeting of services.
- A shift towards preventative services alongside a focus on high level services to meet high care needs.

The 2002 Spending Review suggested that as part of their Public Service Agreement the Department of Health must *'improve the quality of life and independence of older people so that they can live at home wherever possible'*. The Department of Health drew up a plan to increase the numbers of older people receiving intermediate care by 70,000 per year until 2005/6 (Department of Health, 2002a) and highlighted the importance of service integration to form coherent systems of care. Housing providers have begun to develop good practice exemplars.

Good practice example: Leeds City Council, Anchor Housing and Methodist Homes

This partnership are re-modelling four residential care homes as state of the art 'extra care' sheltered housing schemes. Residents will be able to buy, rent, or share ownership of the properties, while receiving 24 hour care from Leeds Social Services. Work on the schemes will begin early in 2005.

Good practice example: Stockport Council

They have developed commissioning strategies linking national, corporate and local objectives for health and housing, characterised by robust planning frameworks and sound knowledge of the local population and its needs.

Housing providers have a huge role to play. Extra care sheltered housing schemes are being re-modelled to provide intermediate care flats for those leaving hospital. The Social Services Inspectorate has reported that councils are starting to reflect on how *Supporting People* could be used to support older people. Extra care sheltered housing was seen to be contributing to the reduced use of residential care and nursing homes during 2002/3 and were planned to continue to fall during 2003/4 (Social Services Inspectorate, 2003). Policy change within the NHS should help establish a distinctive supported housing approach. The NHS and social care planning priorities framework 2003-2006 sets out detailed targets for improving services for older people, which include:

- By 2004, 5,000 more intermediate care beds than in 2000.
- By 2004, 220,000 more people utilising intermediate care than in 2000.
- By 2006, councils to increase their intermediate care places by an extra 70,000 places per year.
- In 2006, 6,900 more extra care places.

Good practice example: St Germains Grange, Marske by the Sea, Anchor Housing

The scheme opened in 2001 and is an example of integrated housing and care. The focus is on promoting and maintaining independence. An on site manager co-ordinates a care team and housing support to 31 flats. It provides an alternative to delayed discharge and has worked to prevent avoidable hospital admissions.

Good practice example: Wolverhampton Council

Had a medium term strategy to maximise the use of extra care sheltered housing, rooted in a joint strategy with health. Key elements included:

- The quality of partnership planning.
- Service user and carer consultation.
- The provision of extra care sheltered housing with preferred providers .
- Other supporting day and community services also developed linked into a substantial residential care de-commissioning programme which reduced the total from 11 to 4.

Moving the agenda forward

Despite the existence of an infrastructure of new and innovative housing with care provision, and a clear policy around joint working, the national picture is still one of variable service provision and fragmentation. A recent district auditor report on the provision of mental health and rehabilitation services for older people, suggests that the key agencies don't always work well together or provide seamless care (Andrews *et al.*, 2002). Research exploring the early days of the delayed discharge mechanism suggests that social services are avoiding fines levied by NHS by providing inappropriate housing and care solutions (Rowland and Pollock, 2004). The Social Services Inspectorate surveyed how well local authorities are working towards improving the quality of older people's services. They concluded the following problems were evident:

- Ineffective or unresponsive referral and assessment systems.
- Disjointed or delayed care management.
- Superficial service led care plans that inadequately reflect user needs.
- Provision of variable quality.
- Serious gaps in provision for older people with dementia, mental illness or sensory impairment.
- Inadequate provision for Black and Minority Ethnic elders.
- Variable quality of intermediate care.
- Variable local arrangements for seamless working between agencies. (SSI, 2003)

The housing sector has responded well to whole systems working. Its achievements include – developing services which cross the housing, care and health divide (such as extra care sheltered housing); moving from institutional and paternalistic services, towards a focus on housing options which provide alternatives to institutional care; new models of support such as forms of floating support; and significantly improved joint working. But significant issues remain to be addressed.

Commissioning mechanisms for housing, health and social care

The challenge to develop the commissioning of specialist and community services on a whole systems working basis remains. Research exploring integration between agencies commissioning health and social care for older people suggests that whilst intermediate care has provided a focus for commissioning; primary care trusts and social services were still providing their own models of intermediate care and not utilising joint funding streams to develop joint responses. Respondents noted they had 'parallel' rather than joint 'agendas' (Davey and Henwood, 2003). The uncertainties of *Supporting People* might also hinder joint commissioning. The obligation of local authorities to promote the well-being of their area (under the Local Government Act 2000) provides an opportunity for Local Strategic Partnerships to develop more effective commissioning structures. Older people's partnership boards (on the lines of children's partnerships) could also take overall responsibility for commissioning.

Governance systems

The NHS Plan suggested either lead or joint commissioning between health and social care, but did not include housing. The Health Acts introduced new flexibilities to enable the creation of care trusts, but this focuses commissioning on specialist health and social care services as opposed to a spectrum of community services. In 2003 the ODPM encouraged primary care trusts and social services departments to draw up local delivery plans for older people's services which included partnership with housing authorities. The housing dimension will become central to the delivery of health and social care strategies and Public Service Agreements targets, but it is not clear that mechanisms exist to contain service developments.

Narrow focus verses whole systems working

Departmentalism is still rife. For example the *National Service Framework* focuses narrowly on *health*, whilst social services are directed towards providing *personal care*. Both appear to marginalise broader approaches to quality of life issues – a focus which brings housing centre-stage. Research found that 75 per cent of primary care trusts contacted about hospital discharge were engaged in activities developing better housing. Yet only 50 per cent had a clear view of housing provision in their area (National Audit Office, 2003).

At frontline service level, sheltered housing providers have warned that older people with dementia or mental health problems are being evicted from sheltered housing because their needs have been incorrectly or inadequately assessed. Research in London, has recently examined the cases of 30 people evicted in a single month from four London sheltered housing schemes. Seven were evicted for anti-social behaviour; others were reported as wandering naked about their housing schemes or throwing wheelchairs around. The failure of whole systems working lies at the heart of the problem. The emerging role of Sheltered Housing Group is calling for protocols to be put in place detailing which information can be shared between health, social services and the police, or the engagement of sheltered housing staff in the development of management of medication, community psychiatric services and care plans (Kenny, 2004).

Supporting People and the health and care landscape

Supporting People offers great potential to consider the strategic development of supported housing across and between localities. Administering authorities will have identified priorities on the basis of how the Supporting People strategy links into other national and local priorities, for example the NHS plan, *National Service Framework* and how schemes might promote joint working. Supporting People could lead to a healthy blurring of boundaries between community care and forms of supported housing. For example, housing providers might develop direct links with health trusts to ensure that housing issues are reflected in planning new intermediate care provision.

The cracks are already evident. It has been reported that over 27,000 older people living in sheltered housing are paying extra for their support because of shortfalls in funding for supported housing. In all 148 providers in 46 local authorities are making charges, other providers are covering the shortfall from their own resources (Stothart, 2004). There are dangers that overstretched budgets will result in the increased targeting of services for frail older people and the most vulnerable, whilst the preventative function of supported housing might be at risk. There are also well founded fears that the budget will be 'colonised' by health and social services to bolster a creaking community budget.

Maintaining preventative services

The services provided by housing agencies can be a means of enabling *supported independence* rather *managed independence*. However, there remains an unhealthy concentration on *institutional solutions* to the care needs of frail older people – to the exclusion of preventative services, domiciliary care and assistive technology. As the numbers of older people needing support grows, there will be increasing tensions around needs based commissioning systems which allocate resources to those most 'in need', to the exclusion of lower level services. The *Independent Inquiry into Inequalities in Health* (1998) found that levels of domiciliary care are insufficient to prevent frail older people entering residential care. The role of preventative services in promoting independence, choice and empowerment, needs to be preserved and enhanced. In 2002 a House of Commons Health Select Committee published the results of its inquiry into delayed discharge. It noted that a third of all delayed discharges were due to the lack of care home places, but this should not mean the development of further care capacity, but should be a spur to the development of adequate home care, aids and adaptations, and the integration of housing into health and social care planning. Preventative services are still under developed and under-funded across the country.

Conversely, the most imaginative responses to working with frail older people, exclude the most disadvantaged. By 2003/4 it is estimated that there will be over 140,000 people receiving intermediate care in one of three forms:

1. in non-residential settings;
2. non-residential housing to facilitate hospital discharge;
3. non-residential to prevent hospital discharge.
   (Social Services Inspectorate, 2003).

An omission has been the absence of older people with mental health problems or dementia. Many areas have not invested sufficient resources to meet the needs of this group, which is still perceived to be a *medical problem* rather than a *consequence of ageing, with both medical and social palliatives.*

Outcomes and performance indicators

An outcome of the 'audit society' has been that each 'sector' has its own goals and objectives, often sustained by individual performance indicators. These can undermine the development of 'joined up' performance indicators which cross health, social care and housing boundaries. Or they can encourage agencies to undermine joint working in the pursuit of performance targets.

For example, the £100 daily fine outside London, and £120 within London and the South East levied for a delayed hospital discharge under the 2003 Community Care (Delayed Discharges) Act. The presence of a fining culture can lead to discharge into inappropriate accommodation. In May 2004 the government announced a drop of 4,000 in the numbers of blocked NHS beds. They attributed this to the implementation of the 2003 act. In *Leaving hospital – the price of delays*, the Commission for Social Care Inspection (2004) reached the conclusion that that although there is good practice, the focus on avoiding fines has been at the expense of older people's needs. The study found that it had led to too many people being expected to accept short term services rather than being offered care that would address their needs. Older people's needs and wishes were seen as secondary to the needs of service providers. In the best performing areas, people were offered a range of options – such as intermediate care and rehabilitation services – which maintained their independence. In poor performing areas, people were sent to care homes and rarely returned to their own homes and half the people were re-admitted within three months. The commission has asked that older people be given more choice. With a shrinking supply of residential care, and extra care sheltered housing slow to come on track, the prospects for speeding up discharge and avoiding fines look bleak.

The Audit Commission brought together information on what older people suggest are factors enabling them to sustain independent lives. These could inform the development of *'well-being outcomes'* (Association Directors of Social Services/Local Government Association, 2003). Rather than focusing on delivering service targets, organisations should be required to reflect on how they are improving the national and local outcomes for older people and work across organisational barriers to do so.

Housing providers and service delivery

Housing providers must increasingly dovetail their services with health and care providers, as access to specialist services will be essential if housing agencies are to meet the accommodation needs of frail older people. Yet some providers remain wary of the responsibilities inherent in working with frail older people, who might be diverted away from residential care into extra care sheltered housing. Two developments offer avenues for housing agencies to participate in developing more 'person centred' services. The *Single Assessment Process* provides opportunities to link assessment to service commissioning, delivery and planning, whilst the *direct payments* scheme (which was extended to older people in 2000) offers older people opportunities to play a part in the direct commissioning and development of their own services. Tenants who have been assessed in need of community care services and are categorised as disabled (under sec. 29, 1948 National Assistance Act) can utilise direct payments, which could be more readily be taken up in supported housing. Take up has been variable around the country, hence in 2002, the government announced under the Community Care (Draft Payments) Act 2002 that it intended to oblige local authorities to offer direct payments to older people, rather than leaving them to come forward.

Can new forms of housing such as extra sheltered housing replace residential care?

A theme of this chapter has been that housing based models of care can provide real change away from 'dependency' towards a 'promoting independence', a cultural change built around quality of life principles and a person centred approach. Much attention has been focused on the closure of residential care places and the potential that extra care sheltered housing offers as an alternative. The future for residential care looks mixed. It is expected to play a role in the local planning of care, but the government continues to signal that the priority should be given to support people living in their own homes and in sheltered housing. At the conference of the National Care Forum Care Services Committee, the Minister for Community Care, Stephen Ladyman suggested he *'did not believe that long term care was synonymous with care provided in care homes, but that there was still a role for residential care in the future'* and announced further funding for supported housing. But the capacity of housing to meet demand is limited. Andrew Stow, chair of the National Care Forum suggested it would take 257 years to replace the current residential stock (*Community Care*, 2004a).

The cost effective nature of extra care sheltered housing should increasingly provide powerful resource incentives to health and social commissioners to consider it as a real alternative to residential care. The Gershon Review, which aimed to release resources more efficiently into frontline services and to inform the 2004 Spending Review (Gershon, 2004) might provide such an incentive. As a response to Gershon, the Department of Health have created the *Care Services Efficiency Delivery Programme*.

Other aspects of the government's programme for adult social care has led to confusion and ambiguity. The Care Standards Act 2000 could include those living in supported housing, although that was not the intention of the act. The government has made it clear that extra care sheltered housing will be unaffected by the act if care is provided by another agency (for example social services) or if care elements are registered separately as a domiciliary provider. In the latter case this would come under domiciliary care regulations of the care standards act. The avoidance of regulation is crucial as it changes the funding regime for sheltered housing and affects the income of tenants.

Policy divergence and older people in the UK

There is currently a major contradiction in policy between health care, available to all, free at the point of use and social care which is rationed and accrues means-tested charges. This issue has been brought into sharp focus by the impact of Scottish and Welsh devolution, and has helped to develop a pluralistic debate about the future shape of services for older people in the UK. Free nursing care has been introduced throughout the UK with variation between countries. However, a key policy divergence has been introduced with the provision of free personal care in Scotland. The decision by Westminster not to introduce free personal care leads agencies back to unseemly disputes about when personal care becomes nursing care, and ombudsman decisions criticising health authorities for failing to meet their obligations to provide continuing care. Introducing free personal and nursing care across the UK would increase public spending on older people from around £8.8 billion to around £10.3. By 2051 this would rise to around £42.6 billion – 1.45 per cent of GDP (Wittenberg, Comas-Herrera and Pickard, 2004). If the numbers of people with dependency do not rise as rapidly as the base data used by Wittenberg *et al.* suggest, then even with free personal care, the percentage spent on long term care might not be any higher than it is today.

However, the debate around free nursing and personal care in Scotland has been re-ignited by figures released by the (Scottish Executive, 2004) showing that in the first nine months, the full year budget of £126 million had already been spent. Local authorities had seen a considerable rise in the number of people claiming free personal care at home. On the basis of these figures the cost of free personal care in Scotland would rise to £2.5 billion by 2020 at today's prices. Population figures for Scotland show that it will have a significantly larger ageing population than the rest of the UK. Therefore it will continue to pay free personal care for much larger numbers of people, which suggests that strategic work will be needed over and beyond the *National Service Framework for Older People* – for example, exploring housing, transport, planning, areas that are not considered central to planning for older people's needs. Wales remains the only UK country which has developed an overall vision and policy framework for an ageing society, which takes account of demographic, social and economic changes that the rest of the UK is experiencing in relation to the older population.

Conclusion: Towards an integrated housing and care policy?

Crucial to the acceptability of new housing options, will be the assurance that independence and autonomy can be attained – *regardless of the setting*. Models of 'collective living' are unusual in Britain, where historically there has been hostility to *'communitaire philosophies'* (Heywood, Oldman and Means, 2002). This poses a challenge for providers of supported housing. Provision might take the form of 'communities of interest' based around religion for example or retirement communities such as Hartrigg Oaks in York.

Increasing numbers of older people are able to buy themselves a retirement lifestyle. Tulle-Winton (1999) argues that this choice represents a deliberate stratagem to cope with the 'declining body' and is a positive way of resisting the ageing process. In Europe new forms of housing are developing on the margins of traditional housing, for example the co-housing model. The Housing Corporation is funding a programme of comparative housing research. Known as the HOPE project, it is searching for more inclusive methods of delivering services, whilst moving away from a 'medical model' of housing which sees ageing as a form of 'sickness' to be cured or alleviated.

As one older person living in co-housing noted, the issue is about making a positive choice to live together with other older people *'it is important to move while you still can to a place you choose before other people move you to a place they choose'* (Brenton, 1998). How housing providers facilitate positive choice; safeguard independence and autonomy, and involve older people in decision-making around care options at both an individual and strategic level will provide a significant challenge in the coming decades.

PART THREE

Looking to the future

CHAPTER 11:
Contested communities? Homelessness, substance misuse and regeneration policy

Anya Ahmed and Julia Lucas

Introduction

The notion of *community* has been placed at the core of current regeneration policy. The very language (or 'discourse') of regeneration centres on community involvement, community empowerment, community (or social) capital and community cohesion. Although debates around the problematic and contested terrain of community are rehearsed elsewhere in this book, it is worth some consideration here, in the context of whether people with community care or support needs can be a part of a community and contribute to decision-making on regeneration issues. To exemplify this, a problematic group with support needs will be the focus of this chapter: homeless people that misuse substances and alcohol. In this sense, we have to consider very basic questions: what is community? Who is 'in' and who is 'out'? And, what are the implications for this particular group with regard to community decision-making around regeneration?

This chapter will consider the above questions before going on to establish the context in which the debate is placed, that is the development of regeneration policies culminating with New Labour's focus on neighbourhoods and communities. It will conclude by revisiting the question of whether a marginalised group within a community can properly engage in local decision-making.

Notions of 'community' and involvement

Historically the study of community has been approached in several ways, although these often overlap:

- Within the confines of a bounded settlement or neighbourhood (Bernard, 1964; McIver and Page, 1961).
- With reference to the significance of 'community feeling' (Milner 1968), so in this sense, community need not be a territorial concept. Nisbet (1973) also emphasises sentiment and relationships between community members over geographical determination. This can also be seen in terms

of mutuality, reciprocity, a sense of belonging or 'social capital' (Putnam, 2000). This refers to the 'social glue' that binds people together.

- The study of a local social system. Gilchrist (2002) asserts that *'people's' sense of community derives from their perception (real or imagined) of being linked into the dynamics of a complex social system of relationships and interactions. It incorporates both objective experience and subjective responses to real life events'*. In this sense an individual's experience of community is an outcome of interaction and engagement with informal (local) networks. Anderson (1987) refers to 'imagined communities', whereby the existence of community lies in the minds of its members.

- The study of a collective identity (status). Glaser (2001) and Dempsy (1990) argue that a community can exist alongside friction and disharmony and that shared values are not always necessary for a community to exist.

The concept of community then may be applied either to place, relationships, collective identity, or to all of these. There are issues however in including people who are homeless and who misuse substances or alcohol within these definitions and these have profound implications for their ability to become involved in any form of decision-making. Cooper (see Chapter 5) discusses the problem of meaningful involvement in decision-making processes for users and carers in general without a system of enshrined rights and effective support structures. People who misuse alcohol and drugs and who are homeless however, face multiple 'jeopardies'. For such people, there is a stigma attached to being homeless and being 'an addict' and this is compounded when these variables intersect. Often there is a lack of support by local residents for schemes catering for this group as they are seen as 'other' than the rest of the population. And, if an individual lives in a place for a short time then it is unlikely that any great attachment (and involvement) will develop. So, in this sense, stability of residence is denied this group. This has clear implications for homeless substance and alcohol misusers since although they may be physically located within a 'bounded settlement', attachment to it, and to other members, will inevitably be limited due to the often temporary nature of their accommodation.

A further significant barrier to community inclusion involves the adverse labelling of whole communities, or groups within a community, as a problem. Again, the implications are clear for homeless substance and alcohol misusers. This leads us to question whether people with support needs can ever be fully part of a community and able as such to engage in local decision-making on key issues, for example, on regeneration. The modernisation agenda has created new channels of dialogue between service providers and service users and there are well-documented reasons as to why this is desirable. For example, there is potential for organisations undertaking regeneration to be more 'efficient, effective and economic' and for residents to have greater control over their environment and the issues affecting them. Both of these factors, if addressed, are associated with a greater commitment to sustainable and successful communities. However, it should be noted that there are difficulties even in involving 'the mainstream': consultation fatigue, apathy and historical legacies of poor communication with neighbourhoods are often put forward as reasons for low levels of resident involvement in decision-making. Added to this is the question of whether this aspect of management should be performance driven. And, although beyond the scope of this chapter, there are inevitably questions about whom such consultation is for, and whether it can in fact become an end in itself rather than a means to effecting change in approaches to regenerating neighbourhoods.

Among the groups eligible for accommodation related support are people with drug and alcohol problems, and it is via these mechanisms that this client group could potentially become visible and engage in consultation around regeneration issues. However, although little research has been carried out in this area, with the only comprehensive guidance being produced by Town (2001), eligibility criteria for general schemes (including hostels and floating support) can *exclude* drug users, again rendering them, and their needs 'hidden' (Flemen, 1999).

The policy context developed

The growth in socio-spatial polarisation in Britain during the 1980s and 1990s has been well documented. Expanded inequalities in income and wealth, changes in employment, population, economic activity and linked changes in housing markets have found spatial expression in increased concentrations of poverty and deprivation in certain localities. Such areas have come to be known among policy-makers as the 'worst estates', the 'poorest neighbourhoods' and the 'most deprived areas'.

Early work carried out by the Social Exclusion Unit identified Britain as being 'marked out' among its European neighbours by high levels of social exclusion, using measures such as the rate of illiteracy, teenage pregnancy, children growing up in workless households and drug misuse among young people. The links between housing, neighbourhood and social exclusion have been extensively explored (Lee and Murie, 1997; Anderson and Sim, 2000; Page, 2000). Over the past few decades the social and economic base of the social housing sector has narrowed considerably, with policies such as the right to buy serving to intensify an already existing movement away from the sector by those most able to access owner occupation (Burrows, 1997). Those remaining are more likely to be economically inactive, to contain dependent children, and to be either younger, or older, than the general population, what Murie, Nevin and Leather (1998) have described as the 'hollowing out' of the sector.

Periodic reviews of poverty and social exclusion have shown that, while there have been some recent successes, notably in reducing levels of child poverty, other indicators such as concentrations of crime and poor quality environments in some areas, levels of homelessness, and problem drug use, have worsened. (Social

Exclusion Unit, 2004; Joseph Rowntree Foundation, 2004). Lupton's (2003) study of the dynamics of neighbourhood decline and renewal shows how, despite measurable improvements in some poor neighbourhoods, feelings of exclusion, and what she calls *'the behaviours of exclusion'* were not significantly diminished, and those with the least ability and opportunity felt further excluded by the focus in regeneration initiatives on work and attainment. As she points out:

> *'What determines neighbourhood fortunes is the 'fit' between their characteristics and the demands of the wider society ... over time, people with choice move away and are replaced by people with no choice ...'*

Over the same period approaches to regeneration have evolved from fairly narrowly conceived 'top-down' policies designed to tackle discrete aspects of decline – particularly those centred on the built environment – to an approach which tries to encompass the complexity of the problems facing such areas and their residents and which places community involvement at the centre. What has emerged is a 'strategic multi-level' approach to regeneration (Hastings, in Imrie and Raco, 2003) that seeks to align and integrate local, regional and central priorities in working towards regenerative ends.

The idea of the community is now firmly embedded in urban policy and can be variously detected in recent initiatives as:

> *'... either an object of policy (in other words a thing to be worked on), a policy instrument (that is, a means by which policies become devised and activated) or a thing to be created (an end in itself)'* Imrie and Raco (2003).

Perhaps encapsulating all three of these notions is the idea of the sustainable community. The active involvement of existing communities in identifying local problems, their causation and potential solutions is seen as key to attempts to revitalise socially excluded neighbourhoods, while concerns with the revitalisation of cities are linked strongly with ideas of social regeneration, and the re-integration of communities which are fragmented and disconnected from the mainstream.

Active citizenship involves communities in rebuilding themselves, utilising their available 'social capital' to increase cohesion and stability, and engaging in processes of policymaking and implementation. This is seen by government as a key way in which to address the 'democratic deficit', a way of rebuilding trust in civic institutions and placing citizens more firmly within the sphere of governance.

Alongside the growing focus on community involvement, pressures towards more customer-oriented public services have been growing since the 1990s, and structures and processes for community involvement are increasingly 'designed in' to regeneration programmes and initiatives. What has been missing though in this conception has been an attempt to articulate *how* and at what *level* community care and supported housing users might be engaged in the rebuilding of communities and localities. One possible vehicle might be the Supporting People 'inclusive forums', which aim to engage service users in debates about the development of services. Another might be the Local Strategic Partnerships. Yet there is evidence that many of these are 'withering on the vine' and falling into disuse (Jerwood, 2004).

Regeneration, housing and communities

During the early 1980s the new Conservative government pioneered ways of dealing with the dereliction and decline of former industrial areas with policies that aimed to create attractive conditions for private sector investment. For the new urban policies, the delivery vehicles of choice were often single purpose non-governmental agencies selected and empowered directly by government. The Urban Development Corporations were charged with the task of facilitating land reclamation, infrastructure and property development to create the right conditions for levering investment into run down areas.

The idea that poor areas and residents would need to be 'joined up' to the newly prosperous developments in order to benefit from them was not really considered, still less any consideration that existing communities in these areas should be included or even consulted. As a result of increasing evidence that such developments were creating islands of prosperity in seas of deprivation, criticisms of the property-led approach to regeneration grew. Though Urban Development Corporations were not charged with overtly tackling the problems experienced by residents of such areas, a recognition grew that a more holistic and inclusive approach was needed to 'join up' solutions to the complex and multifaceted problems associated with deprivation.

A shift in policy involving an increased role for communities (Pacione, 1997) came with the City Challenge and Single Regeneration Budget initiatives which introduced broader-based more inclusive programmes targeted at residential areas and focused on improving outcomes in health, education, housing, crime and so on. These programmes involved a partnership approach led (usually) by local authorities, but required broad-based support from other local interests, in particular business and the community. The performance of such 'one-off special initiatives' has been extensively reviewed; the picture drawn is one of 'limited success' in regeneration. Particular criticisms are that area based initiatives have:

- failed to fundamentally address the problems of neighbourhoods and may displace them to other areas;
- an 'inward looking' (Hall, 1997) focus on developing solutions to local problems without taking account of the impact of macro-economic structural influences on neighbourhoods which indicate that local problems are determined outside of the areas in which they are manifest;
- failed to fully involve and especially to empower communities (Hastings, in Imrie and Raco).

The election of a Labour government in 1997, its promotion of a regional agenda and policies aimed at democratic renewal in government, have led to more fundamental changes in approaches to regeneration. Initially, the Single Regeneration Budget programme was recast to reflect changed priorities, including a longer lead-in to allow time to secure community involvement and sign up, community capacity building projects and an increased emphasis on inclusion and fairness. But a more significant shift in policy towards poor neighbourhoods was to come after the new administration had made its own diagnosis of the problems afflicting them, and of why past policies had made so little difference.

The New Labour strategy for regeneration is summarised in Imrie and Raco (2003) as encompassing:

- A devolution of power.
- Ensuring that communities have greater responsibilities for improving their own lives.
- Improving the capacity of communities.

The Social Exclusion Unit and 18 Policy Action Teams composed of civil servants, local government, and community and voluntary sector interests, were established to investigate the problems of poor neighbourhoods and to make recommendations for policy. The findings and recommendations of the Policy Action Teams were used to inform the production of the framework for a National Strategy for Neighbourhood Renewal. Its 'vision' was that within 10-20 years, *'no-one should be seriously disadvantaged by where they live'* (Social Exclusion Unit, 1998). The long term goals identified were:

- to have lower worklessness; less crime; better health; better skills; and better housing and physical environment in all the poorest neighbourhoods; and
- to narrow the gap on these measures between the most deprived neighbourhoods and the rest of the country.

The need to better co-ordinate the work of agencies and departments engaged in regeneration, and, critically, for community involvement is central to the National Strategy. The 88 most deprived districts have become the focus for change, and the Local Strategic Partnerships set up after the Local Government Act 2000 to help promote 'community well-being' are the vehicles designed to develop and deliver community strategies. Each Local Strategic Partnership is expected to display an 'appropriate balance' of the public, private, and voluntary and community sectors. Indeed a lack of effective engagement would mean failure for a Local Strategic Partnership for whom inclusivity is key. Local Strategic Partnerships are charged to:

- Deliver real improvements in all public services; renew deprived areas; develop strong sustainable economies and healthy, safe communities.

- Focus services on the needs and aspirations of local people – including those who are traditionally excluded – by engaging people in the planning delivery and evaluation of services.

Local Strategic Partnerships are required to actively seek out community involvement, aiding the process by special funding to support it. The government strategy for neighbourhood renewal (Office of the Deputy Prime Minister, 2001a) acknowledged the difficulties of *'representing the differing (and sometimes conflicting) views of communities'*. Whilst guidance issued to Local Strategic Partnerships explores methods for dealing with issues around the selection of community members, the idea of involving hard to reach groups and communities remains expressed chiefly around cultural, religious or language difference.

While acknowledging that the heterogeneity of 'communities' who comprise a multiplicity of groups and individuals with diverse needs and interests may be a significant source of tensions, a problem not acknowledged is the tensions that can exist where the wishes and priorities of government and communities do not coincide. Hence Weaver (2002) notes in the context of a significant under spend on (community led) New Deal for Communities projects:

> *'Money has gone unspent because the government has rejected many of the proposals put forward by communities ... the New Deal is only community-led if the community comes up with the right answers'.*

Critics of the government's approach to regeneration have highlighted a number of concerns: first, that lack of community involvement in regeneration is presented as the problem. This tends to shift the focus from issues such as poverty and social exclusion towards communities themselves and to pathologise them, essentially 'blaming the victim'. Second, that community involvement tends to institutionalise or incorporate community views which effectively further empowers those who already hold power; third, that important decisions are anyway taken by key players behind closed doors; and finally that community views are shoe-horned into initiatives to meet guidelines and targets that have already been set. The needs and interests of the most marginalised, such as homeless drug users, are especially unlikely to be addressed in such circumstances.

Alongside the community-centred policies in current regeneration runs the theme of the urban renaissance. Urban malaise in British towns and cities is linked on the one hand to long term de-population and the selective out-migration of the better off, which results in fiscal problems for cities, concentrated poverty and deprivation and low demand housing areas; and on the other to the prospect of further sprawled development due to an increased rate of household growth and, especially in the south, affordability problems. The vision outlined in the urban white paper *Our Towns and Cities* (Office of the Deputy Prime Minister, 2000) was one of high quality urban environments with high density, mixed use developments to rejuvenate, and re-populate towns and cities.

The *Sustainable Communities Plan* (Office of the Deputy Prime Minister, 2003b) proposed the building of new urban centres in the South East to cope with unmet demand for housing while in the north of England, the failure of housing markets in some areas has led to the Housing Market Renewal Pathfinder projects which aim to restructure and rejuvenate them. Using diversification of tenure and dwelling type the pathfinders aim to attract back or retain better off residents to leaven the social mix of such areas. These programmes involve large-scale clearance and rebuilding by the private sector and housing associations. Atkinson (2004) warns of the dangers of *'state sponsored gentrification'* creating secondary social costs associated with the displacement of poorer and more marginal households and individuals, and of repeating the disintegration and dislocation of communities which resulted from earlier waves of clearance.

While discourses around sustainable communities, in particular the National Housing Federation's 'iN business to support people' which focuses on the role of supported housing in the creation of sustainable communities, are welcome, they clearly have the potential to promote exclusionary policies, particularly for those least able to engage in consultation. So, although *'Community self help is at the heart of renewal ... neighbourhood renewal can only be successful if communities themselves have the power to make things better'* (Boateng quoted in PAT Report 9, Social Exclusion Unit, 1999) it must be acknowledged that there are barriers to community activity in poor neighbourhoods, not least the lack of social capital among marginalised groups, exemplified in this instance by homeless substance misusers.

Homelessness and substance misuse

Homelessness and substance misuse represent two major social problems in England today and while there are regional differences in their prevalence (Aust and Condon, 2003) heroin and crack-cocaine use tend to be concentrated where levels of social deprivation are high (but this can vary considerably across towns and cities). Using heroin/crack cocaine is often associated with disruptive and anti-social activity. The presence of drugs in a neighbourhood leads to fear and insecurity for its inhabitants resulting in neighbourhood decline (Neale, 2002). Of the wider population, it is estimated that 2.2 per cent are dependent on substances and 4.7 per cent on alcohol and there is an increasing trend towards poly-drug use. Further, about one-third of substance misusers have a psychiatric disorder and one-third of psychiatric patients have a substance misuse disorder (Royal College of Psychiatrists London 2001). There is an average of 400 drug related deaths a year, and an estimated 36,000 alcohol related deaths a year in the UK (Alcohol Concern, 2003). In terms of the characteristics of alcohol and substance misusers, CRISIS (2005) suggests that drug problems are as common among single homeless women as men and that the problems are more prevalent among those in their twenties and thirties than in the older age groups. However, rising prevalence affects all age groups and homeless drug users have a tendency to poly drug use which is more hazardous than using one substance. The most commonly used drugs are opiates, such as heroin; stimulants, such as amphetamines, crack and cocaine; cannabis; and benzodiazepines, such as diazepam.

There has been no definitive study undertaken to determine the incidence of substance and alcohol use across homeless households. The only research in this area was undertaken by CRISIS (Fountain and Howes, 2002) and this only looked at rough sleepers. This study however found that 83 per cent of those interviewed used substances, and two-thirds cited drug or alcohol use as a reason for becoming homeless. Four out of five said that they had started using a new substance since becoming homeless. To compound this, there is considerable overlap between drug and alcohol use and mental health problems. In addition, people with addiction problems are among those who are deemed to be more vulnerable to homelessness than the wider population (Fitzpatrick *et al.*, 2000). Significantly, drug use can be an additional factor for homeless people or it can be the root of the problem. Therefore, using substances/alcohol can precede or be a result of homelessness but both represent a significant barrier to accessing housing and support services, and, using substances/alcohol and being without permanent secure accommodation makes this group of people difficult to access in terms of consultation. In addition, people who misuse substances and alcohol face significant barriers when attempting to access social housing and this compounds the nature of their 'hiddeness'. Gaining access to this population is difficult because of factors such as involvement in illegal activities, lack of stable housing and the stigma of being a substance or alcohol misuser. Further, there is no accurate study of the degree and extent of the problem of substance misuse in mainstream social housing. The behaviour of substance users may cause no problems at all, but it can lead to difficulties in:

- accessing and keeping accommodation;
- victimisation by other tenants and neighbours;
- crime and anti-social behaviour;
- contributing to neighbourhood decline.

Substance misuse may be a factor precluding access to permanent accommodation and often, informal 'blanket exclusion policies' operate. Although the numbers of people receiving support has been assessed under the Supporting People arrangements it is thought that this figure is severely under-represented (Office of the Deputy Prime Minister/Home Office, 2005). The extent to which substance misuse contributes to the decline of neighbourhoods is still the focus of contentious debate.

Neale's (2002) study revealed that most of the drug users she interviewed were in run down neighbourhoods, that is, there were high levels of social and economic problems, poor access to services and high levels of crime. However, *'despite such problems, many drug users were anxious to discuss their hopes for the improved housing circumstances for the future'* (2002, p.131). And, when asked what they wanted this did not differ from the rest of the population. In spite of the difficulties in engaging with this heterogeneous group, there are currently a number of projects that attempt to work across agencies to promote inclusion and these are outlined below as 'good practice' examples:

Example 1

Groundswell is a UK wide charity established in 1996 working across 22 cities to include the vulnerable/poor/homeless. They emphasise 'practical solutions' and focus on positive change and community building by attempting to 'deproblematise' this group, maintaining that they are part of the solution to the problem. Activities involve training for agencies/users of homeless services, capacity building, information dissemination and support through a wide range of projects. Their aim is to get marginalised people to play a more effective role in community life and participate in decision-making.

Example 2

Centrepoint is a national charity working with socially excluded young people and communities. In addition to offering support and accommodation, it advises local groups and works in partnership with agencies providing services to young people. A policy and communications team also works in an advisory and research capacity. Centrepoint works with approximately 1,600 young people per year and has established a multiple health needs team which supports young people with substance misuse issues, psychiatric disorders and emotional problems. One remit of this team is to support dually diagnosed young people, who often slip through the system, and bring together a holistic service. There is a hostel in Vauxhall Cross that offers specialist support for up to two years for young people who have slept rough and have complex needs (substance misuse and mental health problems).

Example 3

1-2-1 is an information project based in Sheffield and developed as a result of research commissioned by the Vulnerable People Task Force in 2001. Its premise is that strategic co-ordination, partnership working, longer term income generation and better planning will improve the inclusion of vulnerable groups. There are information sharing arrangements in place to ensure links with initiatives nationwide and a secure information system is currently being developed to monitor patterns of substance misuse and changes in the vulnerable homeless in Sheffield. The idea is that ultimately the planning and development of services will be organised and co-ordinated with input from clients and provider agencies using an information sharing protocol. The project was due to go live on the 1st January 2005.

Conclusion

Throughout this chapter it has been argued that there are significant obstacles to involving homeless substance misusers in community decision-making around regeneration issues. Despite the recent emphasis in regeneration policy on the centrality of community involvement, there are important factors that impede even the mainstream from becoming involved in local decision-making.

On a practical level there are further issues for providers to consider: this is a heterogeneous and hidden group, therefore there are unlikely to be any visible stakeholders for consultation. Using substances often precludes access to tenancies and/or support. If located in the private sector this group would be unknown to providers, similarly if they have a social rented tenancy without accessing support services they remain hidden. As a result, this group is inevitably omitted from community profiling exercises. Further, previous behaviour and convictions for drug use can prevent access to social tenancies.

So far as homeless substance misusers are concerned, there are a myriad of issues which make involvement particularly problematic, not least questions about whether this stigmatised group can be full members of communities. On a fundamental level, there may well be no supported accommodation for these individuals within a community, which renders the debate around their involvement in decision-making academic. The implications of neighbourhood renewal for the least integrated are unclear; if the task of involving individuals and households living in poor neighbourhoods in decision-making in regeneration is difficult, the fate of the least integrated and most stigmatised is likely to be to remain on the margins.

CHAPTER 12:
Housing and community care: a comparative perspective

Tim Brown and Nichola Yates

Introduction

The previous chapters have emphasised that there is a need for a radical step change in thinking on the principles and practice of housing and community care in the United Kingdom. Part One of the book highlighted the context and in particular the move from community care to Supporting People and the associated complex and frequently changing financial and regulatory frameworks. The second part has indicated the challenges from a range of different perspectives including the needs and empowerment of user groups such as people with disabilities and those with mental health difficulties. We believe that a comparative approach can help to take the debate forward by speculating on how the future of housing and community care might look.

The relevance and topicality of a comparative approach cannot be overestimated. The European Year for People with Disabilities in 2003 generated considerable interest with the European Liaison Committee for Social Housing, publishing a guide, *Breaking Down the Barriers*, drawing on examples from many countries (Randall, 2003). In October 2003, the Office of the Deputy Prime Minister announced that the 'Supporting People programme' will be overseen by the Homelessness Directorate. This could lead, as in The Netherlands, to a much stronger relationship between community care and homelessness.

Our approach is based on the need to understand the relevance and challenges of a comparative approach. Drawing in particular on the Dutch experience, we highlight the importance of understanding the broader social policy context as a basis for considering the relevance of a policy transfer approach. We have also provided a guide on sources of further information at the end of the chapter.

The need for a comparative approach

Too often, policy-makers have taken an inward looking approach on housing and community care. There is a tendency to recycle fashionable ideas as they move in and out of vogue and secondly there is a lack of an ability to think radically. For example, multi-agency working between housing, health and the social care sectors was promoted in mid-1970s following local government reorganisation and again in the late 1980s and early 1990s with the 1990 National Health Service and Community Care Act. Yet the evidence suggests a patchy performance on the ground (see, for example, Arnold *et al.*, 1993). Joint working has now been resurrected as a key part of the Supporting People agenda. But have policy-makers really learnt the lessons from previous cycles and could they not benefit from taking a comparative and outward looking approach? The Dutch, for example, have initiated a wide range of innovative proactive multi-agency community care projects through the work of the Netherlands Institute for Care and Welfare (NIZW), the Living and Care Innovation Programme, and the Public Housing Experiment Unit (SEV). A reoccurring theme in many of the innovative experiments is 'domotics' i.e. the use of information communications technology to provide health, social care and housing support in the home.

An inward looking approach results in a poorly developed set of skills amongst policy-makers and service providers in being able to consider a step change in the housing and community care agenda. An outward looking perspective is required that focuses on an awareness of initiatives that have been developed in the community care and housing field elsewhere and, at the same time, there is a need to develop an ability to understand the challenges of policy transfer between countries.

Nevertheless, there is a lack of information and analysis. There is, of course, a wealth of good practice guides for policy-makers and service providers, but much of this material focuses on only a British viewpoint. There is no reference to examples from other countries in the Chartered Institute of Housing's Good Practice Briefing (2003a), or on the Supporting People Website (http://www.spkweb.org.uk). From a community care viewpoint the major text by Means, Richards and Smith (2003) includes only a single chapter on a European perspective on community care. It focuses on both the impact of European Union policies and the relationship between welfare systems (see below) and community care. But there is little attempt to consider the housing and community care agenda from a comparative perspective. From a housing policy standpoint, there has been a growth of interest in a comparative approach. This is illustrated by, for example, Oxley and Smith (1996) and Doling (1997). However, neither of these housing texts considers housing and community care. Instead they focus on a range of so-called mainstream housing issues such as the social rented sector, housing finance and owner occupation. Nevertheless they at least make a start of moving from an inward to an outward looking perspective. In relation to social policy (which provides an important context for community care), there is a much stronger approach on a comparative perspective. For example, Kleinman (2002) focuses on social policy in the European Union. However, although this book considers a comparative approach, it nevertheless fails to trickle down to the policy and practice issues associated with housing and community care.

This brief review has highlighted the considerable variation in the adoption of a comparative approach between various disciplines and policy areas. It is, however, important to appreciate the interlinkages between these four dimensions. The social policy context provides the framework within which the housing and community care agenda is developed. The housing and community care policies form the strategy envelope. Specific initiatives and projects (as promoted through, for instance, good practice guides) are the means by which policy is implemented. It is, therefore, essential that detailed initiatives drawn from an outward orientated comparative approach are located within the broader strategic framework and the social policy context.

Our approach in this comparative chapter is therefore thematic. It is based on the importance of understanding, analysing and being aware of the social policy context as well as the housing and community care strategies in other countries. This, then, allows good practice initiatives to be located within the broader framework so enabling a more robust and rigorous discussion on the possibilities of policy transfer. We also focus much of our material on The Netherlands rather than adopting what is sometimes referred to as a 'Thomas Cook' tour of Western European countries, i.e. a brief descriptive account of housing and community care but with no contextual or strategic policy frameworks.

Justifying a comparative perspective

There are a number of reasons for adopting a comparative approach in housing and community care. We identify four major justifications for its adoption.

The first reason is 'shock therapy'. This involves looking at examples from other countries that might challenge our thinking on the way in which housing and community care is organised and delivered. For example, in The Netherlands there is a much greater role for multi-purpose voluntary sector agencies in community care provision. In Rotterdam, CVD (Centrum Voor Dienstverlening) provides a number of community care services including working with people with drug and alcohol dependency, accommodation and support for older vulnerable people, provision of training and counselling for young disaffected young people and shelters for women fleeing domestic violence. In Amsterdam there is a similar organisation, the HVO Foundation, which again provides a wide range of facilities and services including accommodation, support and personal development plans for vulnerable homeless people. So where is the shock in this? Apart from the enhanced role of voluntary sector organisations, the major challenge is the way in which services are provided. In units that meet the needs of people with alcohol dependency problems there are licensed bars, while in accommodation for people with drug problems there are needle exchange schemes and rooms where assistance is provided with safe injecting methods. In Rotterdam, a homeless project for young vulnerable people (especially from Black and Minority Ethnic communities) involves social workers living on the streets with their clients to help build up confidence and trust (Sheldon, 1996). Compare these initiatives with, for example, the ongoing debate highlighted by organisations in the UK such as Homelessness Link who have pointed out that agencies working with drug users face profound challenges in meeting needs while at the same time taking account of the 'Misuse of Drugs' legislation. The case of the 'Cambridge Two', where the director and manager of a shelter were convicted for failing to prevent the sale of heroin on the premises, left housing providers uncertain about their role.

The second justification for a comparative approach is policy transfer. We have already begun to explore some of the challenges in the previous section. There are, of course, already examples in the housing field of policy transfer. For example there has been the development of choice based lettings in England based on the Delft Model of social housing allocations (Brown, Hunt and Yates, 2000). Policy transfer has operated at a broad strategic level on allocations and lettings as well as at a more detailed operational scale in relation to meeting the needs of vulnerable groups. For instance, the Dutch make extensive use of priority cards for vulnerable households that ensure they take greater responsibility for meeting their needs but with additional support from non-housing agencies. This approach has been used among some of the 27 choice based letting pilots in England between 2001 and 2003. But it is noteworthy that the evaluation of this programme highlighted that one of the weakest areas was the failure of a number of pilots to put in place support for vulnerable people.

The third reason for adopting a comparative approach is opportunities for collaboration. The European Union agenda will gradually lead to housing and community care policies in Britain being more strongly influenced by this broader framework. There will be opportunities for housing and community care organisations to access resources, to work on new policy frameworks, to think about new ideas within this context of the European Union as well as reflecting on the impact of new legislation. For example, the European Year of People with Disabilities in 2003 was based on a framework for action that was agreed in Madrid in spring 2002. The 'Madrid Declaration' called on the nations and citizens of the European Union to focus on, for instance, the rights of disabled people as independent citizens and consumers, empowerment, and the social model of disability. As part of this initiative, the European Liaison Committee for Social Housing commissioned a European Union report on housing and disability (see Randall, 2003).

The fourth and final justification for a comparative approach focuses on the social policy context. Although this may appear to practitioners to be rather unimportant, it is fundamentally linked to the other three reasons for adopting a comparative perspective. 'Shock therapy', policy transfer and greater collaboration need to be considered within the broader social policy context. There is considerable debate over whether there is an increasing convergence of social policy and the nature of welfare in Western European countries (see Kleinman, 2002). Indeed, some researchers argue strongly that there is considerable variation between countries. The key point is that the degree and nature of the appropriateness and relevance of a comparative approach depends on the scale of similarity of welfare and social policy systems that are being compared. For instance, we have already referred to 'shock therapy' and the role of voluntary sector agencies and aspects of provision for people with alcohol and drug dependency issues in The Netherlands. But we need to consider the degree to which the social policy context and the housing and community care strategic frameworks are similar (and these are explored in more depth below).

Challenges of a comparative approach

There are, thus, challenges with a comparative approach. These include:

- a need for a robust framework for comparative analysis;
- a requirement for an objective approach;
- an appreciation of the inter-dependence between the four building blocks that we have referred to already in this chapter.

We believe that it is important to understand the social policy context. The beliefs, values and ideologies underpinning welfare provision vary between different types of welfare regimes and we will explore this issue in more depth in the next section. Nevertheless, it is essential to appreciate that while there is a considerable debate about whether there is a convergence or divergence of welfare systems and the extent to which European Union integration might result in a greater harmonisation of policies, the current reality is one of difference!

Secondly, there is a need to appreciate the different housing policy frameworks by which we mean the structures of provision and role of particular tenures. We also include in this issue, 'terminology', i.e. do things mean the same to people in different countries? In the Netherlands for example, their approach for dealing with homelessness varies quite markedly from that in Britain. Homelessness is not regarded as a bricks and mortar issue and instead it is seen as being about developing life skills among homeless households so that they have better coping mechanisms for maintaining appropriate lifestyles. Housing organisations play a relatively minor role in tackling homelessness.

Thirdly, there is the housing and community care dimension and the degree of linkage between them. For example, in The Netherlands housing organisations tend not to be directly involved in community care or Supporting People provision. As we have already pointed out there is a much bigger role for voluntary sector agencies such as the CVD in Rotterdam and HVO Foundation in Amsterdam. Both of these organisations work with housing associations but there is a clear demarcation between the role of community care providers and housing providers.

Finally, there is the 'good practice' element and by this we mean specific initiatives and projects. This may seem straightforward in relation to a comparative approach, but there can be challenging issues in appreciating the context, aims, objectives and targets of specific projects. For instance, as we have already mentioned, the 'T' team project in Rotterdam for helping young vulnerable homeless households involves social workers building up trust and confidence with their clients by living with them on the streets. The ratio of staff to clients of often less than 1:3 may appear challenging from a British perspective. But the Dutch argue that successful outcomes for highly disaffected young Black and Minority Ethnic people with poor job opportunities requires a sensitive and intense approach over a significant period of time.

Therefore what we are suggesting is that whatever the justification for a comparative approach, it is important that they are not seen in isolation. It is essential that, for example, a focus on shock therapy nevertheless considers the contextual hierarchy of the social policy framework, housing and community care strategies policy, and the housing and community care interface as well as specific projects. For example, from a shock therapy perspective, it is important to understand the social policy context. If this is not appreciated, there is a danger in contributing to what comparative analysis sometimes refers to as the 'Romeo error', i.e. an uncritical appreciation or a 'taken for granted political and cultural assumption'. For instance, recommending the use of a specific Dutch initiative on tackling drug and alcohol dependency (see above) would by itself by naive without an appreciation of the social policy context in The Netherlands.

Nevertheless we believe that these challenges can be overcome if there is a robust approach to the use of a comparative perspective. In the next section we want to begin our more detailed analysis by focusing in on the social policy context by looking at welfare regimes.

The social policy context

Our understanding of the welfare state that underpins housing and community care is based on British experience of the balance between the role of the state, the degree of market influence and the rights and responsibilities of individuals and communities. However, the welfare state is not fixed and varies between countries and over time. Throughout most of the 20th Century, the emphasis in Britain was on the role of the government as provider within a social democratic welfare state that is now often disparagingly referred to by New Labour as the 'first way'. The growing role of the private and voluntary sectors as providers within a more market-orientated system became a central theme of government thinking under the Conservatives in the 1980s and 1990s especially through the National Health Service and Community Care Act. This is now often referred to as the 'second way'. There is now considerable debate on whether a 'Third Way' is emerging under the Labour government post 1997 with a much greater emphasis on the role of customers, citizens and communities. In particular, there is a changing relationship between the state and the individual with a much greater emphasis on the responsibilities as well as the rights of customers and users. For example, there are increased exhortations by the government for individuals to plan ahead financially for their needs in old age. The implications would appear to be that individuals will increasingly be responsible for making choices about long term care provision supported by a basic welfare state safety net.

This pattern, however, is not the same in other countries. Welfare policy is constructed under a different set of relationships between the state, the market and the individual in other Western European countries. For example, in Scandinavia, the welfare state system is characterised by universal social rights, extensive protection against social risks and generous flat rate benefits. The state strives to guarantee full employment and comprehensive public services. This is often referred to as a social democratic model. It can be contrasted with other countries in continental Europe such as Germany and Austria, which have a corporatist approach. Welfare rights are determined according to class and status and make an assumption that the model of society is based on a traditional male breadwinner family. Finally, there are liberal welfare systems. These are based on a residual model of welfare and eligibility is confined to those in greatest need. Universal benefits are frowned upon and means-tested schemes are preferred. Researchers suggest that countries such as the USA, Australia and New Zealand are now examples of this type of welfare system. It, of course, can be argued that Britain was moving towards this type of approach under the Conservative government from 1979-1997. Furthermore, there is considerable debate about whether the Third Way constitutes a shift way from a liberal welfare regime or merely is a modified version of this type of system.

The reason why these debates are important for a comparative approach on housing and community care are threefold. Firstly, there are the socio-legal and regulatory frameworks that underpin each of these types of welfare states. For instance, the rights and responsibilities of individuals will be strongly influenced by the nature of the welfare state. In Sweden, individuals are entitled to a wide range of universal benefits and have a free choice of hospitals. They have, however, to act according to the principles of the Swedish 'folkhome', otherwise there is a strong interventionist approach taken to remedy inappropriate individual and household behaviour. Secondly there are the organisational structures that provide the basis for developing strategies and delivering services. In Britain, under New Labour, there is an increasing emphasis on local authorities acting as strategic enablers in partnership with other agencies, while service delivery is provided by a mix of public, private and voluntary sector agencies. This can be contrasted with the situation in many Scandinavian countries where there is a much greater role for public sector agencies in the provision of services. Finally there is the acceptability issue. The degree to which a radical step change is possible by borrowing policy ideas from other countries will depend in part on the fit between innovative practices and the nature of the welfare state. For example, as we have mentioned, there was a considerable amount of interest in 2003 on tackling the housing needs of disabled people as part of European Year of People with Disabilities. *Breaking Down the Barriers* highlights a range of innovative schemes among social housing organisations with a specific emphasis on user empowerment in a number of countries including Denmark, Ireland and The Netherlands. Although this can provide a useful 'shock therapy' in highlighting new alternative approaches for empowerment for disabled people, it does not necessarily address the challenges of policy transfer between countries with different welfare systems. Indeed, the report notes that although,

> '... meeting the housing needs of disabled people has been slowly moving up the agenda, government priorities over funding vary significantly between countries'.

Housing and community care in The Netherlands

So far in this chapter we have focused on the broad principles of the relevance of a comparative perspective. We will now illustrate these points in relation to a more detailed example drawing on The Netherlands. We have selected this country for two reasons. Firstly, it is an interesting example of a welfare state that has aspects of each of the three types of welfare systems – social democracy, corporatism and liberalism. Indeed most countries in Western Europe do not easily fit into a single ideal type of welfare policy or regime. The Netherlands therefore is a useful example to illustrate the mixture of different ideologies about the role of the state, the market and the individual in relation to welfare. The second reason for selecting The Netherlands is a much more practical justification. There is some familiarity in the UK with a number of aspects of Dutch housing policy. For example, there continues to be considerable interest in the Delft Model of social housing allocations, but the wider policy framework of a less residualised role of social housing is often ignored. We therefore focus on a housing and community care perspective drawing on specific examples within a broader social policy perspective.

This section, therefore, focuses on the four themes highlighted in the early parts of this chapter. These are, firstly, the social policy context, secondly the nature of housing and community care, thirdly the strategic framework and fourthly the issue of policy transfer.

In relation to the political and culture context, there are a number of features that need to be appreciated. The first of these relates to central-local government relations. Municipalities have a relatively greater degree of freedom than their British counterparts. The Dutch government, although providing the legal, regulatory and resource frameworks as well as highlighting good or best practice often leave key decisions to individual local authorities. For example in relation to housing allocations, although the Dutch government favours the use of the Delft

Model, it is not a statutory requirement. Similarly, in meeting the needs of vulnerable groups, the government suggests rather than requires the use of priority cards to enable vulnerable households to gain access to social housing. The second element is the changing political and culture context. Historically, Dutch society has been characterised as a country of minorities divided into an array of religious and class segments that came together through consensus-based multi-party coalition governments. This has resulted in the development of policy frameworks that change infrequently – there tend to be only minor shifts in emphasis following general elections. It, nevertheless, has also resulted in a complex pattern of provision of housing and other welfare services. For example historically there have been different forms of provision by housing associations based on religious divides. Until the mid-1990s, there were the equivalent of two of our National Housing Federations – the NWR covering secular and protestant organisations and the NCIV, which acted as a parent body for catholic-based associations. This pattern of politics is, however, facing strains and tensions. There has been, as in many other Western European countries, a rise of right wing political parties that have challenged some of the status quo policies regarding help and provision for minority groups. The third contextual element is the role of local authorities as strategic enablers rather than providers. In relation to both housing and community care the emphasis has been on the municipalities acting as strategic policy-makers rather than direct providers. Even in the 1970s, for example, the Dutch did not have our system of council housing. Instead they had a range of different types of social housing providers including housing associations and municipal housing companies. Fourthly, there is, as we have already highlighted, a much greater role for voluntary sector agencies, and multi-purpose voluntary organisations in all major Dutch town and cities. Finally, it is important to appreciate the role of housing associations. In The Netherlands, housing associations are primarily focused on their main task of providing social housing and low cost accommodation. There is much less of a debate about the role of housing associations as community development regeneration organisations. In relation to housing and community care, housing associations work in partnership with voluntary sector organisations, but it is the latter that takes the lead on provision for vulnerable groups.

The second aspect that we want to cover in this review of The Netherlands and housing and community care is the nature of provision. The Dutch government has highlighted that housing and care is a major issue. The Ministry of Housing, Spatial Planning and the Environment in 2001 published an equivalent of our green paper, *What People Want Where People Live – Housing in the 21st Century*. It highlighted that the number of people qualifying for assisted housing will increase substantially over the coming decades. The reasons for this are firstly an ageing population with an estimated growth from 14 per cent of the population over 65 in 2000 to 22 per cent in 2050. Secondly there is a trend towards more care in the home with the government calling on municipalities to develop programmes for adapting existing housing. Thirdly there is increasing attention being given to the housing and care needs of street people, the homeless, drug addicts and ex convicts. Other Dutch ministries have also highlighted a number of related issues in their policy statements. For example, the Ministry of Health, Welfare and Sport published a position statement in 2002 on *Choosing with Care*. This argues that the position of care users should be strengthened in line with a general policy of making the health care sector more demand focused. There are, of course, a wide range of care providers and insurers and one of the steps that is being taken is to develop a website portal that will provide reliable, accessible and up-to-date information. There are also proposals to publish information on the quality of services that organisations are providing – reference is made to a possible *'Michelin quality guide for the care sector'*!

These developments highlight the need for the Dutch government, municipalities, housing associations and other organisations to think radically about the type and nature of housing and community care provision and service delivery over the next 30 years. Currently the policy emphasis is on developing life skills among vulnerable groups rather than solely meeting housing needs. Nevertheless as we have just pointed out the nature of the issues and the challenges are changing and society increasingly has to consider how to deal with people and households who have multiple problems. For example there is a major debate in The Netherlands over meeting the needs of people with drug and alcohol dependency who lack necessary social skills and are living on the streets. These are considered as high risk groups in society. This has led to considerable discussions on two related issues. The first of these is the cost of community care and secondly there is the associated issue of community and neighbourhood safety.

From a policy perspective as we have already pointed out municipalities act as a strategic policy-makers rather than providers. Nevertheless the Dutch government argues in its 2001 housing policy paper that many municipalities by themselves are unable to formulate an integrated strategy that links physical aspects with social requirements especially for vulnerable and older households. There is, thus, an even greater need for inter-agency working between, for example, municipalities, the police, health sector, mental health services and voluntary sector agencies. In Rotterdam, for example, the municipality facilitates the input by social care agencies into strategy development by encouraging organisations to identify what actions are needed from the local authority. At the same time, the council undertakes research on the needs of vulnerable groups and monitors the performance of voluntary agencies. Even so, there are major challenges in co-ordinating activities since although the municipality is the main financial provider for many welfare agencies, funding for mental health and addiction care is paid for through insurance schemes.

Innovative projects that operate within the strategic collaborative framework include the recent establishment of community care networks to prevent homelessness in Rotterdam. These entail a collaborative approach involving the police, housing associations, GPs and social work agencies such as CVD. The aim is to be proactive and detect potential problems before they arise. The police are central to this approach and are likely to be the agency that first identifies emerging issues such as nuisance, neighbour disputes, and conflicting and challenging lifestyles that might result later in rent arrears, addiction problems and personal safety concerns. The police will convene a case conference and invite other agencies with appropriate skills to participate. The outcome may be that an outreach case-worker will be appointed to work with an individual and household to prevent homelessness by focusing on improving life and social skills.

An example of an innovative crisis management approach is the 'safety net' team. This is targeted on, for example, households who are already creating major concerns for neighbours and landlords including housing associations. The approach can, thus, be activated by a private individual or an organisation. It involves the health department of the municipality working with a client on tackling issues of inappropriate behaviour on environmental health grounds leading to vermin infestation. Action is taken to tackle the symptoms as well as dealing with the underlying causes.

A final example of emerging collaborative practice is the input by mental health workers into the operation of emergency shelter accommodation especially for homeless people with multiple problems. In Rotterdam, CVD estimates that 40 per cent of the population in shelters (approximately 150-200 people) have a combination of serious problems including psychiatric disorders and addiction problems as well as being homeless. Mental health workers regularly visit shelters and provide a range of services including:

- Training for shelter workers on how to cope with psychotic episodes and medication.
- Negotiating with clinical departments of the health service on behalf of clients for short term courses and treatment including, where appropriate, institutional care.
- Improving the working relationship between shelter workers and their clients.

Lastly, in relation to The Netherlands case study, we want to refocus on an issue that we highlighted in the opening paragraphs of this chapter – 'transferability'. We have identified in the previous paragraphs some of the policies and projects that have been developed in The Netherlands. Clearly these are 'acceptable' to Dutch society and fit in with the current welfare context. The key issue for policy-makers in Britain is whether lessons can be learnt from these types of policies and projects. In order to consider this issue, there is a need to think about four elements. These are firstly whether the pattern of central and local relations in The Netherlands is comparable to the situation in Britain and in particular the extent to which local authorities and their partners in Britain have the flexibility to develop policies that reflect local circumstances. Secondly, there is the role of local authorities as strategic enablers. In The Netherlands this is a well-established and long term tradition. In Britain local authorities have acted as enablers and providers and there are considerable tensions between the provision and enabling role in housing and community care. Much of the emerging practice on collaboration in The Netherlands is based on partnership working between a range of organisations with the municipality acting as the strategic enabler, regulator and funder. Finally, it is important to consider whether the lessons from specific projects such as community care networks and safety net teams are based on key principles such as developing a balance between proactive and reactive initiatives or whether they merely illustrate that there are alternative approaches – what we have referred to as 'shock therapy'.

Conclusions

Many textbooks on housing and welfare issues incorporate a chapter on a comparative or European dimension. Often these appear to be little more than an attempt to describe what happens elsewhere. We, however, believe that a comparative approach can help us to think more radically about how to develop housing and community care and meet the needs of vulnerable groups in the 21st Century. Nevertheless, a comparative approach is not straightforward and borrowing policies and innovative projects from elsewhere without an appreciation of the social policy context can be highly misleading. Even so, if after reading this chapter, it has in any way challenged your views about the British system of housing and community care, then the 'shock therapy' has been useful.

Guide to further sources of information

Comparative community care
The most useful overview can be found in Chapter 8, 'European Perspectives on Community Care', in R. Means. S. Richards and R. Smith (2003) *Community Care – Policy and Practice*, Basingstoke, Palgrave Macmillan, 3rd Edition

European Union programmes
The European Union website is:
http://europa.eu.int

The most useful part of the website is the 'Employment and Social Affairs' section under 'Activities'. This covers social policy.

European housing and community care organisations
These include:
• CECODHAS – European Liaison Committee for Social Housing at:
   http://www.cecodhas.org
   CECODHAS has published a number of reports relevant for housing and community care including social housing allocation systems, social housing

for older people and the recent study, *Breaking down the barriers* as part of European Year for People with Disabilities in 2003

- FEANTSA – European Federation of National Organisations working with the Homeless at http://www.feantsa.org
  FEANTSA publishes a magazine on a regular basis on 'Homelessness in Europe' as well as a wide range of reports (e.g. 'Access to Housing' in 2002) and news and policy updates

The Netherlands

A number of key Dutch organisations have websites with summary material in English. These include:

- The Ministry of Housing, Spatial Planning and the Environment at http://www.vrom.nl/international/
- The Ministry of Health, Welfare and Sport at http://www.minvws.nl
  In addition both CVD and the HVO Foundation are in the process of establishing English summaries on their respective websites:
  - http://www.cvd.nl
  - http://www.hvoquerido.nl

A useful text on Dutch politics and society is:
Anderweg, R. and Irwin, G. (2002) *Governance and Politics of The Netherlands*, Basingstoke, Palgrave Macmillan.

CHAPTER 13:
Not another policy plan:
Supporting People strategies
and community care

**Tim Brown, Jo Richardson and
Jackie Thompson-Ercan**

Introduction

Supporting People strategies represent a determined commitment by the
government to achieve a co-ordinated policy approach at the local level. In
England, they are prepared by the 150 administering authorities (normally
unitary and county councils) with wide ranging consultation and involvement
with local stakeholders including users. 'Shadow' Supporting People strategies
had to be submitted to the government by the end of September 2002, i.e. before
the formal commencement of the Supporting People system in April 2003. The
administering authorities are now either in the process of or have completed a
review of their 'shadow' strategies leading to a formulation of a five year
strategy that were originally supposed to have been submitted in mid-2004 but
have been delayed until spring 2005. The strategies were hailed as an important
step forward at the start of this decade. Guidance published by the Department of
the Environment, Transport and the Regions (2001c) highlighted that:

> *'Supporting People is a new and important way in which local authorities
> and their partner agencies in health and probation can deliver some of the
> local strategic priorities of the community plan, health improvement plan,
> community safety strategy and other local strategies'* (p.11).

The emphasis on joined up thinking was further reinforced in the 'ministerial
foreword' jointly signed by the Deputy Home Secretary, and the Minister of
State for Health as well as the Minister of Housing. This stated that the new
approach would deliver *'integrated strategies at a local and national level where
Supporting People programme facilitates the delivery of key health and
community safety agendas'*. A fundamental principle is that Supporting People
strategies should overcome the fragmentation and confusing pattern of local
policy plans covering housing and support needs.

The aim of this chapter is therefore to review whether these well-intentioned ideas have been delivered in practice – through acknowledging that it takes a considerable period of time for a new forward planning system to bed down into mainstream policy-making. More precisely, the objectives are to:-

- describe and analyse the development of policy-making systems including community care plans and Supporting People strategies;
- locate the challenges of introducing a new strategy system within the changing framework of policy planning such as local housing strategies;
- highlight the impact of the shift towards regional governance and policy-making for housing and Supporting People; and
- speculate on how Supporting People strategies might and should develop.

The focus is, therefore, on the policy-making system rather than substantive policies. Discussions on the latter can be found elsewhere in this book. It should be noted that the intention is to identify the challenges in taking the Supporting People strategy agenda forward rather than merely critically analysing the difficulties that have emerged.

The chapter is based on a wide range of work that the authors have been involved with over the last few years in England. These include an input into the review of the Cornwall Supporting People Strategy, consultancy work on the co-ordination of local policy planning especially local and sub-regional housing strategies, research on the housing needs of vulnerable groups for a number of urban and rural local authorities in the East Midlands, and as a lead officer on Supporting People for a national housing association.

The next section describes and analyses the evolution of policy planning for community care and Supporting People. A key theme is that Supporting People strategies are the latest instalment of a much longer process of planning to meet the housing and support needs of vulnerable groups. This is followed by a discussion of the broader agenda of local policy planning. On the one hand, the government is keen to reduce the unacceptable burden of plan requirements yet at the same time appears to continue to introduce 'new' strategies. A particularly relevant illustration for Supporting People has been the introduction of local homelessness strategies under the Homelessness Act 2002. The penultimate section takes this issue a step forward by investigating the implications of the shift towards regional and sub-regional policy planning for Supporting People strategies. The consequences might include an implicit marginalisation of the housing and support agenda through the focus on integrating the housing and town planning systems by merging regional housing and planning boards. Lastly, the final section draws together the key findings to focus attention on the challenges facing Supporting People strategies.

Developing Supporting People strategies – an overview

The government's vision for Supporting People strategies has been explicit. The Department of the Environment Transport and the Regions (2001c) guidance set out eight criteria and these were:

- Engaging with users including difficult-to-reach groups.
- Forming an integrative approach for local strategic planning purposes.
- Focusing on cross-authority and agency priority groups such as people fleeing domestic violence.
- Involving a wide range of stakeholders in the development and delivery of policies.
- Ensuring, where appropriate, joined up thinking between counties and districts.
- Achieving co-ordination between national, regional and local policy-making on Supporting People.
- Establishing a consensus over policies between housing, social services, health and probation.
- Building on existing structures and policies.

The latter is significant as it implicitly acknowledges that there is a 'history' of policy-making to address the housing and support needs of vulnerable groups. The requirements of a more co-ordinated approach can, in fact, be traced back at least to the late 1960s when studies such as the Cullingworth Report (1969) on 'housing management' and the Seebohm Report (1968) on 'local authority and allied personal services' helped to usher in a period of corporate and inter-corporate policy planning in the post-local government reorganisation era in the mid-1970s. Joint planning between local government departments and the health sector became more commonplace. But the outcomes were disappointing. As Means, Richards and Smith (2003) have pointed out; the plethora of reports on community care in the mid and late 1980s noted amongst other weaknesses the lack of a local strategic vision and the resort to pragmatism and ad-hoc approaches to meeting the needs of vulnerable groups. The advent of community care plans under section 46 of the National Health Service and Community Care Act 1990, was put forward as a way of resolving this problem. Yet just over a decade later, community care plans have been abandoned and there are now Supporting People strategies and health improvement plans. One wonders whether by the early years of the next decade, these will have been replaced by other well-meaning initiatives to achieve a co-ordinated local policy response!

Indeed the guidance on community care plans in the early 1990s mirror the key elements of the vision for Supporting People strategies noted above. A joint circular (Department of the Environment and Department of Health, 1992) emphasised that while social services departments should take the lead in preparing annual community care plans, local authority housing departments and housing associations had a major role to play. The focus was on 'working together' so that these plans reflected key policies in local housing strategies and vice-versa. The reality during the 1990s was often rather different. In fact, a number of studies foresaw major challenges in developing and delivering co-ordinated community care plans. Arnold, Bochel, Broadhurst and Page (1993) famously highlighted that *'housing was a neglected dimension of and a weak link in community care'*. Their call for a housing information base for community care is strikingly reminiscent of current guidance on the better mapping of needs and supply in Supporting People strategies. Similarly, Rao (1990) noted the challenges faced by local authorities in moving towards a strategic enabling role and away from direct provision in community care. From a partnership perspective, she emphasised that collaborative working between many agencies (including local authority housing departments and housing associations) was essential but poorly developed. Nevertheless, the focus was on community care plans as a central component for delivering a mixed economy of housing and support. In practice, the outcome was at best patchy. For example, from a rural perspective there was a small but continuous stream of research complaining about the neglect of the countryside dimension in community care planning (see National Council for Voluntary Organisation, 1995).

The demise of community care planning was, however, primarily a result of new thinking in the Department of Health on local strategies (Means, Richards and Smith, 2003), rather than an outcome of a robust assessment and evaluation of its weaknesses. As early as 1998, the advent of health improvement plans and the growing importance of primary care trusts signalled that social services departments (the lead agency for community care plans) would have a changed and reducing role. During the consultation process in 2001/02 over the removal of the statutory requirement for the production of annual community care plans, the Department of Health stressed that there already existed an adequate range of plans and planning mechanisms including Local Strategic Partnerships and community plans, Joint Investment Plans, and health and modernisation plans. Rather worryingly, no reference was made to Supporting People strategies! The Department of Health also emphasised that *'amalgamating community care plans into health improvement plans could provide a significant vehicle for better co-ordination'*, as would the growing involvement of local authorities in their scrutiny and overview of the health service.

Supporting People strategies in England are, of course, the formal responsibility of the Office of the Deputy Prime Minister rather than the Department of Health. The guidance on these strategies points out that co-ordination with other plans including those produced by the National Health Service is essential (Department of the Environment, Transport and the Regions, 2001c; Chartered Institute of Housing, 2003a). Although this topic is dealt with in more detail in the next section, a crucial link is with the health improvement programme particularly the three year rolling Joint Investment Plans. Indeed it is recommended that this planning process should form a major element of the decision-making for Supporting People strategies.

Clearly this guidance on Supporting People strategies places considerable emphasis on links to broader policy frameworks. However, there is also a focus on a number of other themes. Firstly, there is a requirement for the robust mapping of the need for and supply of local services. Secondly, this mapping should inform the setting of a realistic set of priorities. Thirdly the policy-making process must take account of the needs of difficult-to-reach groups. Finally, the Supporting People strategy document should be accessible and coherent. Detailed guidance on these various requirements was provided in 2001/02 through newsletters, consultation papers and technical notes – the majority of which were made available through the Supporting People website: http://www.spkweb.org.uk. Nevertheless, as a number of commentators have noted, there has been a lack of detailed advice on some key issues such as the mapping of supply and need.

The administering authorities, as has already been pointed out, were required to submit a shadow strategy by September 2002. These have subsequently been evaluated for the Office of the Deputy Prime Minister by Leeds Metropolitan University (2004). The main conclusion appears to be a rather variable performance with 14 per cent of strategies rated as excellent, 32 per cent as good, 36 per cent as fair and 18 per cent as poor. More specifically, the evaluation highlighted from a positive viewpoint that Supporting People strategies:

- achieved a relatively high level of performance in terms of document accessibility and coherence;
- realised a high degree of partnership working on the ground;
- carried out thorough and comprehensive mapping of the supply of services to vulnerable groups; and
- made considerable progress in considering provision for difficult-to-reach groups.

Nevertheless, a number of interlinked weaknesses were identified including:-

- lack of engagement with Black and Minority Ethnic client groups;
- under-researched mapping of local needs;
- failure to link the mapping of need and supply with priorities for action; and
- most surprisingly, because of the guidance, poor links with other local policy planning systems such as Local Strategic Partnerships and community plans.

As the researchers note, the strengths and weaknesses need to be set within the broader context. The development of a 'new' strategy to a tight timetable represented a major challenge. Furthermore, the administering authorities are likely to be able to improve the quality of their strategies by learning the lessons from the first round of shadow plans. Indeed, there are examples of innovation in Supporting People strategies highlighted in the 'Beacon Programme' (which is an annual government scheme to highlight best practice in a range of services). In 2003, as part of round five of the programme, four local authority partnerships were identified as exemplars in Supporting People – Suffolk, Oxfordshire, Salford, and Telford and Wrekin. In each case, aspects of strategy development were praised by the independent panel of assessors:

- Suffolk: Partnership working.
- Oxfordshire: Needs mapping.
- Salford: Needs mapping and health, housing and social services partnerships.
- Telford and Wrekin: Corporate approach.

It is, however, important not to be complacent! A number of the identified problems are precisely those that affected community care planning in the 1990s. For example, there is a rich literature on good practice on mapping the needs of vulnerable groups such as the work on the pathways and prevalence models – see Munro, Lomax, Lancaster, Bramley and Anderson (1996) and Watson (1996). Indeed, the growing interest in the use of Geographical Information Systems in housing needs studies and housing market analysis could prove valuable for mapping needs and supply in Supporting People strategies. But there is little evidence that Supporting People teams drew on this available material or have understood the potential of Geographical Information Systems for improving decision-making. Similarly, the lack of links to other strategies is inexcusable given the guidance on Supporting People strategies and the lessons that could have been learnt from community care plans.

The 150 administering authorities in England have been in the process of updating and reviewing their policies for the spring 2005 deadline for submission of the five-year strategies. The minister responsible for Supporting People, Yvette Copper, has pointed out in her foreword to the Supporting People strategy toolkit (see http://www.spstrategytoolkit.org.uk/) that there is a *'need to look beyond the implementation process and on to the medium and longer term'*. This toolkit and guidance stress that the five year strategies should focus on:

- existing supply analysis;
- review process for each service supplied;
- current and future needs analysis; and
- justified and robust five year strategies and annual plans.

The guidance (which in some respects parallels that for local housing strategies) provides detailed advice to the administering authorities including recommendations on the format and structure of the strategies. There has, however, been a strong tendency to marginalise this activity. There is, in fact, little up-to-date advice on the Supporting People website and the Office of the Deputy Prime Minister (2004b) guide on Supporting People makes only a single reference to strategies. The Supporting People strategy website (http://www.spstrategytoolkit.org.uk/) has still to be fully populated. The emphasis has been, instead, on funding for specific services and projects. This is perhaps understandable given the uncertainty during 2004 following the independent review by RSM Robson Rhodes that highlighted the lack of value for money, unexplained variations in costs between similar local authorities and the confusion over what project elements were eligible for funding through Supporting People. This has been compounded by a series of announcements in autumn 2004. These included, firstly, a study for the Office of the Deputy Prime Minister by Matrix Research and Consultancy who found that nearly 5 per cent of the Supporting People budget was spent inappropriately on non-housing-related services and that local authorities were uncertain whether a further 30 per cent of services were housing-related. Secondly, and more significantly, Office of the Deputy Prime Minister announcements on funding following the government's Spending Review in July 2004 intensified local debates on how the process of responding to cuts in funding would be achieved. This is leading to an inevitable focus on pragmatic decisions on the future of existing schemes and the lack of forward planning. A number of local authorities have commented that they have yet to complete their service reviews and therefore have found it challenging to make reasoned decisions on funding specific projects. But have we not been here before in both the mid-1980s and 1990s? There is a fundamental need already to re-emphasise the importance of, and reinvigorate, strategic policy-making!

Local policy planning

However, improving the quality of strategic policy-making is not straightforward. Learning the lessons from the evaluation of the shadow strategies and making more effective use of good practice guidance on, for instance, mapping local needs is useful. But the complexity and changing nature of the local policy planning framework provides a fundamental challenge. On the one hand, the government is committed to reducing the burden on local authorities of policy planning, but at the same time it appears to be increasing the number of annual statements and plans. From a Supporting People perspective, a decrease in the number of overlapping plans is generally to be welcomed as it makes policy co-ordination more straightforward. But there is a dilemma that reducing the number of plans might marginalise the needs of difficult-to-reach groups.

Table 13.1 lists the Supporting People client groups highlighted by the Office of the Deputy Prime Minister (2004b) and examples of specific plans.

Table 13.1: Supporting People client groups and strategies

Supporting People client groups	Examples of client group strategies prepared by local authorities
Homeless households and rough sleepers	Local homelessness strategies/rough sleepers' strategies
Ex-offenders and people at risk of offending	Crime and disorder strategies/community safety plans
People with a physical or sensory disability	Joint investment plan on welfare to work for disabled people
People at risk of domestic violence	Crime/disorder strategies
People with alcohol or drug problems	Drugs action plan
Teenage parents	Teenage pregnancy strategies
Older people	Older people's strategies Joint investment plans for older people
Young people at risk	Area child protection committee business plan Behaviour support plan Children's services plan Youth justice plans
People with HIV and AIDS	HIV/AIDS grant plan
People with learning difficulties	Valuing People strategies Joint investment plans for people with learning disabilities
Travellers	Development plan under town and country planning legislation DoE Circular 1/94 on *'gypsy sites and planning'*
Homeless families with support needs	Local homelessness strategies

This shows the difficulties faced by Supporting People teams in effectively integrating specific service plans. It should, however, be noted that the reality is even more complex, for example:

- The table highlights examples and is not comprehensive – for instance, development plans under the town and country planning legislation are likely to have policies for ensuring the provision of Lifetime Homes and hence be of relevance to people with physical and sensory disabilities.

- Schemes are constantly undergoing modification – reference has already been made to the demise of community care plans. The Planning and Compulsory Purchase Act 2004, sets out a revised framework for development plans, while the emerging 'strategy for children and young people' will encompass a number of more specific policies such as Children's Services Plans and Youth Justice Plans.
- The table excludes strategies required through the National Health Service.

Added complexity is created by the existence of broader policy plans such as local authority housing strategies. Supporting People teams should take account of local homelessness strategies that are part of a sub-set of housing plans. But, in addition, the overarching housing strategy includes an assessment of the housing needs of vulnerable groups as well as incorporating relevant policies. Similarly, there are 'better care, higher standards' charters that focus on the co-ordination of social services, health and housing provision. This will include agreed performance standards that will be of relevance for Supporting People strategies.

Finally, at a strategic level, local authorities are required under the Local Government Act 2000, to prepare a community plan that sets out the priorities for achieving economic and social well-being. It is expected to be closely associated with the work of Local Strategic Partnerships and the local authority's Best Value performance plan. It can be argued that this framework provides an opportunity to co-ordinate the diverse array of local policy plans including Supporting People strategies. Nevertheless, it is another challenge for Supporting People teams in ensuring effective collaboration especially in localities where there is a county council and district councils with both tiers producing community plans.

The bewildering and changing number of local policy plans has been identified by many researchers. The Chartered Institute of Housing (2004) has noted, there is a *complex portfolio of strategies and plans which local authorities, health authorities and other bodies prepare'*, and these should be co-ordinated through Local Strategic Partnerships. The Department of Transport, Local Government and the Regions (2001b) found in their review of this issue that the number of plans required of local authorities (depending on the tier of local government) could be as high as 48. It also noted that this was an under-estimation as local authorities may use their discretionary powers to produce additional strategies. Furthermore, each plan may have its own subset of requirements such as statistical returns and sub-plans – the local housing strategy system is a good illustration of this situation. This burden of plan making on local government has been acknowledged by the Office of the Deputy Prime Minister as unacceptable as part of its modernising government strategy. It has set out a number of inter-related steps to improve the situation. These include:

- Reducing the overall number of local policy plans required by central government departments through administrative and statutory changes by 75 per cent – this proposal was highlighted in 2002.

- By 2006, local authorities will only be required to produce six major service plans as well as a community plan and a Best Value performance plan.
- For excellent local authorities under the comprehensive performance assessment system, the possibility that by 2006 they will be *'freed from the requirement of producing any major service plan'*.

Rather significantly, the Office of the Deputy Prime Minister and Local Government Association in a letter to local authority chief executives in summer 2003 indicated the possibility of Supporting People strategies being integrated and subsumed within community strategies. Nevertheless, the commitment to reducing the burden of plan making should not be over-stated. The requirement for local homelessness strategies in 2002 was emphasised by the Office of the Deputy Prime Minister at the same time that it was stressing its commitment to reducing plan requirements. Recently it has announced that local authorities will be required to produce annual efficiency statements – clearly these will have relevance for Supporting People teams given the growing emphasis on value for money and efficiency savings.

This section has highlighted the bewildering range of local policy plans relevant for Supporting People strategies. It has not been the intention to provide the reader with a definitive guide especially as any such attempt would quickly become out-of-date. The commitment by the government to reduce local plan requirements is generally to be welcomed. However, the detailed consequences present a dilemma. Supporting People strategies may become a sub-section of the community strategy while service plans for specific groups may be abandoned. Will this result in a marginalisation of strategic planning for housing and support purposes?

The regional and sub-regional dimensions

This marginalisation may be increased because of the growing focus on regional and sub-regional policy-making in housing. The Labour government has put considerable emphasis on the regional dimension. Since 1997, there has been a plethora of initiatives such as the establishment of regional development agencies, a greater role for government offices for the regions and the establishment of Regional Housing Boards charged with producing regional housing strategies. Nevertheless, the rejection of the establishment of an elected regional assembly in the North East in a referendum in November 2004 shows that progress has not been straightforward. Even so, the government appears committed to continue the development of regional governance.

From a housing perspective, the emergence of regional housing strategies has raised important questions about the long term future of local housing strategies. The latter, although now a statutory requirement under the Local Government Act

2003, appear to be of decreasing significance. Key resource allocation decisions are now made by the Regional Housing Boards guided by their regional housing strategies, though these also have to be approved by the Office of the Deputy Prime Minister. The emphasis in these strategies is on 'mainstream' policies such as affordable housing provision, meeting the Decent Homes Standard, tackling low demand and delivering the four new growth areas. A strong driver is the *Sustainable Communities Plan* (Office of the Deputy Prime Minister, 2003b). There is implicitly a low priority attached to housing and support in both this plan and the regional strategies – a criticism that has been frequently aired by local authorities and housing associations in the consultation processes in 2003/04 on the development of regional housing strategies.

The neglect of the housing and support agenda at the regional level could intensify. The government has consulted on the merger of regional and planning boards with a view to this taking effect in mid-2005. Organisations such as the Chartered Institute of Housing have raised concerns that one of the unintended consequences will be an increasing focus on numbers of new housing units and residential land allocations at the expense of issues such as the Supporting People agenda. At best, it is argued that regional housing strategies may focus on less controversial client groups such as older people.

In late 2004, both the Treasury and the Office of the Deputy Prime Minister issued consultation papers on regional resource allocation processes, and again the paucity of references to Supporting People is worrying. Indeed, the proposed reformulation of a housing needs index for allocating resources to the regions is based on the affordable housing requirements, meeting the Decent Homes Standard and tackling multiple deprivation. Although it is acknowledged that Supporting People funding is through a separate mechanism to the regional housing pot, these proposals implicitly continue to relegate this issue in the debates on regional housing strategies.

Of course, it can be argued that these worries will be alleviated because of the commitment by the Department of the Environment, Transport and the Regions (2001c) and the Supporting People strategy toolkit to emphasise cross-boundary issues through regional planning groups. But this initiative has only been focused on a number of specific client groups such as those fleeing domestic violence. Overall, there is little if any evidence that such planning groups have contributed to, or commented on, draft regional housing strategies in either 2003 or 2004, despite the acknowledgement in the Supporting People strategy toolkit that a closer working relationship is needed with Regional Housing Boards and the Housing Corporation.

It might also be suggested that especially in areas with two tier local government, county councils have had the opportunity to act strategically and co-ordinate housing and social care strategies. This, however, has not materialised for a number of reasons. Firstly, there is an uncertain future for social services departments (see above). Secondly, the patchwork quilt of local authority administrative boundaries (as well as primary care trusts) with counties and districts often intermingled with unitary authorities does not reflect local housing markets. And lastly, and most importantly, counties have had an extremely small scale role in relation to housing strategies limited to the planning aspects of residential land allocations and numbers of housing units.

Moving forward

This chapter has presented a pessimistic perspective on Supporting People strategies. The quality of the shadow strategies was, at best, variable. This was disappointing as important lessons on partnership working and co-ordinating policies could have been learnt from community care planning in the 1990s. Similarly, there is a wealth of material on the key issue of mapping need and supply but again little use has been made of techniques and methods such as Geographical Information Systems and pathways approaches. It will be interesting to examine in 2005/06 whether there has been a marked improvement in the quality of policy-making in the new five year strategies.

More importantly, of course, strategies are only a 'means to an end' rather than an 'end in itself'. The crucial issue is whether Supporting People strategies are resulting in more appropriate housing and support services for users and carers. Our conclusions are not promising. We have emphasised throughout this chapter the tension between strategic planning and the pragmatic responses required to react to changing funding envelopes and government guidance. There is clearly a gap between policy and action!

We consider there are two possible trajectories for tackling this issue. Firstly, there is a case for enhancing the relevance and quality of strategies by:

- Developing a shared long term vision with other local policy planning systems such as housing and health strategies.
- Co-ordinating policies and investment strategies for vulnerable groups.
- Ensuring that community plans and Local Strategic Partnerships reflect the importance of addressing health and social care agendas.
- Tackling the challenges posed by different administrative geographical boundaries.
- Improving the mapping of needs and supply.

At the same time, it is essential that Supporting People strategies feed into regional and sub-regional housing strategies. This requires an advocacy approach by Supporting People teams and the recognition by Regional Housing Boards of the importance of housing and support.

Secondly, and more radically, the existence of Supporting People strategies as separate documents could be abandoned in favour of their incorporation into community plans and Local Strategic Partnerships. Specific and detailed annual service plans for the Supporting People client groups could be prepared that would co-ordinate the delivery of projects. In some cases, these already exist – see Table 13.1. This approach would fit in with the modernising government agenda and dovetail with the stated commitment of the Office of the Deputy Prime Minister to reduce the local authority planning burden. It would not represent an abandonment of policy-making. There would still be a requirement to map needs and supply and to develop strategies that reflect the outcome of this type of analysis. But it would feed directly into community plans and strategies and present a real opportunity for joined up thinking.

CHAPTER 14:
'Social capital': a systems approach to housing and community care

Paul Simic

Plato (Cratylus 402A): *'Heraclitus, you know, says that everything moves on and that nothing is at rest; and, comparing existing things to the flow of a river, he says that you could not step into the same river twice.'*

Douglas Coupland: *'Historical overdosing: to live in a period of time when too much seems to be happening.'*

Introduction

What I'm aiming to do here is draw together some of the threads of recent social policy on housing, social care and health covered by the preceding chapters and to try to point some comprehensible way forward for the collaborative working agenda that underpins the new approaches required.

The main conclusion, I'll say in advance, is that the rhetoric on meeting people's housing, health and social care needs involves an inexorable logic: a systems approach through reshaping services and through more collaborative approaches. Most importantly, we are talking of a complex system with a multitude of inter-relating and changing variables. Policy which is too narrow, particularly that relating to 'top down' performance management driven activity, will do the opposite of what is required. It will shore up the walls acting as barriers between services, an issue that has been the subject of so much criticism and that was given so much prominence in the 'Berlin Wall' between health and social care. The problem implicit in the reference, and the challenge implicit within the problem, is the fact that there is not one wall, but many, between and within organisations charged with planning and providing services. Dealing with these interfaces, particularly the housing role, requires a *'fundamental shift in thinking'* (Bochel, Bochel, and Page, 1999) and a challenge to the dysfunctional repetition implicit in *'new boundaries around old behaviour'* (Platt, 2004).

The recognition of the 'social capital' yield, that should be the product of the new collaborative agenda, challenges the narrow performance management approach which is representative of a partial view; departmentally-led or led by a narrow sectional interest: this is the way backwards not forwards. The requirement is – switching my philosophical mentors from Plato – for some Archimedean point from which to view the 'whole picture'. This provides some means of measuring the value-added aspects of an improved system, the development of 'social capital' (Putnam, 2003; OECD, 2001), that is the ultimate outcome of diverse but interconnected approaches to a diverse range of problems.

The main challenge, implicit in the title and the quotes above, is managing the constant change that characterises the relationship between the main actors and their environment and which is the key feature of latter-day health and social care policy.

Deconstructing 'care' and 'support'

Health care, social care and housing support are built over fault lines. These are the ever-shifting 'tectonic plates' of health, housing and social care practice and policy. The 'new' idea in policy (implicitly and sometimes explicitly) is that of a systems approach; straddling historical boundaries and obstacles (such as that famous health and social care 'Berlin Wall'). This is embedded in some of the new rhetoric of the Third Way's, 'post-ideological', approach to policy (e.g., joined up government, tackling social exclusion, central-local rebalancing, communitarianism). The challenge for workers and managers in the frontline is to make sense of this in the real world of the ever tightening screw of 'efficiencies' and continuous organisational change, and the shifting boundaries of what is and what is not in your province.

Housing

Housing policy over the last quarter of a century has seen the re-creation of a divide between those who own property and those who don't (Murie, 2003) after a period which saw an intent to pull in the opposite direction. The period seeing the impetus towards increasing ownership of property also saw the counterveiling transformation of 'public housing' as a mainstream activity, to 'social housing', something for the marginalised (Lund, 1996). In a nation of property owners, those who could not enter that market either rented from what was called, and which now sounds oddly anachronistic, the 'public sector' (councils), from housing associations (the voluntary sector) or (private sector) landlords; usually with some support from the social security system. Housing provided by the public sector ('social housing') diminished substantially over the last quarter of the twentieth century (Audit Commission, 1998). Over that period succeeding administrations have pursued policies which show a clear heritage line back to Margaret Thatcher's 1979 commitment to a *property owning democracy* – to accompany the other, then revolutionary goals, of trade union reform and the deconstruction of nationalisation as a model for public service delivery of public 'goods', all in the context of a individualistic narrative: *'there is no such thing as society'* (quoted in Keay, 1987).

There have been *'dramatic shifts in policy and the role of the state'* in relation to housing (Murie, 2003). The main changes Murie identified were the centralisation of policy and the reduction of *'the direct influence of the state'* as a consequence of privatisation (ibid). That housing stock devoted to those not in the housing market has increasingly been used for 'social housing' – shorthand for housing aimed at people who are more likely to have at least low level care and/or support needs (Means *et al.*, 2003). This change has been characterised through two concepts: residualisation and marginalisation: in a nutshell, social housing for the poor and excluded rather than housing as a mainstream, universal, public 'good' (see also Lund, 1996; Glennerster, 2000, pp.180-81). *'Structural forces in housing policy have resulted in the concentration of socially excluded groups, such as disabled people and the poor, in low quality social and, increasingly, private sector housing'* (Hawtin, 2000). 'Public housing' is now the province of housing associations and councils who have been redirected from the provider function towards a commissioning/planning function. Such housing is no longer a universal service but one targeted at those who are excluded from the market.

This shift has meant that 'housing', as a concept, and in the context used in this book, sits on the territory also occupied by social care services and health services: where need is addressed through assessment, in a necessary relationship with professional 'gatekeepers', who control and manage access and who operate in a structure where the funded bodies are managed through cost containment techniques such as 'capping' and 'efficiency' requirements.

Controlling expenditure, working out new relationships between public and private sectors, assessing need and allocating care/support on the basis of that assessment – trying to balance preventive interventions with meeting greatest need – are now parallel processes occurring across the three sectors we are discussing in this chapter.

There is also a discourse on user voice/empowerment, expressed in different language in different circumstances, but essentially attempting to redraw some traditional boundary lines between service sectors, between organisations, and between the 'laity' ('users', 'carers', 'consumers', 'customers', 'citizens') in receipt of services and the professional providers or gatekeepers. Each sector has its own history, its own discourse as to what it is, what it should be, and where it has come from, but the one essential shared truth about these discrete areas of policy and practice is that they are interlinked in a way never before so clearly recognised, at least, in rhetoric.

The factors that influence the sectors and how they work together include not only sectoral boundaries themselves (e.g., what is and isn't 'your' territory), and the challenges brought on by reinterpretation of those boundaries, but also the balance between primary and secondary aspect of services as they are organised within those boundaries. 'Primary' interventions are those that aim to 'get in' before the fact, before the problem, whatever it is, presents itself needing a solution. They are directed at the general population, or possibly some part of that population judged to be more at risk, rather than those who are judged to need, and judged to be eligible for, a specific service or intervention.

Housing services are in a critical position in relation to this interface between primary and secondary, and timely and effective interventions from housing services can impact on the career paths of 'service users' and 'citizens'.

The *Leeds Declaration* (Long, 1994), from a public health perspective, talked of 'upstream' (early prevention) and 'downstream' ('secondary' and specialist 'tertiary' care) services and called for a refocusing 'upstream': concentrating on social structures and processes that influence health and on factors that enable some people to remain healthy in adverse circumstances. Upstream services are preventive services which aim to prevent people falling into the river and downstream services are aimed at pulling out those who have fallen in. A fixed pot of money to tackle both ends of the needs spectrum creates a fundamental tension in decisions on resource allocation. Indeed, an implicit aim of 'community care' was to refocus public care services (and their funding) on those in greatest need (downstream) leaving those with lower care needs to look to kith and kin, the community, and the private sector (if they could pay) to meet those needs. Some authors have argued that this shift in care is little more than a shift towards maintaining the burden of care on women rather than in more general terms on the 'community'.

Community care

There is no 'social care' policy as such in the way there have been attempts at articulating health care or housing policy. 'Community care' has been the label attached to changes aimed at re-engineering the social care sector.

This sector is made up of care in residential settings and other specialist settings, and in home settings, for the groups defined by the *Caring for People* white paper (ibid) as the 'elderly', the 'disabled' (physical and sensory), the 'mentally ill' and those with 'mental handicap' (Department of Health, 1989a) as being the groups in need. The sector was largely the province of public sector providers but just as *Caring for People* emphasised alternatives to residential care it brought in the obligation to develop the 'independent' sector in a 'mixed economy' of care.

Modern policy can, somewhat arbitrarily but with some logic, be seen to start with the Audit Commission report, *Making a Reality of Community Care* (1986) which was a response to Treasury concerns over the expansion of the DSS budget for care homes. There was a concern over the lack of development of alternative care models that could populate a true 'spectrum of care'. To what extent this was Treasury driven rather than driven by other considerations (e.g., quality of care) is a moot point. The structural tension was in the view that support needs which could be met 'upstream' were being met by 'downstream' services which weren't really required (given available alternatives) and which were overly costly. The Audit Commission identified a number of fundamental problems with the system: it was characterised by *'organisational fragmentation and confusion'*, a lot of money was spent on it, and the cost to the Treasury was running away exponentially (£10 million to £1 billion 1979-89; and a further doubling by 1991-2). The report concluded: *'If this opportunity is not taken, a new pattern of care will emerge; based on private residential homes rather than a more flexible mix of services ... The result will be a continued waste of scarce resources.'* Others have argued that while there may have been some perverse incentive, what the DSS route gave people who were not so well off was the same option ('choice') as the better off, and they exercised that choice, albeit for residential care, to the Treasury's displeasure. Community care was a solution for bringing the focus back to the point of the 'need' rather than 'want' through the vehicle of 'assessment', thus leading away from 'choice'. This can be a dangerously unbridled concept, not only for the Treasury but for the parties (government and people) complicit in the big illusion that we can have good quality care services as well as low taxes and that someone or something else can pay for it (the individual, the family, the future).

In the Care in the Community pilots conducted by PSSRU at the University of Kent in the mid-80s, while they covered a range of client groups and initiatives (Challis, 1993), a core theme was both targeting resources at those most in need and, logically, redistributing those resources away from so-called 'low level' services. This was exactly the kind of 'upstream', low level continuing support services that may function preventatively and which are now increasingly the concern of the Supporting People policy. This was most evident in Kent's re-targeting of home help provision, leaving – and this is a crucial point, too – those who had low level needs with the options of either paying privately for the care that now wouldn't be paid for publicly or being looked after by the 'informal' sector: family carers, most usually women carers.

The original Care in the Community projects were presented as targeting resources at those most in need, rather than taking them away from people who needed them but not as much as others. However, by the mid-90s the consequences of this were being recognised and another perspective was being articulated (e.g., Arblaster *et al.*, 1996). The authors found *'significant gaps for vulnerable people living in ordinary housing [with] insufficient accommodation of an appropriate type and standard.'* They also found *'serious shortfalls in care support for people with medium and low levels of need who are not given priority in community care provisions.'* This was a dynamic rather than static situation and housing management staff were concerned about their capacity to cope with the growing number of vulnerable people living in unsuitable areas where there is little other support.

'Low intensity support can prevent people reaching crisis point' (JRF, 1999a) but targeting resources can mean that *'people get little or no support until their needs become acute'* (ibid). The challenge relates to how, with finite resources needing to address upstream and downstream needs, those in charge of those resources target them to best effect and, especially, do not see resources consumed by the majority, while only the minority would ever need 'rescuing'. Every service manager knows that all their budget could be allocated on preventive services and all could be allocated on meeting greatest need; the trick is how to get the balance right. The 'x factor' in upstream funding is that a substantial proportion of those to whom services might be allocated upstream would anyway, by one means or another, get themselves out of trouble and thus the funding allocated to their rescue (continuing the analogy to complete the argument). A review of low intensity support services (Quilgars, 2000) showed how crude the process was still, of articulating outcomes and objectively measuring impact (a limitation echoed elsewhere, e.g., Cameron *et al.*, 2001).

With this background in mind – sectoral boundaries (between health and social care and housing) and their morphic nature, the challenge of balancing prevention with addressing greatest need, and the emphasis on budgetary control – the start of the new century has seen the arrival of an new initiative 'Supporting People' to balance the 'community care' policy launched in the early 1990s (Department of Health, 1989a) aimed at dealing with that famous foundling: Griffiths' 'nobody's baby' (Griffiths, 1988).

Supporting People

The Supporting People programme went 'live' in April 2003, ten years after community care went 'live', at least in its post-Griffiths, local authority-led, persona. Ostensibly, the programme can be seen to be a means to plug the gap left by the refocusing of community care services on those with greatest need (those who are 'downstream'), leaving no parallel national strategy focusing on preventive services other than a reliance on the, as it is called, 'informal' sector, most commonly women. Indeed, much of the critique of community care as a policy from the inception of the 'Care in the Community' projects evaluated by PSSRU in the 1980s onwards was the shift of the hidden burden to the informal sector as an implicit (perhaps even hidden) aim of policy.

The problem needing to be fixed, in order to try and move towards 'seamlessness' in service provision, ('seamlessness', and its relations, being a high value piece of rhetorical currency over recent times) was outlined by Watson (Watson, 1997). Watson and colleagues highlighted the marginalisation and residualisation of housing stock, something which resulted in the fact that often the only housing available to those in need was poor quality and in undesirable areas while, on the other hand, the 'narrow reach' of community care assessments meant that those who could benefit from a lower level of support either were unable to access services or had inappropriate services 'thrust on them'.

Health

The interface is not, though, merely between community care and housing. Complex enough though that is, would that it were so simple. One of the core philosophical ideas influencing modern policy (as expressed under the rubric 'modernisation') is interconnectedness of things and many ministerial statements use this rhetoric. It is impossible to talk of 'care' and 'support' as a social or housing-related discourse solely; it must include health services and the even broader issue of 'health' as opposed to merely health (really 'illness') services. The calls for a systems approach (See Patton, 1990, for a simple introduction to systems theory) to understanding care.

Post war policy on health has been characterised by two features, firstly, a concentration on illness services rather than on health more broadly: *'Health policy in recent times has been dominated by an unhealthy concentration on health services'* (Harrison *et al.*, 1991) and secondly, by kaleidoscopic change not unrelated to the fact that the NHS, in particular, is the politician's favourite electioneering territory. Latterly, pooled budgets are the most recent innovation aimed at introducing some centripetal forces and thereby improving the potential for joint working between social services and health (Health Act, 1999). Under the Health Act money can be pooled between health bodies and health-related local authority services, and resources and management structures can be integrated. The arrangements, which have been in use since April 2000, allow the joining up of existing services and the development of new, co-ordinated services. This is an explicit recognition of the need to work across existing boundaries and for funding to track and facilitate that work.

Upstream and downstream

Just as 'community care' and 'Supporting People' can be seen to occupy different places along the bank of the river, we have seen some parallel rebalancing (up and down stream) of NHS services. The 'primary care led NHS' is its current form, with the creation of PCTs as the main health care commissioners of secondary care (GP fundholding having been rejected by New Labour although, as this chapter is written, aspects of that innovation may be revisited). The big issue faced by modern government at a macro level is cost containment. Governments across all developed countries are trying to rein in health spending, stalked by the fear of the unsupportable costs associated with technological advance, consumer power and choice, and an ageing population. An NHS driven by primary care end purchasers is, it is supposed, is likely to be cheaper than that led by secondary and tertiary end providers just as there is an implicit assumption (erroneous, I'd argue) that community care is cheaper than its alternatives.

It is also, though, a recognition of the need to re-engineer and rebalance the service sector subject, as it is, to the pressures of demographic, technical and social forces impelling change. The direction of change, the view of which seems shared across political perspectives, was towards a rebalancing involving more of a 'mixed economy' in the model of services. The rebalancing of care sectors is discussed further below (Symonds and Kelly, 1998).

Citizen and state: care and support: who pays?

The shift, then, has been towards a systems perspective, upstream towards proactive approaches and prevention, and away from the administrative model where cost trailed activity and government stumped up the money, to one where cost is King of the Jungle and cost and funding issues (at the macro and micro levels) are to the fore. The last quarter of a century in policy-making from government(s) has witnessed a fundamental debate around costs, both in terms of cost containment (which derives from concerns over the proportion of GDP spent on public services) and in terms of 'who pays?' (the spread of the cost burden and the relationship between individual and state).

Melanie Henwood (Henwood, 1999) outlined the issue between of citizen and state in relation to who pays?

> *'Major reforms to the structure of community care in the early 90s ... were concerned largely with improving management and accountability of local services and with promoting community rather than residential based models of care. These failed to address the larger underlying question about the balance of responsibilities between individuals and the state'.*

Just as 'community care', as an articulated policy, was seen as the means to limit and cap the open ended DSS commitment to funding residential care as much as rebalancing care towards the 'community', so Supporting People's aim, whatever else it might be in terms of plugging the 'low level support' gap, has been to consolidate and control a number of funding streams (including supported housing management grant, DSS Resettlement Grant, transitional housing benefit, and income support) into one mechanism for funding 'housing-related support services' and to cap that funding.

What exactly 'housing-related support services' are is unclear (see, for example, online discussions on spkweb.org.uk) as is the exact boundary between these and other care services, mimicking the interminable debates in health and social care about when nursing care stopped and social care began (the infamous 'nursing bath' vs. the 'social bath'). As argued elsewhere in this collection (see Foord's introduction) we now seem to have nursing (personal care around the 'body') and social care/support (around housing) each with its own financial drivers and regulation processes (although between health and social care there is some convergence).

There were also some clear parallels between the community care and Supporting People initiatives and the use of language in their respective launches. The most obvious comparison is the disjunction critics highlight between the rhetoric, focused around needs and choice (the 'manifest' function), and the real or underlying driver ('latent' function) as those critics see it, of Treasury concerns regarding public spending. Just as Oldman argues elsewhere in this chapter, that 'independence' is code for 'cost saving' so one can see the same contrast in the 'needs' and 'choice' rhetoric in Supporting People.

The February 2004 press release by the housing minister, following the 'Independent Review' of the Supporting People programme, illustrates the point clearly: *'Supporting People is an extremely important programme which aims to help some of the most vulnerable people in society live independently with the support they need.'* She continues, with no development of that theme or pause, *'It is important that the programme delivers value for money'* adding a reference to the Independent Review being clear *'that value for money can be improved and the variations between local authorities should be addressed'* and further adds that *'the government has asked the Audit Commission to conduct detailed inspections of some of the high cost authorities so these problems can be dealt with and valuable services for the vulnerable can be safeguarded and sustained.'*

This little vignette serves to raise into view the contrast between those manifest and latent aspects of policy-making we refer to. The emphasis on meeting need is written large on the banners at the front of the march but the ranks behind the banners are mainly concerned about costs. Their concern about costs is also somewhat skewed as only high costs are identified as problematic; low costs are, implicitly, of no notable concern. So 'invisibles', people not receiving a service or receiving an inadequate level of service, prompt no equivalent and vigorous audit.

The Independent Review itself was set up not because of quality concerns but of cost: *'The Independent Review was commissioned after significant late growth in costs for 2003/4.'* Anyone asked, 'what is this essentially about?' would have to say 'it's about money'. The fact that needs analysis was expressly excluded from the inception phase of Supporting People (although the Independent Review calls for a future focus on just such a needs-led approach) indicates that 'needs-based' remains a highly qualified concept at the policy centre. We have, in contemporary policy, an attempt to join up housing with health and social care into some comprehensible policy framework, a framework linking sectors (health, housing and social) with stages in care, or what can be termed 'orientation' (primary and secondary; upstream/downstream).

Behind these concerns, the question may be asked as to whether policies like 'community care' and 'Supporting People' are not authentic attempts at new ways of funding and delivering care and support at the turn of the 21st century? That is, services that are more appropriate, more flexible and sensitive, more inclusive, as well as affordable; and affordability is itself a perfectly valid aim for commissioners and both local and central government to seek. It is also right to remain sceptical about the disjunction between rhetoric that emphasises 'choice', 'needs', local decision-making, while policy seems to give a preference to top down management tools such the performance indicator movement and league tables (in 2005 already being discarded, having been so recently lauded, as a tool for monitoring hospital performance) and the budget-capping structures in place for community care and Supporting People budgets.

Key points

- The relevance of systems theory and a holistic approach to care.
- Integration involves: linking across sectors, aligning orientation (primary and secondary).
- The importance of the 'Who pays for care?' question and the balance of responsibility between the individual and the family, the insurance industry, and 'the state' (local and central government).
- The main policy drivers in health care, social care and in housing: primary end emphasis, cost awareness, holistic approach.
- The changing positions of 'social care', 'health care' and 'housing support' and the common territory they inhabit.

Deconstructing the policy context – 'modernisation': some key terms and directions

Six elements in the politics of recent policy on health and social care:

- Pace of change, 'continual revolution'.
- Cost containment, cost burden sharing.
- Modernisation, managerialism and marketisation.
- Reframing 'community care' and institutional care models.
- 'Upstream' and 'downstream' issues.
- 'Public' and 'private' issues.

What is policy? I shan't pause too long, but it is necessary to stop and 'smell the flowers' en route even if only for a minute or two. The best account of what is and what isn't 'policy' is still by Booth:

'Social policy can best be seen as encompassing all policies which affect the distribution of resources and life-chances among individuals, groups and classes in society, including cash incomes, benefits in kind, capital assets,

public services and status and power. It may be explicit and deliberately formulated or implicit and accidental. It includes not only policies which are framed and implemented by central and local government, but also those of non-state institutions such as voluntary organizations, trade unions, private companies and firms' (Booth, 1988).

The value of his account stresses the role of government, but also the role of other players, the role of intended and unintended consequences, the inclusion of the irrational and messy along with the rational, and the role of power in defining the discourse and shaping what is latent with what is manifest.

The period covering the last two decades has seen a tremendous, indeed mind-boggling, amount of change in health and social care with governments of different colours that have seen themselves as radical (no longer a concept synonymous with the left of the political spectrum), crusading and interventionist. The focus for that intervention has broadly been the 'public purposes' involved in meeting social need and the agents and agencies involved.

'Modernisation' is the label for a suite of approaches across a range of policy areas (such as health, education, and transport) and structures (e.g., central government, local government, health authority governance) that have common features: the requirement for an increased responsiveness in public services, more joined up and strategic approaches, a focus on cost-control (aka 'efficiency') and a clear view on outcomes measurement ('quality'). This is clearly outlined in the *Modernising Social Services* white paper (Department of Health, 1998b) for just one example. Change and how to manage it, whether as instigator, sufferer or surfer is one of the biggest features of our age. Bauman (2003) recognised the mutability of organisations and jobs. Just as Bauman's solid walls melted away, so health and social care bodies shape-shift as if sculpted in plasticene or as if they were oil in a lava lamp. Seebohm-heralded social services departments came and went. Now they are absorbed into education departments, or combined social services and housing departments, or with core functions absorbed by new health and social care bodies. They now must look like distant relatives to the post-Seebohm creations. Housing, too, has shifted shape so as to be unrecognisable from the local authority housing departments that straightforwardly provided housing, while the voluntary housing sector has been similarly characterised by dynamic and substantial change (Malpass, 2000). The constantly shifting boundaries in the post war tripartite structure of the NHS and latterday experiments in internal markets and GP fundholding have seen the same processes in action in health.

For the professionals involved much has changed. Those nurses, social workers and housing officers who've been around the jobs long enough to acquire some overview will recognise how much their jobs, and the context for those jobs, has changed.

The impact of general management and 'new managerialism' (DHSS, 1983; Farnham and Horton, 1993; Symonds and Kelly, 1998) has represented a major shift as the context for practice, as has the care management processes that have impacted on frontline practitioners in nursing and housing as well as social work (e.g., the amount of paperwork involved, the emphasis on accountability rather than direct care, increased assimilation of budgetary awareness and costs into routine practice, practitioner as gatekeeper rather than advocate).

There has been something of a vacuum left in the repositioning of practice away from direct, hands-on care or help. Borrowing a couple of sociological terms, 'social distance' and 'status', it is of note that the lowest status activity is that care and support which is closest to the patient or client. Professional status has an inverse relationship with direct client or patient care. The low status accorded 'care' and 'support' when compared with 'treatment' within the health service is an example as is the generally low status accorded, and reward given to, social care staff. There has been a greater emphasis on a 'customer' focus and the accommodation of business models and thinking to what was once referred to as 'public service'. There has, too, been another push factor so that workers, of whatever professional or occupational creed, are more aware of the need to work with others from dissimilar backgrounds. One example of this is the now common model of social work as part of the community mental health team and the attendant disappearance of mental health social work 'territory' from social services.

These changes in service sectors were occurring while in the broader political local context, 'modernisation' attempted to reshape local democracy through 'modernising' local government, directing it towards 'responsibility' and 'efficiency' on the surface but, some argue, in order to shift more power to the centre (Rao, 2000). Challis (Challis *et al.*, 1994) identified the general trends in care across a range of 'developed' countries:

- A move away from institution based care.
- The enhancement of home based care.
- The development of mechanisms of co-ordination.

In parallel to these changes was an ever-increasing awareness of cost and the need for governments to control public sector expenditure at the turn of the 21st century; quietly locking the door on the distant mad relative no one should speak of (income tax). The changes Challis referred to were designed to produce 'downward substitution' in the provision of care from:

- High to low cost.
- High to low restrictive environments.
- Institution-based to home based care (Challis, ibid).

An especial concern with cost permeates policy, whatever clothes it is dressed up to go out in ('needs', choice', 'independence'). The ageing population and the 'demographic timebomb' exercises planners and forecasters greatly and has been a driver of recent policy. Some basic statistics fuel this panic: the amount of NHS expenditure 'consumed' by older people, particularly the last year of life figures (approximately 40 per cent of NHS expenditure goes on over-65s and at any one time two-thirds of general and acute hospital beds are taken up by people in this age band); the over 85s population has seen 'exponential growth' with forecasts of a 50 per cent increase in over 65s to 13 million by 2030; the ratio of working people to retired is set to move from 3.7:1 in 1999 to 2.1:1 by 2040; 11 per cent of 'elderly' require daily care but this figure rises to 40 per cent of those over 85; the prevalence of dementia in over 85s is about 25 per cent (for a range of accessible information on population and service usage see www.statistics.gov.uk).

An apparent inability to relate cost to desired outcome, and the wide variation in those costs is also a concern for those working in the care system as well as for those trying to find out how to fund it. Using international comparisons of health spending as the example, there is a wide variation in spending with no apparent difference in benefit to the population. OECD countries' health care spending ranges from 5.7 per cent to 11.2 per cent (2002 figures) with the US as the top end outlier at 14.2 per cent. The UK spends 7.7 per cent of GDP on health care. The problem that politicians and planners have is that if you look at health outcomes across these different countries there is little or no significant difference found in mortality and morbidity by those widely varying health spending levels. So, how does anyone answer major questions such as where spending should go and how we know where to have the greatest impact (or indeed any impact) on need, and how do we make meaningful comparisons between alternative spending options?

This theme – spending and demonstrable impact – is a core theme of modern government. Rhetoric is not enough; ideology is not enough. The political backdrop has changed and first principles no longer inform us to the extent they did. The health services are called on to show some impact on population health status. Social care is directed to impact, in some recognisable and *measurable*, way on 'quality of life' or 'functioning', or other key concept. This set of fundamental concerns has shown itself, in one way, through the development of 'evidence based practice'. Notwithstanding the actual models used, there is an increasing emphasis on 'measurable outcomes' as a mechanism for evaluating practice and services.

Underlying all the changes has been a managerialist discourse (Symonds and Kelly, 1998) that has shifted debate, at the level of grand theory, away from structural concerns (e.g., equity), at middle range, has reframed what services are and what practitioners do within a consumerist paradigm, and at ground level, has reshaped organisations and their control systems. Examples are, the separating of functions (separating purchasing from providing and from inspecting and from quality assurance), the increase of central control through changed funding mechanisms (increasingly short term, targeted, funding towards specific initiatives) and increasing use of 'performance management' to control and direct activity, increasingly from the centre (Henwood, 2000). The shift in the centre of gravity from provider-led models of care to consumer-led models show an increasing concern with demonstrable impact asking practitioners 'what difference do you make?' while commissioners are required to seek the biggest bang for the littlest buck.

Conservative (and later New Labour) philosophies, following Enthoven (1985) sought to use the market as a management mechanism. The *Working for Patients* white paper in 1989 (DoH, 1989b) recommended an 'internal market' through the separation of purchasers from providers – the purchaser-provider split. This concept was later used to cleanse the different organisational functions (providing, inspecting and commissioning) as if they were ethnic territories, so that each area is horizontally pure (providers' organisations provide, inspectors inspect and commissioners' commission) whatever the vertical consistency. Part of the 'marketisation' of health and care services involved a different tack for personal social services, as managers of an external market as opposed to an internal one. From 1993, local authorities were obliged to contract out their care homes for older people starting a 'low-key privatisation'.

The impact of markets and marketisation was the rebalancing of care sectors. Symonds (Symonds, 1998) used a typology that distinguished the 'public', 'private', 'voluntary' and 'informal' sectors. The history of care shows a rebalancing of these sectors at different times. The 'Fordist' post war analysis saw a prime role of the state as care and protection (ibid).

Indeed, Hardy and Wistow (2000) remind us that one of the presumptions of the changes following Seebohm and local authority social services authorities in the early 70s was that care should be state funded and state provided and the private sector's profit motive was seen as *'incompatible with the provision of care for vulnerable people'*. However, they note that *'The private sector has become firmly established in the late 90s as the dominant provider of residential and nursing home care and has been rapidly moving to a position of similar dominance in the domiciliary sector.'*

The 'market' is seen as a good influence now, as opposed to a pernicious influence, as before. It is held, almost without question, that the market is, in '1066 and all that' terms, a 'good thing'. In practice, though, governments don't always want the political consequences of true markets in the social and health care context. For example, in a review of the NHS reforms, Enthoven, founding father of markets in health care, reflected on the fact that *'Above all, the government was not willing to accept the logic of a competitive system – which is to allow failing institutions to close'* (quoted in Klein, 1999).

The backdrop to the stage, the context in which these debates occurred, was of a debate between 'left' and 'right'. The (aspirationally) ideology-free 'Third Way', the New Labour 'big idea' (Giddens, 1998; 2000) has sought to assert that it does not matter, indeed, which 'sector' (public, private or voluntary) does what, so long as governance affords the opportunity of proper accountability and oversight by external bodies and government.

The Third Way debate blurs the 'public' and 'private' distinction in relation to providers of goods and services. It also has made quite invisible the notion of 'the public good' as a concept. It leaves questions such as: to what extent is social care (or health care, or housing) a public or private good? Who is responsible for it and who should pay and who benefit? These questions remain, not so much unanswered as excluded from any resolvable debate.

This vacuum chimes in nicely with another contemporary convex-shaped concept: the hollowing out of the state (Roberts and Devine, 2003). Lund says of housing policy that *'Housing policy has been dominated by the attempt to roll back the state, allowing the "neutral judge" of the market a dominant role in the supply and distribution of housing'* (Lund, 1996). The authors would argue that the same point can be made, without contention, of health and social care policies.

Cutting across this discourse is the contrast drawn between 'community care' and 'institutional care'. Wagner (1988) noted, in relation to care in a residential homes setting, that there was no positive discourse on residential care, which was seen, as a reflex, to be a term of condemnation and mutable, to boot: *'"community", a term is "notorious for its shiftiness"'* (Mayo, 1998). Nonetheless, it carries with it the implicit notion that it is automatically a good thing and particularly when compared with alternatives, e.g., hospitals or residential care homes. It is also assumed to be cheaper, a questionable assumption when comparing like with like. This debate, even when conducted at the most elevated levels, often does not seem get beyond a level more subtle than community is a 'good thing' and institutions are a 'bad thing' (after '1066 and all that'), and that's enough said. More recently 'independence' is used similarly as a term no one could argue with and a defining feature of care in the community or 'your own home'. It is portrayed as if there were some simple continuum from independence to support and thence to care as opposed to some more complex mix of inter-dependence. The analysis one might extract from policy as expressed in *Modernising Social Services* and Supporting People papers indicates just such a linear relationship. The 'social model' of care challenges these notions through a critique of the latent concepts lying behind the terminology. Looking through the lens of power the social model attacks the 'medical paradigm' implicit in the rhetoric on health and social care, with its locus of power and control beyond the individual. Looking through the budgetary keyhole, Oldman, for instance, argues that we can see, in 'independence', the same trap as was set by the term 'community': it is a secret way of primarily saving money, and maintaining the tryst between public and government that we can have a good quality service sector and a low tax economy (Oldman, 2003). The immediate impact of restraining Supporting People's budget might also challenge the notion that Supporting People is what it says it is on the tin.

On policy there is a murky mix of truth and partial truth, of intended and unintended consequence, of political drivers and social change and organisational adaptation. The big ideas of the last decade line up behind the general rubric of 'modernisation'. Health, social care and housing, as sectors, are all experiencing substantial and fundamental change and each are faced with the challenge of working better together within the ever-tightening discipline of 'efficiencies' and cost-capping.

Drivers, philosophical:
- the Third Way;
- re-engineering services, greater emphasis on prevention;
- central government – local government relations;
- marketisation and 'Consumerism' qua philosophies;
- hollowing out the state;
- collaboration (as main course not side dish!);
- the new consensus on 'the market'.

Drivers, practical:
- technical innovation;
- costs: need to cap, need to link to outcome;
- 'demographic timebomb fears';
- changing expectations and attitudes;
- fashion;
- greater consumer knowledge and consumerist attitudes.

Shapeshifting – the continual evolution of care: social capital and collaborative working

We are seeing the reshaping of things and there is a laudable move, as articulated by Charles Handy (1994), towards the organisation *of* things as opposed to organisations *as* things. This is implicit in an outcomes oriented evaluation of services such as has featured so significantly in the 'modernisation' agenda. I think Handy's is a powerful but simple articulation of a critical focus for modern organisational theory as applied to care and support agencies. But it isn't just of interest for theoreticians. It also creates some impelling force at practice level to constantly challenge and re-evaluate organisational activity, focus, and boundaries.

Collaborative and partnership approaches are key to the way forward. *'Globally, partnership is the new language of public government [it] is about sharing responsibility and overcoming the inflexibility created by organizational, sectoral and even national boundaries'* (Sullivan and Skelcher, 2002).

Cozens emphasises the amount social services has evolved over recent times, the increased pooling of budgets (£2.5 billion of services now in pooled budgets), and more integrative care models (Cozens, 2004).

'The all-purpose care trust has been seen to be too narrow and prescriptive. It removed one boundary (with primary care trusts) and introduced new problems with accountability, governance, and ... the loss of flexibility to move money around ... to meet unexpected patterns of demand. Instead of such limited organizational changes, we have seen real progress with joint commissioning, joint teams, health and social care centres and creative partnerships around housing and the Supporting People programme" (ibid).

This is a perfect example of where organisational structures, organisations *as* things get in the way of the need being addressed by other forums: the organisation *of* things. His suggestion is that the children's trust vehicle is the way forward offering a federal approach to commissioning care that can cross borders.

Denise Platt has lately referred to the 'knocking down' of service barriers (Platt, 2004) as have policy movers and shakers since Frank Dobson coined the 'Berlin Wall' metaphor. The mission of the ODPM has been to work across departmental boundaries within government. But the question remains: can funding and audit mechanisms keep pace with organisational change? Those who want collaborative outcomes, and the knocking down of walls that inhibit movement and communication, need to recognise how those very walls may be maintained by performance management and audit processes associated with the oversight of a managerialist government. The challenge is, can the performance target culture, and the increasing use of targeted, time-limited, funds be free enough in format to allow the necessary networks and partnerships spanning organisational and sectoral boundaries to be able to deliver the desired outcomes?

For example, what problem is there in 'cost-shunting' (the issue dogging the debate on the early stages of Supporting People), if the overall costs meet overall need appropriately and do so proportionately (which is a different question altogether, based on accurate assessment of need and accurate measurement of impact)? The problem only arises because of the solid walls erected to protect budgets and individual organisational and departmental performance. Cost-shunting is seen a an inhibitor whereas it should be seen as an opportunity to shift away from traditional ('legacy') funding towards outcomes oriented funding, and away from funding based around organisations towards funding based on needs.

But budgets and performance measures and a managerialist ethic inhibit flexibility. Collaboration is about sharing, innovating, involving, while organisational boundaries are about looking after your own, meeting your key performance indicators, improving your place in the league table (Painter and Clarence, 2000). This is an impossible tension to resolve in order to please the insatiable parent figure that is managerialist government.

The debate about 'public good' has disappeared in this managerialist and individualistic age. Organisations are hidebound by performance monitoring just as governments are frightened of the consequences of the sheer cost to the treasury of public 'goods' (e.g., health, education, social care). Government seeks to occupy a territory where the state ceases to be a direct provider but is rather a facilitator and, ideally, (seen as) 'honest broker'; the political yield presumably being a lower profile enabling more efficient blame avoidance particularly at election time. During the 2005 general election, the main parties gathered their forces for battle on the territory of public services, particularly the NHS, and they chanted and jeered 'choice' across the battlefield at each other.

'Social capital' has lately entered the lexicon and may help raise the level of debate. It has been referred to as *'the norms and networks that enable collective action'* (NESF, 2003). It has arrived from a Third World discourse but is perhaps able to fill the void left by the death of the notion of 'public good' as opposed to the individual and private good obtainable by successful 'consumers' that political debate so focuses on.

> *'Increasing evidence shows that social cohesion – social capital – is critical for poverty alleviation and sustainable human and economic development'* (ibid).

> *'A web of interpersonal relationships which arise through networking ... often supports the formality of a partnership. These constitutute a type of social capital'* (Sullivan and Skelcher, 2002).

The concept of the development of social capital as an organisational aim, as part of the governance structure, is a recognition of wider concerns beyond the narrow organisational focus. An example is Diane Henderson, of the National Housing Federation, who said (quoted in *Community Care*, 2nd October 2003) *'We are in the business to do more than bricks and mortar. Part of being a good social landlord is being a good partner in your neighbourhood'*. This wider perspective echoes the importance of the shared context of social care and support and, shifting the stance from static to active, she adds *'It's moving from being led by needs to being led by aspirations ... [and] breaking the boundaries'*.

If there is an implicit acceptance of a holistic systems-based approach to care at the philosophical level, and a recognition at a pragmatic level that joint working, collaboration, co-operation (and however many other terms you might want to list) is necessary, not optional, then the juncture we are at just as Supporting People enters stage right, is the start of a new collaborative act in the play. Holmes calls for the integration of housing within wider strategies for economic development (Holmes, 2003). He identifies the issue of housing poverty as the *'most extreme form of social inequality in Britain'* the answer to which is to *'make housing markets work for more mixed and sustainable communities'*. This is an example of the broadening of focus required by collaborative approaches that look and reach beyond narrow organisational or departmental boundaries.

'The pre-existing and rigid boundaries between public and private sectors, different tiers of government and voluntary and community agencies are becoming more permeable as actors reach across these organisational divides and explore new ways of developing and delivering public purposes ... Collaborations for public purpose ... are both about the formal structures that emerge and the micro-politics of individual actors as their roles intersect across organisational, sectoral and geographical boundaries' (Sullivan and Skelcher, 2002).

This activity yields an output; this output can be seen as a means of investing in 'social capital', the measurable social good arising from collaborative interventions towards desired goals.

Looking ahead: social capital

'Tous les jours, a tous points de vue, je vais de mieux en mieux.' Emile Conce. Also as: *'Every day, in every way, I get a little better.'* Frank Spencer.

'The future is not business as usual.' Jim Coulter, CEO, NHF (October 2003).

As has been said here and elsewhere, the importance of housing to care services has been recognised for a long time. There has been progress. Since the Griffiths' report, housing services have felt marginalised in the planning process (Hawtin, 2000) but there is some evidence, Hawtin goes on to add, they have been coming in from the cold through greater involvement in community care planning, locality planning forums and special needs forums. Progress in achieving integration remains slow, however (Cameron *et al.*, 2001). Addressing the challenges of integrating housing with social care, and additionally with health care, can be traced back, at least in the relatively recent policy discourse, to *Caring For People* in 1989 (DoH, 1989a). That housing-related services have been pulled, through the Supporting People initiative, increasingly onto a shared territory with health and social care – and a territory with three levels, being 'independent', needing 'support', and needing 'care' – merely reflects the verity that in social policy, as in science, nature abhors a vacuum. As community care services were pulled away from prevention and low level continuing support there was a vacuum created that had to be filled. The concern is whether at policy level, at the centre, there is the commitment to fund services when they discover 'need', which has a price tag and which cannot be soaked up by the 'sponge buffer' of informal care (Peryer, 1997).

One can look at the issue from the point of view of grand policy, from the professional and inter-professional perspectives or from the point of view of organisations, singly or in an inter-agency guise. One can also look at it from the point of view of the consumer/user. Through whichever filter one looks, reflective policy-making requires some Archimedean point from which to view.

Obtaining this vantage point, and seeing the links between things and the impact on one part of a system from changes in other parts, is a challenge that latter-day housing and care policies again bring us to face.

The policy emphasis in recent years on 'joined up-ness', whatever its label and there have been many (e.g., joint working, joined up government, working together, collaborative working, seamlessness), requires this vantage point and places the emphasis on connections. The challenge for social science is to address the multifaceted nature of need. We need to conceive of a lattice-work structure, conceptual and practical, stretching across organisations, professions and occupations, sectors, and communities, unbound by monolithic structures; and some forum or individual with responsibility for this 'warp and weft' of things. The role of the ODPM at government level and the increasing use of so-called Tsars over specific policy areas is a recognition of this problem.

Implicit in the emphasis on interconnectedness and the complexity of that interconnectedness, is a challenge to a reductionist viewpoint focusing on the parts rather than the whole and an affirmation that systems are open to, and interact with, their environments, and are in a state of continual evolution. Systems theory focuses on the arrangement of, and relations between, the parts which connect them to a whole. It recognises the multivariate nature of the relationship between relevant variables in the system. Too often only bivariate relationships are examined (e.g., the relationship between cost and service levels with the Supporting People programme, excluding linked costs in other parts of the system as well as unintended consequences).

The phase we are in now (whatever 'post' it is that comes after 'post-modern') shows – a post-Fordist intellectual crisis in centralism – a loss of faith in the ability to control (as a provider) – coupled with, paradoxically, a command and control model from the centre via performance management, inspection and audit.

This is where we are now and this is the context into which Supporting People is born. The context is the attempt to meet the challenge of re-integrating primary care (aka 'support') with secondary care and to establish a mechanism for bridging the historical divides of health, housing and social care sectors.

Sullivan and Skelcher point to the challenges faced by this approach. They highlight the tensions between performance management, democratic renewal and standards in decision-making in the public interest and go on to say,

> *'The analysis of collaboration needs to be undertaken with an acute awareness of this wider context. Yet ... academic analysis frequently omits to locate collaboration and partnership in the context of other forces acting on public services ... presenting partnership working as something that can be delivered through the adoption of a toolkit of techniques rather than the negotiation of powerful and sometimes contradictory forces'* (ibid, p.209).

Perhaps there is something in the notion of 'social capital' as an articulation of a potential payback, a demonstrable return on social investment in the context of organisational governance, that can help us reflect on how we shape and fund services, span boundaries, and limit the constricting effects of narrow performance management models. This concept may help signpost a path back to the more general social good – the 'public good' – that care and support services, whether health, social or housing-related care, are meant to address rather than the narrow focus implicit in consumerist models of the 'citizen' and 'state'. How we take forward the rebalancing of those services towards the new future, the one that is not 'business as usual', depends on how the powerful and contradictory forces referred to are negotiated.

'L'esprit d'escaliers'

- **Funding:** Who pays for social care and support? What should the balance be between the individual, the family, the state and the insurance industry?
- **Sectoral:** How do health, housing and social care bodies work together if they have different drivers? How does central control and oversight mesh with local need and flexibility? (Sullivan and Skelcher, 2002)
- **Orientation:** How do the primary and secondary services interface effectively across their own and intersectoral boundaries? As evidenced by primary Supporting People and secondary (and tertiary) community care services?
- **Critical awareness:** Will we ever have a proper debate on the Wagner issues (bringing the 'community' and 'independence' into the critical ambit rather than outside it as they are now?
- **The market:** What role does the market have?
- **Users and professionals:** How do we resolve the 'user led' rhetoric with a valid role for professionals?
- **Individual needs and public goods:** Can 'social capital' fill the void left by a consumerist and individualist ethos that has excluded the notion of 'public good' from the discourse?

'Nothing in the world can one imagine beforehand, not the least thing.' Rainer Maria Rilke.

Contributors

Anya Ahmed
Anya has been a lecturer in housing studies at the University of Salford since 1998. Prior to this she taught at Liverpool John Moores University. She worked in housing practice for four years both for a local authority and RSL in housing management and policy. She has research interests in the construction of communities, ethnicity, gender and homelessness and substance misuse.

Deborah Bennett
At the time of writing this chapter, Deborah was a senior lecturer/practitioner teacher in housing studies with the Centre for Comparative Housing Research at De Montfort University. She taught in areas of housing management and social policy, with a particular interest in homelessness and the interface between housing and social care. Previously she worked in local authority housing for 15 years holding a wide variety of posts including urban renewal officer, development manager and manager of housing advice and rehousing and homelessness services. She has recently returned to local government housing as a strategy and enabling officer.

Tim Brown
Tim is a corporate member of the Chartered Institute of Housing and has a qualification in town planning. He is director of the Centre for Comparative Housing Research at De Montfort University (see http://www.dmu.ac.uk/cchr). Tim is joint co-ordinator of the Housing Quality Network's Strategy Excellence Network, and is on the board of Leicester Housing Association's Social Enterprise Agency. His research and consultancy interests include local housing strategies, allocations and lettings, comparative housing and social policy, rural policy and local policy planning. He has published widely on housing issues including co-authoring *Developing Housing Strategies in Rural Areas* for the Chartered Institute of Housing.

Charlie Cooper
Is a lecturer in social policy at the University of Hull. In the mid- to late-1970s he worked for Doncaster Women's Aid. This was followed by a period working for housing associations – initially at Portsmouth and then, for almost a decade, in London. At the end of the 1980s, disillusioned by the neo-liberal reforms to 'social housing', Charlie moved into higher education where he has primarily taught on courses in housing studies, social policy and criminology. His current research interests are primarily around conditions of domination within British social policy and the harms these generate. He also holds avid affections for Sheffield United F.C. and 'world' music.

Jackie Thompson-Ercan

Jackie is currently a senior lecturer in housing at De Montfort University, where she teaches on both postgraduate and undergraduate courses in Housing. During an eight year career in housing management, Jackie has held a variety of positions, the most recent being the head of supported housing for Orbit Housing Association. Prior to this, she worked as a lecturer in a further education college and a teacher in a number of language schools in Turkey. Wider involvement in the housing field includes working with a charitable supported housing organisation, Mayday Trust, as a board member, since 2002.

Mark Foord

Mark is a principal lecturer in social policy at the University of Central Lancashire. Formerly, he was course leader for the MSc in housing management at the University of Salford. Prior to becoming an academic, he worked for many years in supported housing and homelessness projects in London. He has wide research interests around the housing-care interface; older people and housing; and rough sleepers. Currently he is researching the conflict between the role of local authority social services family and children teams, and housing providers around the implementation of anti-social behaviour legislation. He is a board member of the Adactus Housing Group in the North West.

Murray Hawtin

Murray is senior policy analyst at the Policy Research Institute, Leeds Metropolitan University. He is a qualified social worker and has practised as a residential worker, social worker and community worker in Scotland and England. He has an MA in housing and has worked as a project worker for a large housing authority. He currently researches and writes widely on a range of social care and housing issues including inter-agency co-operation in community care and research around Supporting People strategies and homelessness.

Julia Lucas

Julia is lecturer in, and director of, housing studies at the University of Salford. She has teaching and research interests around regeneration and sustainable communities.

Marcus Ormerod

Marcus is a principal carer for someone with a learning disability and a senior lecturer at the University of Salford. He is the director of the SURFACE inclusive design research centre within the School of Construction and Property Management. Marcus has been involved in major government funded research projects on the Disability Discrimination Act and the built environment. He has written a Best Practice Note for English Partnerships on inclusive design that will influence all new developments. Marcus trained as a surveyor gaining chartered status and worked in the construction industry for 12 years before moving into academia and has actively contributed to the research arena for the past 10 years. More information on the work of Marcus and SURFACE can be found at www.inclusive-design.it

David Race

David has worked in the field of disability, especially learning disability, since 1973, in various countries, as a researcher, consultant, writer and teacher. As an academic, he has worked for the universities of Reading (in a joint appointment with Berkshire Social Services Department), Sheffield, Hong Kong, and currently Salford. The two most recent of a number of books are *Learning Disability – a Social Approach* (Routledge, 2002) and *Leadership and Change in Human Services: Selected Readings from Wolf Wolfensberger* (Routledge, 2003). David Race's continuing personal experience of disability comes from having both a sister-in-law (who died in May 2004) and a son with Downs' Syndrome, and as a trustee in the independent living fund of a person with major physical impairments.

Jo Richardson

Jo is a corporate member of the Chartered Institute of Housing. She is course leader of the CIH Undergraduate and Postgraduate Professional Diploma in the Centre for Comparative Housing Research at De Montfort University. Jo has a practitioner background and has worked in a local authority, a housing association, and latterly for the Chartered Institute of Housing. Jo's research and consultancy interests include allocations and lettings, and housing and customer services. She has managed a major project for Cornwall County Council on Supporting People strategies, and has completed a part time PhD on Travellers and Gypsies.

Julie Savory

Julie Savory is a lecturer in housing studies at the Housing and Urban Studies Unit, University of Salford. She is a corporate member of the Chartered Institute of Housing and a member of the HE Academy for Teaching and Learning. She has experience of working in both local authority and housing association sectors and is currently a board member of a large housing agency in the North West. Her research interests are in housing policy and practice, particularly the links between housing, health and social care.

Paul Simic

Paul is the chief executive of the Lancashire Care Association; previously he was a mental health social worker and manager before developing an academic career. Formerly, he was director of the Applied Research and Consultancy Centre at Manchester University and Lecturer in Social Work at the University of Salford. He has written and published widely on social care issues, the interface between housing and social services and mental health policy.

Bogusia Temple

Bogusia Temple is reader in the Housing and Urban Studies Unit at the University of Salford. She has worked with minority ethnic communities across health, social care and housing research. She is particularly interested in how to ensure that the perspectives of service users as well as service providers are included in service audit and research. Her most recent work includes a project funded by a Joseph Rowntree Foundation around user views of accessing services via interpreters. She is currently working on views of community cohesion and has run workshops at the Home Office 2004 National Integration Conference. She is also working on a national evaluation of services for disabled children aged 0-3.

Pam Thomas

Pam Thomas is a freelance disability equality consultant, trainer and researcher. She is a disabled woman who has extensive experience of involvement with disabled people's own organisations, which have campaigned for equality and provided services to disabled people. Pam has also worked as a social worker and strategic planner in social services. She has an MA in disability studies. Pam is part of the SURFACE team at the University of Salford and has just been awarded a PhD for her work on disabled people's experiences of home ownership.

Nichola Yates

Nicola Yates has worked in the public sector for the last 15 years. Originally trained as a housing professional, Nicola studied social sciences with the Open University, where her interest in community care issues began. She is a corporate member of the Chartered Institute of Housing and also has an MSc in housing studies. She has had extensive involvement with housing organisations delivering care services in the Netherlands and is a regular visitor to Dutch projects. Now a service director at Harborough District Council she has responsibility for a wide range of customer facing services but still retains an interest in her professional background.

Bibliography

Abbott, P. and Wallace, C. (1990) *An Introduction to Sociology: Feminist Perspectives,* London, Routledge.

Ahmed, A. and Sodhi, D. (2000) *The Housing and Support Needs of Women Especially Those From Ethnic Minorities,* Rochdale, Rochdale Womens Housing Aid Group.

Alcock, P., Erskine, A., and May, M. (eds) (2003) *The Student's Companion to Social Policy,* 2nd edition, Oxford, Blackwell.

Alcohol Concern (2003) *Drink Deaths Double,* at: http://www.alcoholconcern.org.uk/servlets/doc/498, Alcohol Concern, London.

Allen, C. (1998) 'Post-modernism and knowledgeable competence – social work, housing management and community care needs', in I. Shaw, S. Lambert, and D. Clapham (eds) *Social Care and Housing Research Highlights in Social Work 32,* London, Jessica Kingsley.

Allen, C., Milner, J. and Price, D. (2002) *Home is where the start is: The housing and urban experiences of visually impaired children,* Bristol, The Policy Press.

Allott, M. and Robb, M. (eds) (1997) *Understanding Health and Social Care: An Introductory Reader,* London, Sage.

Anderson, B. (1987) *Imagined Communities: Reflections on the Origin and Spread of Nationalism,* London, Verso.

Anderson, I. (1994) *Access to Housing for Low Income Single People,* York, Centre for Housing Policy.

Anderson, I. and Sim, D. (eds) (2000) *Social Exclusion & Housing,* Coventry, Chartered Institute of Housing.

Andrews, F., Burdon, P. and Huggins-Cooper, K. (2002) 'Slow progress', *Community Care,* 21st February 2002.

Apte, R. Z. (1968) *Halfway Houses: a new dilemma in institutional care,* London, Bell.

Arblaster, L. and Hawtin, M. (1993) *Health, Housing and Social Policy,* London, Socialist Health Association.

Arblaster, L., Conway, J., Foreman, A. and Hawtin, M. (1996) *Asking the Impossible? A study of interagency working to address the housing, health and social care needs of people in general needs housing,* Bristol, Policy Press/Community Care.

Arnold, P. and Page, D. (1992) *Housing and Community Care,* York, Joseph Rowntree Foundation.

Arnold, P., Bochel, H., Broadhurst, S. and Page, D. (1993) *Community Care – The Housing Dimension,* York, Joseph Rowntree Foundation.

Association of Directors of Social Services/Local Government Association (2003) *All Our Tomorrows: Inverting the Triangle of Care,* London, Association of Directors of Social Services/Local Government Association.

Atkins, E. (2004) 'I don't buy it', *The Guardian*, 15th November 2004.

Atkinson, R. (2004) 'The evidence on the impact of gentrification: New lessons for the urban renaissance?' *European Journal of Housing Policy,* 4(1) April, pp.107-131.

Audit Commission (1986) *Making a Reality of Community Care,* London, HMSO.

Audit Commission (1994) *Finding a Place: A Review of Mental Health Services for Adults,* London, HMSO.

Audit Commission (1997) *The Coming of Age: Improving care services for older people,* London, HMSO.

Audit Commission (1998) *Home Alone: The role of housing in community care,* London, HMSO.

Audit Commission (2000) *Fully Equipped: The provision of equipment to older or disabled people by the NHS and social services in England and Wales,* London, Audit Commission.

Audit Commission (2002) *Integrated Services for Older People – building a whole systems approach in England*, London, Audit Commission.

Audit Commission (2004a) 'Supporting People', at the Audit Commission website at: http://www.audit-commission.gov.uk/reports, accessed 20th September 2004, pp.1-4.

Audit Commission (2004b) *Supporting People Review: Liverpool City Council,* London, Audit Commission.

Audit Commission and Better Government for Older People (2004) *Supporting Frail Older People: Independence and Well Being Report 3,* London, Audit Commission.

Aust, R. and Condon, J. (2003) *Geographical Variations in Drug Use: key findings from the 2001/02 British Crime Survey: England and Wales*, London, The Home Office.

Baldwin, M. (2002) 'New Labour and social care: continuity or change?', in M. Powell (ed) *Evaluating New Labour's Welfare Reforms*, Bristol, Policy Press.

Balloch, S. and Taylor, M. (2001) *Partnership Working Policy and Practice,* Bristol, Policy Press.

Barclay Report (1982) *Social Workers, their Role and Tasks*, London, Bedford Square Press.

Barker, L. (1998) 'A liberal lesson in homelessness', *Roof,* September/October, p.14.

Barnes, C. (1991) *Disabled People in Britain and Discrimination*, London, British Council of Disabled People.

Barnes, C. and Mercer, G. (1995) 'Disability: emancipation, community participation and disabled people', in Mayo, M. and Craig, G. (eds) *Community Empowerment: A Reader in Participation and Development,* London, Zed Books, pp.46-59.

Barnes, C. and Mercer, G. (eds) (1997) *Doing Disability Research*, Leeds, The Disability Press.

Barnes, M. (1997) *Care, Communities and Citizens,* London, Longman.

Barnes, M. and Walker, A. (1996) 'Consumerism versus empowerment: a principled approach to the involvement of older service users', *Policy and Politics*, 24(4), pp.375-393.

Barr, A., Drysdale, J., and Henderson, P. (1997) *From Rhetoric to Reality, Community Development and Community Care,* Brighton, Pavilion.

Barron, D. (1996) *A Price to Be Born: My Childhood and Life in a Mental Institution,* Harrogate, Mencap Northern Division.

Barrow, J. (1999) *If I Had No Choice: The housing needs of ethnic elders,* Scotland, Age Concern.

Bartlett, P. and Wright, D. (eds) (1999) *Outside the Walls of the Asylum: The History of Care in the Community 1750-2000,* London, The Athlone Press.

Barton, R. (1959) *Institutional Neurosis,* Bristol, Wright.

Bauman, Z. (2003) *Liquid Love,* Cambridge, Polity Press.

Baumann, G. (1996) *Contesting Culture: discourses of identity in multi-ethnic London,* Cambridge, Cambridge University Press.

Bayley, M. (1973) *Mental Handicap and Community Care: A Study of Mentally Handicapped People in Sheffield,* London, Routledge and Kegan Paul.

Beresford, P. (2001) 'Service users, social policy and the future of welfare', *Critical Social Policy,* 21(4), pp.494-512.

Beresford, P. (2004) *A New Day Dawning: Our rights, our hopes, our futures,* London, MIND.

Bernard, J. (1964) 'Community disorganisation', in *The International Encyclopaedia of the Social Sciences,* Vol. 3, New York, Macmillan-Free Press.

Bernard, M. and Phillips, J. (2000) 'The challenge of ageing in tomorrow's Britain', *Ageing and Society,* Vol. 20, pp.33-54.

Bertalanffy, L. Von (1971) *General Systems Theory,* London, Penguin Press.

Biggs, S. (1997) 'Interprofessional collaboration: problems and prospects', in J. Ovretveit, P. Mathias, and T. Thompson (eds) (1997) *Interprofessional Working for Health and Social Care,* Basingstoke, Macmillan.

Blunden (1975) *The Development and Evaluation of Services for the Mentally Handicapped – An Outline Research Plan: Discussion Paper No. 2,* Cardiff, Mental Handicap in Wales – Applied Research Unit, Welsh National School of Medicine.

Bochel, C., Bochel, H., and Page, D. (1999) 'Housing: the foundation of community care?' *Health and Social Care in the Community,* 7, 6, pp.492-501.

Booth, T. (1988) *Developing policy research,* London, Gower.

Bowes, A. and Dar, N. (2000) 'Researching social care for minority ethnic older people: implications of some Scottish research', *British Journal of Social Work,* 30, pp.305-321.

Bowes, A., Dar, N. and Sim, D. (2000) 'Housing preferences and strategies: an exploration of Pakistani experiences in Glasgow', in F. Boal (ed) *Ethnicity and Housing: Accommodating differences,* pp.170-178, Aldershot, Ashgate.

Bowes, A., Dar, N. and Sim, D. (2002) 'Differentiation in housing careers: the case of Pakistanis in the UK', *Housing Studies,* 17(3), pp.381-399.

Bowling, B. (1995) *Elderly People from Ethnic Minorities: A Report on Four Projects,* London, Age Concern Institute of Gerontology.

Boyle, G. (2004) 'Facilitating choice and control for older people in long term care', *Health and Social Care in the Community,* 12(3), pp.212-220.

Bramley, G., Pawson, H., Satsangi, M. and Third, H. (1999) *Local Housing Needs Assessment: a review of current practice and the need for guidance*, Research Paper No. 73, Heriot-Watt University, Edinburgh.

Brenton, M. (1998) *We're in Charge: Co-housing Communities of Older People in the Netherlands: Lessons for Britain?* Bristol, Policy Press.

Bright, L. (2003) 'Home sweet home?', *Property People*, 21st August 2003.

Bright, L. and Clough, R. (2003) *Homing in on Housing*, London, Centre for Policy on Ageing.

Brindle, D. (1998) '£1bn to end care in the community', *The Guardian,* 25th July 1998, p.1.

British Association of Social Work (1985) *Housing and Social Work*, Birmingham, British Association of Social Work.

Brown, T., Hunt, R. and Yates, N. (2000) *Lettings – A Question of Choice,* Coventry, Chartered Institute of Housing.

Burden, T., Cooper, C. and Petrie, S. (2000) *Modernising' Social Policy: Unravelling New Labour's Welfare Reforms,* Aldershot, Ashgate.

Burrows, R. (1997) *Contemporary Patterns of Residential Mobility in Relation to Social Housing in England*, Centre for Housing Policy, University of York.

Bytheway, W.R. (2001) *Understanding Care, Welfare and Community: a reader,* London, Routledge.

Cabinet Office (1999) *Modernising Government*, London, The Stationery Office.

Cameron, A., Harrison, L., Burton, P. and Marsh, A. (2001) *Crossing the Housing and Care Divide,* Bristol, Policy Press.

Campbell, J. (2002) 'A critical appraisal of participatory methods in development research', *International Journal of Social Research Methodology*, 5(1), pp.19-29.

Care Standards Tribunal (2003) *Alternative Futures v the National Care Standards Commission*, 11th July 2003: case no (2002) 101-111 NC.

Carr, S. (2004) *Has Service User Participation Made a Difference to Social Care Services?* SCIE Position Paper no 3, March 2004, London, Social Care Institute for Excellence.

Carter, M. and El-Hassan, A. (2003) *Between NASS and a Hard Place*, London, HACT.

Carvel, J. (2004) 'Abscess of NHS racism exposed', *The Guardian*, 6th February, p.1.

Castles, S., Korac, M., Vasta, E., and Vertovec, S. with the assistance of Hansing, K., Moore, F., Newcombe, E., Rix,. and Yu, S. (2002) *Integration: Mapping the Field: Report of a Project carried out by the University of Oxford Centre for Migration and Policy Research and Refugee Studies Centre contracted by the Home Office Immigration Research and Statistics Service*, Home Office Online Report 28/03.

Challis, D. (1993) *Care Management: Observations from a programme of research,* PSSRU, Bulletin 9, Canterbury, University of Kent.

Challis, D. and Davies, B. (1986) *Case Management in Community Care,* Gower, Aldershot.

Challis, D., Davies, B. and Traske, K. (1994) *Community Care in the UK and Overseas: New agendas and challenges,* London, Arena.

Challis, L., Fuller, S., Henwood, M., Klein, R., Plowden, W., Webb, A., Whittingham, P. and Wistow, G. (1988) *Joint Approaches to Social Policy: Rationality and Practice,* Cambridge, Cambridge University Press.

Chaney, P. and Drakeford, M. (2004) 'The primacy of ideology – social policy and the first term of the National Assembly for Wales', in N. Ellison, L. Bauld and M. Powell (eds) *Social Policy Review 16 – Analysis and Debate in Social Policy 2004,* Bristol, Policy Press and the Social Policy Association, pp.121-142.

Chartered Institute of Housing (2003a) *Supporting People – Good Practice Briefing No. 25,* Coventry, Chartered Institute of Housing.

Chartered Institute of Housing (2003b) *Providing A Safe Haven – Housing Asylum Seekers And Refugees,* Coventry, Chartered Institute of Housing.

Chartered Institute of Housing (2004) *Health and Housing – Good Practice Briefing No. 29,* Coventry, Chartered Institute of Housing.

Clapham, D. and Franklin, B. (1994) *Housing Management, Community Care and Compulsory Competitive Tendering: A good practice guide,* Coventry, Chartered Institute of Housing.

Clapham, D. and Smith, S. J. (1990) 'Housing policy and special needs', *Policy and Politics* 18 (3) pp.193-205.

Cloke P., Milbourne P., and Widdowfield, R. (2001) 'The local spaces of welfare provision: responding to homelessness in rural England', *Political Geography* 20, pp.493-512.

Cobbold, C. (1997) *A Cost Benefit Analysis of Lifetime Homes,* York, Joseph Rowntree Foundation.

Cocks, E. (2002) 'Evaluation of quality in learning disability services', in D. G. Race, (ed) *Learning Disability – a Social Approach*, London, Routledge.

Cohen, S. and Young, J. (1973) *The Manufacture of News: Deviance, Social Problems and the Mass Media,* London, Constable.

Commission for Social Care Inspection (2003) '*What the new Commission will mean for the people who use social services',* at the CSCI website at: http://www.doh.gov.uk/csci/users.pdf, accessed 23rd January 2004, pp.1-2.

Commission for Social Care Inspection (2004), *Leaving Hospital – the price of delays,* London, Commission for Social Care Inspection.

Community Care (2003) 'Platt outlines her plans for social care's new independent regulator', *Community Care*, 9th October 2003.

Community Care (2004a) 'No cash for shift to supported housing', *Community Care,* 22nd April, 2004.

Community Care (2004b) 'News in brief', *Community Care*, 2nd September, 2004.

Cooper, C. and Hawtin, M. (eds) (1997) *Housing, Community and Conflict: Understanding Resident 'Involvement'*, Aldershot, Arena.

Cooper, C. and Hawtin, M. (eds) (1998) *Resident Involvement and Community Action: Theory to Practice*, Coventry, Chartered Institute of Housing.

Cooper, K. (2004) 'Providers face upheaval', *Inside Housing,* 28th May 2004.

Cooper, M. (1981) 'The Normanton patch system', in L. Smith and D. Jones (eds) *Deprivation, Participation and Community Action*, London: Routledge and Kegan Paul, pp.168-180.

Cooper, R. and Watson, L. (1995) 'Housing and the homely environment', *Housing,* July/August p.42.

Cope, H. (1999) *Housing Associations* (2nd edition), Basingstoke, Macmillan.

Corrigan, P. W. (2004) 'Don't call me nuts: an international perspective on the stigma of mental illness', *Acta Psychiatrica Scandinavica,* Vol. 109, Issue 6, p.403 June 2004.

Corrigan, P. W. and Penn, D. L. (1999). 'Lessons from social psychology on discrediting psychiatric stigma', *American Psychologist, 54,* pp.765–776.

Cowans, J. (1999) *Inclusive Housing: The role of low cost home ownership,* York, Joseph Rowntree Foundation.

Cox, C. and Pearson, M. (1995) *Made to Care: The Case for Residential and Village Communities for People with a Mental Handicap*, London, Rannoch Trust.

Cozens, A. (2004) 'Our social secret', *The Guardian*, 10th March 2004.

Crabtree, A. and Hemmings, T. (2001) *The Sociality of Domestic Environments: A paper for the Accords project* at: http://www.sics.se/accord/plan/del/D11.doc

CRISIS (2005) *Homelessness Factfile*, at: www.crisis.org.uk/research/factfile_index.php, CRISIS, London.

Croft, S. and Beresford, P. (1992) 'The politics of participation', *Critical Social Policy,* 35, pp.20-44.

Cuff, E.C., Sharrock, W.W. and Francis, D.W. (1998) *Perspectives in Sociology*, 4th edition, London, Unwin Hyman.

Dalgleish, M. (1983) 'Environmental constraints on residential services for mentally handicapped people: some findings from the Sheffield Development Project', *Mental Handicap*, 11, pp.102-5.

Daly, G. (2001) 'Citizenship, public accountability and older people: User involvement in community care provision', *Education and Ageing*, 16(1), pp.55-75.

Darton, R. (2004) 'What types of homes are closing? The characteristics of home which closed between 1996 and 2001', *Health and Social Care in the Community,* 12(3), pp.254-264.

Davey, V. and Henwood, M. (2003) 'Loose connections', *Community Care*, 15th May 2003.

Davies, K. (1993) 'The crafting of good clients', in J. Swain, S. French, C. Thomas and C. Barnes (eds), *Disabling Barriers Enabling Environments,* London, Sage.

Davies, K. (1999) *A Social Barriers Model of Disability: Theory into practice. The Emergence of the "Seven Needs",* Paper prepared for the Derbyshire Coalition of Disabled People, February 1990.

Davis, J.M. (1980) 'Antipsychotic drugs', in H.I. Kaplan, B.J. Sadock and A.F. Freedman (eds) *Comprehensive Textbook of Psychiatry,* 3rd edition pp.2257–89. Baltimore, MD: Williams and Wilkins.

Dean, M. (2003) *Growing Older in the 21st Century,* Swindon, Economic and Social Research Council.

Dempsey, K. (1990) *Smalltown: A study of Social Inequality, Cohesion and Belonging,* Oxford, Oxford University Press.

Department of the Environment (1980) *Housing Requirements: A Guide to Information and Techniques,* London, HMSO.

Department of the Environment (1993) *Housing Welfare Services and the Housing Revenue Account: A Consultation Paper 2/93,* London, Department of the Environment.

Department of the Environment/Department of Health (1992) *Housing and Community Care – Circular 10/92 and LAC (92) 12,* London, HMSO.

Department of the Environment, Transport and the Regions (1998a) *Modernising Local Government: Improving local services through Best Value,* London, Department of the Environment, Transport and the Regions.

Department of the Environment, Transport, and the Regions (1998b) *Supporting People: A new policy and funding framework for support services,* London, Department of the Environment, Transport and the Regions.

Department of the Environment, Transport and the Regions (2000a) *Quality and Choice: a decent home for all*, London, Department of the Environment, Transport and the Regions.

Department of the Environment, Transport, and the Regions (2000b) *Supporting People – Together Towards 2003,* London, Department of the Environment, Transport, and the Regions.

Departments of the Environment, Transport and the Regions (2001) *2000/01 Survey of English Housing: Preliminary results,* London, Department of the Environment, Transport and the Regions.

Department of the Environment, Transport and the Regions/Department of Health (2000) *Best Value in Housing Care and Support: Guidance and Good Practice,* London, Department of the Environment, Transport and the Regions/Department of Health.

Department of Health (1989a) *Caring for People – Community Care in the Next Decade and Beyond*, London, HMSO.

Department of Health (1989b) *Working for Patients,* London, HMSO.

Department of Health (1991) *Care Management and Assessment: The practitioners' guide,* London, HMSO.

Department of Health (1997) *The New NHS: Modern, Dependable,* London, The Stationery Office.

Department of Health (1998a) *Modernising Mental Health Services: Safe, sound and supportive,* London, The Stationery Office.

Department of Health (1998b) *Modernising Social Services: Promoting independence, improving protection, raising standards*, London, The Stationery Office.

Department of Health (1998c) *Partnership in Action,* London, The Stationery Office.

Department of Health (1998d) *Our Healthier Nation: A contract for health,* London, The Stationery Office.

Department of Health (1999a) *Facing the facts – services for people with learning disabilities: A policy impact study of social care and health services,* London, Department of Health.

Department of Health (1999b) *Saving Lives: Our healthier nation,* London, The Stationery Office.

Department of Health (1999c) *Better Care, Higher Standards: A charter for long term care,* London, The Stationery Office.

Department of Health (2000) *The NHS Plan – A Plan for Investment, A Plan for Reform*, London, The Stationery Office.

Department of Health (2001a) *National Service Framework for Older People,* London, The Stationery Office.

Department of Health (2001b) *Safety first: 5 year report of the National Confidential Inquiry into Suicide and Homicide by People with Mental Illness,* London, Department of Health.

Department of Health (2001c) *Valuing People: A strategy for Learning Disability for the 21st Century*, London, The Stationery Office.

Department of Health (2001d) *Building Capacity and Partnership in Care,* London, The Stationery Office.

Department of Health (2001e) *Residential Care, Housing, Care and Support Schemes and Supporting People: A Consultation Paper*, London, Department of Health.

Department of Health (2002a) *Intermediate Care – Moving Forward*, London, Department of Health.

Department of Health (2002b) *The Single Assessment Process Guidance for Local Authorities,* London, Department of Health.

Department of Health (2002c) *The National Confidential Inquiry into Suicide and Homicide by People with Mental Illness Update,* London, Department of Health.

Department of Health (2003a) *Community Care Assessment Directions – Consultation on proposed draft Directions 2003*, London, Department of Health.

Department of Health (2003b) *Community Care Statistics 2001-02,* www.doh.gov.uk (Accessed 27th October 2003).

Department of Health (2004a) *Developing and Implementing Local Extra Care Housing Strategies,* London, Department of Health.

Department of Health (2005) *Independence, Well-being and Choice: Our vision for the future of social care for adults in England*, London, Department of Health.

Department of Health and the Health and Social Care Change Agent Team (2003) *Defining a Whole System Approach.* Accessed at: www.doh.gov.uk/changeagenteam/housing-lin.htm on 13th October 2003.

Department of Health and Social Security (1971) *Better Services for the Mentally Handicapped,* London, HMSO.

Department of Health and Social Security (1981) *Growing Older*, London, HMSO.

Department of Health and Social Security (1983) *NHS Management Enquiry* (the Griffiths' Report), London, HMSO.

Department of Social Security (1998) *Supporting People: A new policy and funding framework for support services,* London, HMSO.

Department of Transport, Local Government and the Regions/Department of Health (2001a) *Quality and Choice for Older People's Housing: A strategic framework,* London, The Stationery Office.

Department of Transport, Local Government and the Regions (2001b) *A Review of Local Authority Statutory and Non-Statutory Service and Policy Planning Requirements,* London, DTLR.

Department of Transport, Local Government and the Regions (2001c) *Supporting People: Policy into Practice*, London, The Stationery Office.

Department of Transport, Local Government and the Regions (2002a) *Reflecting the Needs and Concerns of Black and Minority Ethnic Communities in Supporting People,* London, DTLR.

Department of Transport, Local Government and the Regions (2002b) *Further findings from the English House Condition Survey; The registered social landlord stock*, Housing Research Summary 159, London, DTLR.

Dewsbury, G. (2001) *Designing the Home to Meet the Needs of Tomorrow Today*, Open House International Special Edition Summer 2001.

Doling, J. (1997) *Comparative Housing Policy,* Basingstoke, Macmillan.

Dominelli, L. (1997) *Sociology for Social Work*, London, Palgrave Macmillan.

Douglas, A. (2000) 'Going beyond lip service', *Community Care*, 13th July, at: www.communitycare.co.uk , accessed 15th December 2003, 13.45, pp.1-3.

Doyal, L. and Gough, I. (1991) *A Theory of Human Need*, Basingstoke, Macmillan.

Easterbrook, L. (2003) *Moving on From Community Care – the treatment, care and support of older people in England,* London, Age Concern.

Edwards, S. (2000) *Good Practice Briefing: Housing and Services for People with Support Needs,* Coventry, Chartered Institute of Housing.

Ellison, N., Bauld, L. and Powell, M. (2004) 'Introduction', in N. Ellison, L. Bauld and M. Powell (eds), *Social Policy Review 16 – Analysis and Debate in Social Policy 2004*, Bristol, Policy Press and the Social Policy Association, pp.1-10.

Emerson, E. (1992) 'What is Normalisation?' in H. Brown and H. Smith H. (eds), *Normalisation: A Reader for the Nineties*, London, Routledge.

Emerson, E., Robertson, J., Gregory, N., Hatton, C., Kessissoglou, S., Hallam, A., Knapp, M., Jarbrink, K., Netten, A., and Walsh, P. (1999) *Quality and costs of residential supports for people with learning disabilities: A comparative analysis of quality and costs in village communities, residential campuses and dispersed housing schemes,* Manchester, Hester Adrian Research Centre, University of Manchester.

Enthoven, A.C. (1985) *Reflections on the management of the National Health Service,* Oxford, Nuffield Provincial Hospitals Trust.

Farnham, D. and Horton S. (1993) *Managing the new public services,* London, Macmillan.

Finkelstein, V. (1980) *Attitudes and Disabled People: Issues for Discussion,* New York, World Rehabilitation Fund.

Finkelstein, V. (1991) 'Disability: An Administrative Challenge? The Health and Welfare Heritage', in M. Oliver (ed) *Social Work Disabled People and Disabling Environments,* London, Jessica Kingsley.

Finkelstein, V. (1998) *Re-Thinking Care in a Society Providing Equal Opportunities for All,* Discussion Paper, The Open University, Milton Keynes.

Finkelstein, V. (2001) A Personal Journey into Disability Politics – a talk given at Leeds University Centre for Disability Studies, 7th February 2001, accessed at: http://www.leeds.ac.uk/disability-studies/archiveuk/archframe.htm

Fisher, K. and Collins, J. (1993) 'Access to Health Care', in K. Fisher and J. Collins (eds) *Homelessness, Health Care and Welfare Provision,* London, Routledge.

Fitzpatrick, S., Kemp, P. and Kinker, S. (2000) *Single Homelessness: A review of research in Britain,* Bristol, Policy Press.

Flemen (1999) *Room for Drugs,* London, Release.

Fletcher, P. (1999) 'Services for the next generation – planning for the future', *Housing, Care and Support,* 2.1 March.

Fletcher, P. and Spencer, S. (2002) *Working with the New Health and Social Care Agenda*, London, National Housing Federation.

Flynn, R.J. and Lemay, R.A. (eds) (1999) *A quarter-century of normalization and Social Role Valorization: Evolution and Impact,* Ottawa, Canada, University of Ottawa Press.

Foord, M. and Simic, P. (2001) 'A Sustainable Approach to Planning Housing and Social Care: If Not Now, When?' *Health and Social Care in the Community,* vol.9 (3), pp.168- 176.

Foord, M., Savory, J. and Sodhi, D. (2004) 'Not everything that can be counted counts, and not everything that counts can be counted – towards a critical exploration of modes of satisfaction measurement in sheltered housing', *Health and Social Care in the Community,* vol. 12 (2), pp.126-133.

Foord, M., Young, F. and Huntington, A. (2004) 'No Room for Nuisance', *Community Care* 22-28 April 2004 pp.42-44.

Forrest, R. and Kearns, A. (1999) *Joined-Up Places? Social cohesion and neighbourhood regeneration,* York, Joseph Rowntree Foundation.

Foucault, M. (1967) *Madness and Civilisation: A History of Insanity in the Age of Reason*, London, Tavistock.

Foucault, M. (1972) *The Archaeology of Knowledge*, Routledge, London.

Fountain, J. and Howes, S. (2002) *Home and Dry? Homelessness and substance abuse,* London, CRISIS.

Francis, E. (2004) 'Too little, too late', *Society Guardian*, 1st February 2004, p.9.

Franklin, B. (1998) 'Discourses and Dilemmas in the Housing and Support Debate', in I. Shaw, S. Lambert, S. and D. Clapham (eds) *Social Care and Housing Social Care and Housing,* London, Jessica Kingsley.

Freeman, K. (2004) 'Vital Statistics', *Housing Today,* 3rd September 2004, pp.26-28.

Gann, D., Barlow, J. and Venables, T. (1999) *Digital Futures – Making Homes Smarter*, York, Joseph Rowntree Foundation.

Gatward, J. (2004) 'Age Concerns', *Inside Housing,* 20th February 2004.

Gauldie, E. (1974) *Cruel Habitations; a history of working class housing, 1780-1918,* London, George Allen and Unwin.

Gershon, P. (2004) *Releasing Resources to the Front Line – Independent Review of Public Sector Efficiency,* London, HM Treasury.

Giddens, A. (1998) *The Third Way,* Cambridge, Polity Press.

Giddens, A. (2000) *The Third Way and its Critics,* Cambridge, Polity Press.

Gilbert (2004) 'Capital faces crisis over care homes', *Care and Health,* 6th April

Gilchrist, A. (2002) 'The well connected community; networking to the 'edge of chaos', *Community Development Journal*, Vol. 35 no 3.

Glaser, J. (2001) 'Producing Communities as a Theoretical Challenge', in the *TASA Annual Conference Proceedings; TASA, Sydney, Australia.*

Glendinning, C. (2002) 'Building a United Front', *Community Care,* 14th November 2002.

Glennerster, H. (2000) *British Social Policy since 1945*, Oxford, Blackwell, 2nd edition.

Goffman, E. (1961) *Asylums. Essays on the Social Situation of Mental patients and other Inmates,* Harmondsworth, Penguin.

Goodby, G. (1998) *The Case for Sheltered Housing amongst Black and Minority Ethnic Elderly Communities in West London,* London, Inquilab Housing Association.

Goodwin, S. (1989) 'Community Care for the Mentally Ill in England and Wales: Myths, assumptions and realities', *Journal of Social Policy*, Vol. 18(1), pp.27-52.

Goodwin, S. (1990) *Community Care and the Future of Mental Health Service Provision,* Aldershot, Avebury.

Griffiths, R. (1988) *Community Care: Agenda for action. A report to the Secretary of State for Social Services,* London, HMSO.

Guardian (2003a) 'Ageing baby boomers set to rock society', 1st September 2003.

Guardian (2003b) 'Antenatal checks to be reduced', 22nd October 2003.

Guardian (2003c) 'He'll be weighing brains next', 14th November 2003.

Guardian (2003d) 'Does a cleft palate justify abortion? Curate wins right to challenge doctors', December 2nd 2003.

Guillebaud Report (1956) *Report of the Committee of Enquiry into the Cost of the National Health Service (Cmd 9663)*, London, HMSO.

Hadley, R. and Clough, R. (1996) *Care in Chaos: Frustration and Challenge in Community Care*, London, Cassell.

Hadley, R. and Hatch, S. (1981) *Social Welfare and the Failure of the State: Centralised Social Services and Participatory Alternatives*, London, George Allen and Unwin.

Hall, P. (1997) 'Regeneration policies for peripheral housing estates: inward and outward looking approaches', *Urban Studies*, Vol. 34, No. 5-6, pp.873-890.

Handy, C. (1994) *The Empty Raincoat: Making Sense of the Future*, London, Hutchinson.

Hanover Housing Group (1998) *Housing Options for Ethnic Elders,* London, Hanover Housing Group.

Hanson, J. (2001) *From Sheltered Housing to Life Time Homes: an inclusive approach to housing*, accessed at: http://3rdagehomes.bartlett.ucl.ac.uk/homepg/xplore-fold/InclusiveApproachToHousing.pdf

Hardy, B. and Wistow, G. (2000) 'Changes in the private sector', in B. Hudson (2000) *The changing role of social care*, London, Jessica Kingsley.

Harker and King (1999) *An ordinary home: Housing and Support for People with Learning Disabilities*, London, Local Government Association.

Harrison, M. (1998) 'Theorising exclusion and difference: Specificity, structure and minority ethnic housing issues', *Housing Studies*, 13(6), pp. 793-806.

Harrison, M. with Davis, C. (2001) *Housing, Social Policy and Difference: Disability, ethnicity, gender and housing*, Bristol, The Policy Press.

Harrison, M. with Phillips, D. (2003) *Housing and Black and Minority Ethnic Communities: Review of the evidence base,* London, Office of the Deputy Prime Minister.

Harrison, S., Hunter, D.J., Johnston, I., Nicholson, N., Thunhurst, C. and Wistow, G. (1991) *Health before health care*. Social Policy Paper no. 4, London, Institute of Public Policy Research.

Hastings, A. (2003) 'Urban Renaissance?' in R. Imrie and M. Raco (eds) *Urban Renaissance? New Labour, Community and Urban Policy,* Bristol, Policy Press.

Hatton, C. and Emerson, E. (1996) *Residential Provision for People with Learning Disabilities: A Research Review*, Manchester, Hester Adrian Research Centre, University of Manchester.

Hawtin, M. (2000) 'Social care and housing', in B. Hudson (2000) *The changing role of social care*, London, Jessica Kingsley.

Hawtin, M. and Kettle, J. (2000) 'Housing and Social Exclusion', in J. Percy-Smith (ed) *Policy Responses to Social Exclusion – towards inclusion?* Buckingham, Open University Press, pp.107-129.

Health and Social Services Statistics (HPSSS), accessed at:
http://www.performance.doh.gov.uk/HPSSS/INDEX.HTM

Henwood, M. (1999) *Home and away: reflections on LT care in the UK and Australia*, SPRC Discussion Paper 101, June.

Henwood, M. (2000) 'Central – local relations: the changing balance of Direction vs Discretion in social care', in B. Hudson (2000) *The changing role of social care*, London, Jessica Kingsley.

Heywood, F., Oldman, C. and Means, R. (2002) *Housing and Home in Later Life*, Buckingham, Open University Press.

Higham, P. (2001) 'Changing practice and an emerging social pedagogue paradigm in England: The Role of the Personal Adviser', *Social Work in Europe*, 8(1), pp.21-28.

Hill, J. (2004) 'Hub of the Matter', *Society Guardian*, 24th March 2004.

Holmes, C. (2003) *Housing, equality and choice*, London, Institute of Public Policy Research.

House of Commons Health Committee (1994) *1st report – Better off in the Community? The Care of People who are Seriously Mentally Ill. Vol.1,* London, HMSO.

House of Commons Health Select Committee (2002) *Delayed Discharge: Report and Proceedings of the Committee*, HC617-1, Report together with formal minutes, oral and written minutes, 2002, London, The Stationery Office.

House of Commons Housing, Planning, Local Government and the Regions Select Committee (2004) *Supporting Vulnerable and Older People: The Supporting People Programme 10th Report of session 2003-04,* HC 504-1, Report together with formal minutes, oral and written minutes, 2004, London, The Stationery Office.

Housing Associations' Charitable Trust at: www.hact.org.uk

Housing Corporation (1997) *A Housing Plus Approach to Achieving Sustainable Communities,* London, The Housing Corporation.

Housing Corporation (2003a) *National Investment Policy 2004/05-2005/06*, Issued 24th October 2003 at www.housingcorp.gov.uk.

Housing Corporation (2003b) *Strategy for Housing Older People in England,* London, The Housing Corporation.

Housing Corporation/Anchor Housing (2002) *Implementing Supporting People – A Guide for Support Providers*, London, The Housing Corporation and Anchor Housing.

Houston, F. (1955) 'A project for a mental health village settlement', in *The Lancet*, 1955, pp.1133-44 quoted in G. Thornicroft and G. Strathdee (1994) 'How many psychiatric beds?' *British Medical Journal,* 309, pp.970-971.

Hoyes, L. and Means, R. (1993) 'Quasi Markets and the Reform of Community Care', in J. Le Grand and W. Bartlett, (eds) *Quasi Markets and Social Policy*, London, Macmillan.

Huber, J. and Skidmore, P. (2003) *The New Old,* London, DEMOS/Age Concern.

Hudson, B. (1987) 'Collaboration in Social Welfare: A Framework for Analysis', *Policy and Politics,* Vol. 15(3) pp.175-182.

Hudson, B. (2001) 'Standards bearers?' *Community Care*, 20th September 2001,

Hudson, B. (2002) 'Interprofessionality in Health and Social Care: the Achilles' Heel of Partnership', *Journal of Interprofessional Care*, Vol.16 (1).

Hudson, B. (ed) (2000) *The Changing role of social care*, London, Jessica Kingsley.

Hudson, B. and Henwood, M. (2002) 'NHS and social care: The final countdown', *Policy and Politics*, Vol. 30(2) pp.155-166.

Hunter, D. and Wistow, G. (1987) *Community Care: Variations on a Theme*, London, King Edward's Hospital Fund for London.

Hutton, W. (1996) *The State Were In: Why Britain is in crisis and how to overcome it*, London, Vintage.

Huxham, C. (ed) (1996) *Creating Collaborative Advantage*, London, Sage.

Illich, I. (1975) *Medical Nemesis: The Appropriation of Health*, London, Calder and Boyars.

Imrie, R (2003) *The Impact of Part M on the design of new housing*, Egham, Royal Holloway University of London.

Imrie, R. and Raco, M. (eds) (2003) *Urban Renaissance? New Labour, community and urban policy*, Bristol, Policy Press.

Independent Inquiry into Inequalities in Health (1998) *The Independent Inquiry into Inequalities in Health*, Chairman Sir Donald Acheson, London, The Stationery Office.

Information Centre about Asylum and Refugees at www.icar.org.uk

Inman, K. (2003) 'Building Blocks', *Community Care*, 25th September 2003.

Inside Housing (2004) 'Budget cuts will force councils to make big supporting people savings', *Inside Housing*, 10th December 2004, p.7.

Inside Housing (2004) 'Supporting people cuts delayed', *Inside Housing*, 3rd December 2004, p.4.

Jack, R. (1998) 'Institutions in Community', in R. Jack (ed) *Residential Versus Community Care: The role of institutions in Welfare Provision*, Basingstoke, Macmillan.

Jan-Khan, M. (2003) 'Community Cohesion: Myth or Reality', paper presented at the ESRC Seminar Series '*Eliciting the views of refugees and asylum seekers*', Salford, University of Salford.

Jarvis, D., Hancock, R., Askham, J. and Tinker, A. (1997) *Getting Around After 60 – a profile of Britain's Older Population*, London, HMSO.

Jay Committee (1979) *Report of the Committee of Enquiry into Mental Handicap Nursing and Care*, Cm 7468, London HMSO.

Jenkins, R., McCulloch, A., Friedli, L, and Parker, C. (2002) *Developing a national mental health policy*, Maudsley Monographs no. 43, London, Psychology Press Ltd.

Jerwood, K. (2004) 'Where have all the forums gone?' *SITRA Bulletin*, June 2004, no. 172.

Jones, A. (1994) *The Numbers Game: Black and minority ethnic elders and sheltered accommodation*, Oxford, Anchor Housing Trust.

Jones, A. (1998) *The Invisible Minority: The Housing Needs of Chinese Older People in England,* Birmingham: Centre for Urban and Regional Studies, University of Birmingham.

Jones, G. (1986) *Social Hygiene in the Twentieth Century*, London, Croom Helm.

Jones, K. (1972) *A History of the Mental Health Services*, London, Routledge and Kegan Paul.

Jones, M. (1968) *Social Psychiatry in Practice*, Harmondsworth, Penguin.

Jordan, B. (1998) *The New Politics of Welfare: Social Justice in a Global Context*, London, Sage.

Joseph Rowntree Foundation (1999a) *Low intensity support: preventing dependency,* JRF 'Foundations' 159, York, Joseph Rowntree Foundation.

Joseph Rowntree Foundation (1999b) *Response to Consultation on Supporting People*, York, Joseph Rowntree Foundation.

Joseph Rowntree Foundation (2004) *Monitoring Poverty and Social Exclusion,* York, Joseph Rowntree Foundation.

Karn, V., Mian, S., Brown, M. and Dale, A. (1999) *Tradition, Change and Diversity: Understanding the Housing Needs of Minority Ethnic Groups in Manchester,* London, The Housing Corporation.

Keay, D. (1987) 'Aids, education, and the year 2000', *Women's Own*, pp.8-10, October 31, interview with Margaret Thatcher.

Kenny, C. (2004) 'Housing Group Says Providers Failings Lie Behind Evictions', *Community Care,* 26th August 2004.

Khan, S. (1997) *'Today's Concerns and Bleak Tomorrows': A national study of the housing and health needs of older people from West Indian, Bangladeshi and Indian communities,* London, Service Access To Minority Ethnic Communities.

King, R. D., Raynes, N. V. and Tizard, J. (1971) *Patterns of Residential Care: Sociological Studies in Institutions for Handicapped Children*, London, Routledge and Kegan Paul.

King's Fund (1980) *An Ordinary Life – Comprehensive Locally Based Services for Mentally Handicapped People,* London, King's Fund Centre.

King's Fund/Banks, P. (2002) *Partnerships under Pressure*, London, King's Fund.

Kinsella, P. (1993) *Supported Living: A New Paradigm*, Manchester, National Development Team.

Kirkwood, T. (2001) Reith Lectures 2001: *The End of Age*, at: www.bbc.co.uk/radio4/reith2001/

Klein, R. (1999) 'Markets Politicians and the NHS', *British Medical Journal,* 319, pp.1383-4.

Klein, R. and Maynard, M. (1998) 'On the way to Calvary', *British Medical Journal,* 317: 5.

Kleinman, M. (2002) *A European Welfare State? European Union Social Policy in Context*, Basingstoke, Palgrave.

Knutt, E. (2003) 'Our Grey Future', *Housing Today*, 1st August, 2003, pp.22-18.

Kretzmann, J. and McKnight, J. (1993) *Building Communities From The Inside Out: A Path Toward Finding And Mobilizing A Community's Assets,* Illinois, Center for Urban Affairs and Policy Research, Northwestern University.

Kugel, R. and Wolfensberger, W. (eds) (1969) *Changing Patterns in Residential Services for the Mentally Retarded,* Washington, D.C., President's Committee on Mental Retardation, US Government Printing Office.

Kuhn, T. (1962) *The structure of scientific revolutions,* Chicago, University of Chicago Press.

Kumar, S. (2004a) 'Councils urged to pool funds with Supporting People to meet needs', *Community Care,* 16th September 2004, p.12.

Kumar, S. (2004b) 'Inspectors uncover core services funded by housing support money', *Community Care,* 21st October 2004, p.9.

Ladyman, S. (2004) Speech to the National Care Homes Association, 27th October, 2004 (transcript provided by the National Care Homes Association) London, National Care Homes Association.

Laing and Buisson (2003) 'Value of the home care market: Care of the Elderly People Market Survey 2003', *Community Care Market News,* accessed at: www.laingbuisson.co.uk on 27th October 2003.

Laing, R.D. (1965) *The Divided Self,* London, Pelican Books.

Laing, W. (2002) *Calculating a Fair Price for Care: A toolkit for residential and nursing care costs,* Bristol, Policy Press.

Le Grand, J. (1990) *Quasi-markets and Social Policy,* Bristol, School of Urban Studies, Bristol University.

Leason, K. (2003) 'English care watchdog must apply consistency and cut bureaucracy', *Community Care,* 27th March 2003.

Leathard, A. (1994) *Going Inter-professional,* London, Routledge.

Lee, P. and Murie, A. (1997) *Poverty, Housing Tenure and Social Exclusion,* Bristol, Policy Press.

Leeds Metropolitan University (2004) *Supporting People – Shadow Strategy Analysis 2002-3,* London, Office of the Deputy Prime Minister.

Leff, J. (ed) (1998) *Care in the community: illusion or reality?* London, Wiley and Sons.

Leff, J. (2000) 'TAPS Phase II: The evaluation of the transfer of care from psychiatric hospitals to district based services', *The Research Findings Register,* Number 174.

Leigh, C. (1994) *Everybody's Baby: Implementing Community Care for Single Homeless People,* London, Campaign for the Homeless and Rootless.

Leishman, C., Aspinall, P., Munro, M. and Warren, F.J. (2003) *Preferences, quality and choice in new-build housing,* York, Joseph Rowntree Foundation

Lewis, J. and Glennerster, H. (1996) *Implementing the New Community Care,* Buckingham, Open University Press.

Local Government Association (1997) *Budget facts No.4,* London, Local Government Association.

London Federation of Housing Associations (1995) *Managing Vulnerability: The Challenge for Managers of Independent Housing,* London, London Federation of Housing Associations.

London Research Centre and Lemos and Crane (1998) *Assessing Black and Minority Ethnic Housing Needs*, London, The Housing Corporation.

Long, A. (1994) *Directions for health: the Leeds Declaration*, Radical Statistics, 57, pp.39-42.

Lund, B. (1996) *Housing problems and housing policy,* London, Longman.

Lund, B. and Foord, M. (1997) *Housing Strategies and Community Care: Towards Integrated Living?* Bristol, Policy Press.

Lupton, M., Patel, A. and Wong, J. (2004) 'Serious players', *Inside Housing*, 23rd January, pp.20-22.

Lupton, R. (2003) *Poverty Street,* Bristol, Policy Press.

Macfarlane, A. and Laurie, L. (1996) *Demolishing Special Needs,* Derby, British Council of Disabled People.

Maginn, P. (2004) *Urban Regeneration, Community Power And The [In]Significance Of 'Race',* Aldershot, Ashgate.

Malpass, P. (2000) *Housing associations and housing policy: a historical perspective,* London, Palgrave Macmillan.

Marshall, M. (1999) 'Modernising mental health services', *British Medical Journal*, 318, pp.3-4.

Martin, G., Phelps, K. and Katbamna, S. (2004) 'Human motivation and professional practice: of knights, knaves and social workers', *Social Policy and Administration*, Volume 38 (5), October 2004, pp.470-488.

Mathias, J. (2001) *Meeting the Needs of Black and Minority Ethnic Communities,* London, The Housing Corporation.

Mayo, M. (2002) 'The shifting concept of community', in M. Allott and M. Robb, M. (eds), *Understanding Health and Social Care*, London, Sage.

McCafferty, P. (1994) *Living Independently: A study of the housing needs of elderly and disabled people*, London, HMSO.

McEwan, P. and Laverty, S. (1949) *The Chronic Sick and Elderly in Hospital,* Bradford, Bradford Hospital Management Committee.

McIver, R. and Page, C. (1961) *Society: An Introductory Analysis,* New York, Holt, Rinehart and Winston.

McKie, R. (2004) 'Living with Britain's population time bomb', *The Observer*, 25th January 2004.

McKnight, J. (2003) *De-Clienting society – New Directions in Community Building (Lessons from the USA on asset-based community building)*, paper presented at the *From Client to Citizen Conference*, London.

McNally, D., Cornes, M. and Clough, R. (2003) 'Implementing the Single Assessment Process: Driving change or expecting the impossible?' *Journal of Integrated Care*, Vol. 11, Issue 2, pp.18-29, April 2003.

Means, R. (1992) 'From the Poor Law to the Marketplace', in C. Grant (ed) *Built to Last? Reflections on British Housing Policy*, London, Roof.

Means, R., Brenton, M., Harrison, L. and Heywood, F. (1997) *Making Partnerships Work in Community Care: a Guide for Practitioners in Housing, Health and Social Services,* Bristol, the Policy Press.

Means, R. and Smith, R. (1994) *Community Care Policy and Practice,* London, Macmillan.

Means, R., Morbey, H. and Smith, R. (2002) *From Community Care to Market Care? The development of services for older people,* Bristol, Policy Press.

Means, R., Richards, S. and Smith, R. (2003) *Community Care – Policy and Practice,* 3rd edition, London, Palgrave Macmillan.

Mental Health Alliance (2004) *MHA submission to the Joint Scrutiny committee on the Draft Mental Health Bill*, London, Mental Health Alliance.

Mental Health Foundation (2004) *Draft Mental Health Bill Memorandum from the Mental Health Foundation and the Foundation for People with Learning Disabilities*, London, Mental Health Foundation.

Miller, E. and Gwynne, G. (1972) *A Life Apart,* London, Tavistock.

Milner, H. M. (1968) 'Community-Society Continua', *International Encyclopaedia of the Social Sciences*, Vol 3, New York, Macmillan Free Press.

Ministry of Health (1968) *Social Work (Scotland) Act 1968,* London, HMSO.

Mooney, G. and Poole, L. (2004) 'A land of milk and honey? Social Policy in Scotland after devolution', *Critical Social Policy,* Vol. 24 (4), pp.458-483.

Moran, R. and Butler, D. (2001) 'Whose health profile?' *Critical Public Health*, 11(1), pp. 59-74.

Morris, J. (1989) *Able Lives,* London, The Women's Press.

Morris, J. (1991) *Pride against prejudice: transforming attitudes to disability*, London, The Women's Press.

Morris, J. (1993) *Independent Living or Community Care*, Basingstoke, Macmillan.

Morris, P. (1969) *Put Away: A Sociological Study of Institutions for the Mentally Retarded,* London, Routledge and Kegan Paul.

Munro, M., Lomax, D., Lancaster, S., Bramley, G. and Anderson, K. (1996) *Estimating the Housing Needs of Community Care Groups*, Edinburgh, Scottish Office Central Research Unit.

Murie, A. (2003) 'Housing', in P. Alcock, A. Erskine and M. May, *The Student's Companion to Social Policy*, 2nd edition, Oxford, Blackwell.

Murie, A., Nevin, B. and Leather, P. (1998) *Changing Demand and Unpopular Housing Working Paper 4,* London, The Housing Corporation.

National Audit Office (2003) *Ensuring the Effective Discharge of Older Patients from NHS Acute Hospitals*, London, National Audit Office.

National Council for Voluntary Organisation (1995) *Still Just a Sideshow – A Second Review of Shire County Community Planning for Rural Areas*, London, National Council for Voluntary Organisations.

National Economic and Social Forum (2003) *The policy implications of Social Capital Forum,* Report No. 28, NESF, Dublin.

National Housing Federation (1997) *Management Options: Tenant Support in General Needs Housing,* London, National Housing Federation.

National Housing Federation (2001) *Working with the New Health and Social Care Agenda (revised edition),* London, National Housing Federation.

Neale, J. (2002) *Drug users in Society,* Hampshire, Palgrave.

Neighbourhood Renewal Unit (2003) *Review of Community Participation: Report for Public Consultation Report for Public Consultation,* accessed at: www.renewal.net July 2003.

Nichter, M. (1984) 'Project community diagnosis: participatory research as a first step towards community involvement in primary health care', *Soc.Sc.Med.,* 19(3), pp.237-252.

Nisbet, R. (1973) *The Social Philosophers: Community and Conflict in Western Thought,* New York, Thomas Y. Cromwell.

North-West Regional Health Authority (1982) *A Model District Service,* Manchester, North-West Regional Health Authority.

O'Brien, J. and Lyle, C. (1986) *Framework for Accomplishment,* Decatur, GA., Responsive Systems Associates.

Office for National Statistics (2004) *Social Trends,* 34, London, HMSO.

Office of the Deputy Prime Minister (1999) *Local Housing Needs Assessments: a review of Current Practice and the Need for Guidance,* accessed at: www.odpm.gov.uk July 2003.

Office of the Deputy Prime Minister (2000) *Our Towns and Cities,* London, Office of the Deputy Prime Minister.

Office of the Deputy Prime Minister (2001a) *A New Commitment to Neighbourhood Renewal: National Strategy Action Plan,* London, Office of the Deputy Prime Minister.

Office of the Deputy Prime Minister (2001b) *Housing in England 2001,* London, Office of the Deputy Prime Minister.

Office of the Deputy Prime Minister (2002a) *Delivering Affordable Housing Through Planning Policy,* accessed at: www.odpm.gov.uk.

Office of the Deputy Prime Minister (2002b) *2000/2001 Survey of English Housing: Preliminary Results,* London, Office of the Deputy Prime Minister.

Office of the Deputy Prime Minister (2002c) *The Homelessness Act: Code of Guidance.* London, The Stationery Office.

Office of the Deputy Prime Minister (2003a) *News Release: £1.8 Billion for Supporting Vulnerable People,* accessed at: www.odpm.gov.uk

Office of the Deputy Prime Minister (2003b) *Sustainable Communities – Building for the Future,* London, Office of the Deputy Prime Minister.

Office of the Deputy Prime Minister (2004a) *Benefits Realisation of the Supporting People Programme,* London, Office of the Deputy Prime Minister.

Office of the Deputy Prime Minister (2004b) *What is Supporting People?* London, Office of the Deputy Prime Minister.

Office of the Deputy Prime Minster (2004c) *Review of the Supporting People Programme,* London, Office of the Deputy Prime Minster.

Office of the Deputy Prime Minster (2004d) *Supporting People: Review of the Policy and Costs of Housing Related Support Since 1997,* London, Office of the Deputy Prime Minster.

Office of the Deputy Prime Minister/Department of Health (2003) *Preparing Older Peoples Strategies: Linking housing health, social care and other local strategies,* London, Office of the Deputy Prime Minister/Department of Health.

Office of the Deputy Prime Minister/The Home Office (2005) *Housing Options for People who Misuse Substances: Guidance for Supporting People Commissioners and Officers,* London, Office of the Deputy Prime Minister.

Oldman, C. (2000) *Blurring the Boundaries – a fresh look at housing provision and care for older people,* Brighton, Pavilion.

Oldman, C. (2003) 'Deceiving, theorizing and self-justification: a critique of independent living', *Critical Social Policy,* 23(1) pp.44-62.

Oldman, C., Quilgars, D. and Oldfield, N. (1995) *Housing Benefit and Service Charges: DSS Research Report No.55,* London, HMSO.

Oliver, M. (1983) *Social Work and Disabled People,* London, Macmillan.

Oliver, M. (1990) *The Politics of Disablement,* Basingstoke, Macmillan.

Organisation for Economic Cooperation and Development (2001) *The Well-being of Nations: The role of human and social capital,* Organisation for Economic Cooperation and Development, London.

Organisation for Economic Cooperation and Development (2004) Health data OECD-IRDES, accessed at: www.oecd.org/health/healthdata

Ovretveit, J., Mathias, P. and Thompson, T. (eds) (1997) *Interprofessional Working for Health and Social Care,* Basingstoke, Macmillan.

Oxley, M. and Smith, J. (1996) *Housing Policy and Rented Housing in Europe,* London, E and F N Spon.

Pacione, M. (1997) 'Urban restructuring and the reproduction of inequality', in M. Pacione (ed) *Britain's Cities: Geographies of Division in Urban Britain,* London, Routledge.

Padgham, M. and Spencer, P. (2003) *An Engaging Process: Relationships Between the Statutory and Independent Health Care Sectors in London and the South of England,* London, Department of Health/Social Care Change Agent Team.

Page, D. (2000) *Communities in the balance,* York, Joseph Rowntree Foundation.

Painter, C. and Clarence M. (2000) 'New Labour and intergovernmental management: flexible networks or performance control?' *Public Management,* 2, 4, pp.477-498.

Parry, R. (2002) 'Delivery structure and policy development in post devolution Scotland', *Social Policy and Society,* Vol. 1 (4), pp.315-24.

Pascall, G. (1997) *Social Policy: A New Feminist Analysis,* London, Routledge.

Pastalan, L. A. (1997) 'An introduction to international perspectives on shelter and service issues for ageing populations', *Journal of Housing for the Elderly,* 12(1/2), pp.1-8.

Patton, M. Q. (1990) *Qualitative Evaluation and Research Methods,* London, Sage.

Peace, S. and Holland, C. (eds) (2001) *Inclusive Housing in an Ageing Society: Innovative Approaches,* Bristol, Policy Press.

Peryer, D. (1997) *Human Resources for Personal Social Services,* The Local Government Management Board, London.

Petch, A. (2000) 'UK Variations in Social Care', in R. Hudson (2000) *The Changing Role of Social Care*, London, Jessica Kingsley Press.

Phelan, J., Link, B., Stueve, A., and Pescosolido, B. (1997) *Public conceptions of mental illness in 1950 in 1996: Has sophistication increased? Has stigma declined?* Paper presented at the meeting of the American Sociological Association, Toronto, Ontario.

Pickard, L., Wittenberg, R., Comas-Hererra, A., Davis, B. and Darton, R. (2000) 'Relying on informal care in the new century? Informal care for elderly people in England to 2031', *Ageing and Society* 20(6) pp.745-772.

Platt, D. (2004) 'How we'll knock down service barriers', *The Guardian,* 10th March 2004.

Platt, L. (2002) *Parallel Lives: Poverty Among Ethnic Minority Groups in Britain,* London, Child Poverty Action Group.

Poggi, G. (1965) 'Main Theme of Contemporary Sociological Analysis: Its Achievements and Limitations', *British Journal of Sociology* 16 (4), pp.283-94.

Popple, K. and Redmond, M. (2000) 'Community development and the voluntary sector in the new millennium: the implications of the Third Way in the UK', *Community Development Journal,* 35(4), pp.391-400.

Powell, M. (2000) 'New Labour and the third way in the British welfare state – a new and distinctive approach?' *Critical Social Policy,* Vol. 20 (1), pp.39-60.

Pratt, J., Gordon, P. and Plamping, D. (1998) *Working Whole Systems: Putting Theory into Practice in Organisations,* London, King's Fund.

Property People (2003) *Relentless BME research 'of no help to anyone',* 19th June 2003.

Putnam, R.D. (2000) *Bowling Alone: The Collapse of American Community,* New York, Simon and Schuster.

Putnam, R.D. (2003) *Better together: restoring the American community,* Simon and Schuster, New York.

Quilgars, D. (2000) *Low intensity support services: a systematic review of effectiveness,* Bristol, The Policy Press.

Race, D.G. (1999a) *Social Role Valorization and the English Experience,* London, Whiting and Birch.

Race, D.G. (1999b) 'Hearts and Minds – Social Role Valorization, UK Academia and Services for People with Learning Disabilities', *Disability and Society,* Vol. 14(4), 1999.

Race, D.G. (2002a) 'The Historical Context', in D.G. Race (ed) *Learning Disability – a Social Approach*, London, Routledge.

Race, D.G. (2002b) 'The Normalisation Debate – Time to Move On', in D.G. Race, D.G. (ed.) *Learning Disability – a Social Approach*, London, Routledge.

Race, D.G. (2003) *Leadership and Change in Human Services: Selected Readings from Wolf Wolfensberger,* London, Routledge.

Race, D.G. and Race D.M. (1979) *The Cherries Group Home – A Beginning*, London, HMSO.

Radia, K. (1996) *Ignored, silenced, neglected: Housing and mental health care needs of Asian people in the London Boroughs of Brent, Ealing, Harrow and Tower Hamlets,* York, Joseph Rowntree Foundation.

Ramsden, S. (2002) *Response to residential care, housing care and support schemes and supporting people,* Housing Management and Support Team Advice and Information Note, January 2002, London, National Housing Federation.

Randall, B. (2003) *Breaking Down the Barriers*, Paris, European Liaison Committee for Social Housing.

Rao, N. (1991) *From Providing to Enabling – Local Authorities and Community Care Planning*, York, Joseph Rowntree Foundation.

Rao, N. (2000) *Reviving local democracy: new labour, new politics,* Bristol, The Policy Press.

Ratcliffe, P. (1996) *'Race' and Housing In Bradford: Addressing the needs of the South Asian, African and Caribbean communities,* Bradford, Bradford Housing Forum.

Ratcliffe, P. (1998) '"Race", housing and social exclusion', *Housing Studies*, 13(6), pp.807-818.

Ratcliffe, P. with Harrison, M., Hogg, R., Line, B., Phillips, D. and Tomlins, R. (2001) *Breaking Down The barriers: Improving Asian Access to Social Rented Housing*, Coventry, Chartered Institute of Housing.

Rickets, A. (2005) 'Support provider to axe 250 jobs after funding cut', *Inside Housing*, 10th June 2005.

Ritchie, J., Dick, D. and Lingham, R. (1994) *Report of the Inquiry into the Care and Treatment of Christopher Clunis,* London, HMSO.

Robb, B. (1967) *Sans Everything: A case to answer,* London, Nelson and Co.

Roberts, J.M. and Devine, F. (2003) 'The hollowing out of the welfare state and social capital', *Social Policy and Society*, 2, pp.309-318.

Robson, D., Nicholson, A.M. and Barker, N. (1997) *Homes for the Third Age – A Design Guide for Extra Care Sheltered Housing*, London, Spon.

Roulstone, A. (1998) *Enabling Technology, Disabled People, Work and new technology*, Buckingham, Open University Press.

Rowland, D.R. and Pollock, A. (2004) 'Choice and responsiveness for older people in the "patient centred" NHS', *British Medical Journal*, 328, pp.4-5.

Royal College of Psychiatrists (2001) *The Role of Consultants with responsibility for substance misuse – position statement by the faculty of substance misuse,* Council Report CR97, London, Royal College of Psychiatrists.

Royal College of Psychiatrists, British Medical Association and Society of Medical Officers of Health (1972) *The Mental Health Service After Unification.* London, British Medical Association.

Ryan, J. and Thomas, F. (1987) *The Politics of Mental Handicap 2nd Edition,* Harmondsworth, Penguin.

Sainsbury Centre for Mental Health (2002) *Breaking the Cycles of Fear,* London, Sainsbury Centre for Mental Health.

Sainsbury Centre for Mental Health (2004a) *Briefing Paper 26: the Supporting People Programme and Mental Health,* London, Sainsbury Centre for Mental Health.

Sainsbury Centre for Mental Health (2004b) *So what's the future for mental health?* London, Sainsbury Centre for Mental Health.

Sayce, L. and Morris, D. (1999) *Outsiders coming in? Achieving social inclusion for people with mental health problems,* London, MIND.

Schwabenland, C. (2002) 'Towards A Paradigm Shift: lessons from anti-oppression movements', in J. Merrifield, R. Tandon, C. Flower, and C. Schwabenland (eds) *Participation – North and South: New ideas in Participatory Development from India and the UK,* pp.5-17, London, Elfida Society.

Scottish Executive (2004) *First Report of the Range and Capacity Review: Projections of Community Care and Service Users, Workforce and costs,* Edinburgh, The Scottish Executive.

Scull, A., MacKensie, C. and Hervey, N. (1996) *Masters of Bedlam: The Transformation of the Mad-Doctoring Trade,* Princeton, NJ, U.S.A., Princeton University Press.

Secker, J., Hill, R., Villeneau, L. and Parkman, S. (2003) 'Promoting independence – but promoting what and how?' *Ageing and Society,* 23, pp.375-391.

Seebohm Committee (1968) *Report of the committee on local authority and allied personal social services,* London, HMSO, Cmnd 3703.

Sharkey, P. (2000) 'Community work and community care: links in practice and in education', *Social Work Education,* 19(1), pp.7-17.

Sheldon, T. (1996) 'Going Dutch', *Inside Housing,* 29th March 1996, p 13.

Shelter (2002) *The Homelessness Act: an Introduction* (unpublished information sheet), London, Shelter.

Sim, D. (1993) *British Housing Design,* Harlow, Longman Group.

Simons, K. (2001) *Strategies for change – implementing 'Valuing People' at the local level: Developing Housing and Support Options – Introduction and context setting,* Norah Fry Centre, Bristol, University of Bristol.

SITRA (February 2004) *The Robson Rhodes Independent Review of the Supporting People Programme – A Briefing for Practitioners,* accessed at: www.sitra.org.uk/publications

Smith, J. (1994) 'Shopping for the right stuff', *Care Weekly,* 10th March, 1994.

Soares, T. (2004) 'Black-led associations have a right to exist', *Inside Housing*, 6th February 2004, p.15.

Social Exclusion Unit (1998) *Bringing Britain Together: A National Strategy for Neighbourhood Renewal*, Cm 4045, London, HMSO.

Social Exclusion Unit (1999) *Policy Action Team Report 9 'Community Self-help '*, London, Social Exclusion Unit.

Social Exclusion Unit (2001) *A New Commitment to Neighbourhood Renewal: National strategy action plan*, London, Social Exclusion Unit.

Social Exclusion Unit (2004) *Breaking the Cycle of Social Exclusion*, London, Social Exclusion Unit.

Social Services Inspectorate (1998) *They Look After Their Own Don't They?* London, Social Services Inspectorate.

Social Services Inspectorate (2003) *Improving Older Peoples Services – an overview of performance,* London, Social Services Inspectorate.

Sodhi, D. and Ahmed, A. (2001) *Asian Elders: Housing and social care needs in Rochdale and Oldham,* Salford, Salford Housing and Urban Studies Unit, University of Salford.

Spencer, S. and Fletcher, P. (2002) *Working with the New Health and Social Care Agenda*, London, National Housing Federation.

Stedman Jones, G. (1971) *Outcast London,* Oxford University Press, Oxford.

Steele, A. (1999) *The Housing and Social Care Needs of Black and Minority Ethnic Older People in Derby,* Salford, Salford Housing and Urban Studies Unit, University of Salford.

Steele, A. (2001) *The Housing and Social Care Needs of the Asian Community in Bury,* Salford, Salford Housing and Urban Studies Unit, University of Salford.

Steele, A. and Sodhi, D. (1999) *The Housing and Related Needs of BME Communities in Luton,* Luton, Luton Borough Council.

Stewart, J. (2004) 'Scottish solutions to Scottish problems? Social welfare in Scotland since devolution', in N. Ellison, L. Bauld and M. Powell (eds), *Social Policy Review 16 – Analysis and Debate in Social Policy 2004*, Bristol, Policy Press and the Social Policy Association, pp.101-120.

Stewart, J., Harris, J. and Sapey, B. (1999) 'Disability and dependency: origins and futures of 'special needs' housing for disabled people', *Disability and Society* Vol.14, No.1. pp.5-20.

Stone, D. A. (1984) *The Disabled State*, Macmillan, London.

Stothart, C. (2003) 'Who Cares?', *Housing Today,* 31st October 2003.

Stothart, C. (2004) 'Supported housing cuts push elderly into debt', *Housing Today*, 15th October 2004.

Subhra, G. and Chauhan, V. (1999) *Developing black services: Evaluation of the African, Caribbean and Asian Services Funded Under Alcohol Concern's Grants Programme,* London, Alcohol Concern.

Sullivan, H. and Skelcher, C. (2002) *Working across boundaries: Collaboration in public services,* London, Palgrave Macmillan.

Sumner, K. (2001) 'Real choice in later life living arrangements – radical solutions to make this a reality', *Journal of the British Society of Gerontology*, Vol. 11, No.3.

Symonds, A. and Kelly, A. (1998) *The Social Construction of Community Care,* London, Macmillan.

Szasz, T. S. (1970) *The Manufacture of Madness: A Comparative Study of the Inquisition and the Mental Health Movement,* New York, Harper Row.

Tandon, R. (2002) 'Overcoming disability: lessons from participatory development', in J. Merrifield, R. Tandon, C. Flower, and C. Schwabenland (eds) *Participation – North and South: New ideas in Participatory Development from India and the UK,* pp.33-40, London, Elfida Society.

Taylor, M. (2003) *Communities at the heart? Approaches to inclusion in the UK,* paper presented at the From Client to Citizen Conference, London.

Taylor, P.J. and Gunn, J. (1999) 'Homicides by people with mental illness: myth and reality', *British Journal of Psychiatry*; 174, pp.9-14.

Temple, B. (2002) 'Interpreters, translators and bilingual workers in cross language research', *Qualitative Health Research*, 12(6), pp.844-854.

Temple, B. and Chahal, K. (2002) 'The salience of terminology: housing research with older people from minority ethnic communities', *International Journal of Social Research Methodology: Theory and Practice*, 5(4), pp.353-369.

Temple, B. and Moran, R. with Fayas, N., Haboninana, S., McCabe, F., Mohamed, Z., Noori, A. and Rahman, N. (2005) *Learning to Live Together: Developing communities where there are dispersed refugee people seeking asylum,* York, Joseph Rowntree Foundation.

Temple, B. and Steele, A. (2004) 'Injustices of Engagement: Issues in Housing Needs Assessments with Minority Ethnic Communities', *Housing Studies*, 19(4), pp.541-556.

Temple, B., Glenister, C., and Raynes, N. (2002) 'Prioritising home care needs: research with older people from three minority community groups', *Health and Social Care in the Community,* 10(3), pp.179-186.

Thane, P. (1982) *The Foundations of the Welfare State,* London, Longman.

Thomson, M. (1996) 'Family, Community and State: the Micro Politics of Mental Deficiency', in A. Digby and D. Wright (eds) *From Idiocy to Mental Deficiency: Historical Perspectives on People with Learning Difficulties,* London, Routledge.

Tinker, A. (1997) *Older People in Modern Society,* London, Longman.

Tizard, J. (1964) *Community Services for the Mentally Handicapped,* London, Oxford University Press.

Tomlins, R. (1999) *Housing Experiences of Minority Ethnic Communities in Britain: an academic literature review and annotated bibliography*, Bibliographies in Ethnic Relations No. 15. Warwick: Centre for Research in Ethnic Relations, University of Warwick.

Tomlins, R., Johnson, M. and Owen, D. (2002) 'The resource of ethnicity in the housing careers and preferences of the Vietnamese communities in London', *Housing Studies*, 17(3), pp. 505-519.

Town, H. (2001) *Tackling Drugs: Reading and resources*, London, Sage.

Townsend, P. (1962) *The Last Refuge*, London, Routledge and Kegan Paul.

Tredgold, A. F. (1947) *A Text Book of Mental Deficiency,* 7th edition. London, Bailliere Tindall.

Tredgold, A.F. (1909) 'The feebleminded – a social danger', *Eugenics Review,* 1, 97-104.

Tulle-Winton, E. (1999) 'Growing old and resistance: Towards a new cultural economy of old age?', *Ageing and Society,* 19(3), pp.281-300.

Turning Point (2003) *A Hospital is not a Home: Time to move on*, London, Turning Point.

Twigg, J. (2000) *The Changing Role of Users and Carers,* in R. Hudson (2000) *The Changing Role of Social Care*, London, Jessica Kingsley Press.

Twine, F. (2000) 'Racial Ideologies and Racial Methodologies', in F. Twine and J. Warren (eds) *Racing Research, Researching Race: Methodological Dilemmas in Critical Race Studies*, pp.1-34, New York and London, New York University Press.

Union of Physically Impaired Against Segregation (1976) *The Fundamental Principles of Disability*, London, Union of Physically Impaired Against Segregation.

Venables, T. and Taylor, C. (2001) *Smart Homes – A specification guide*, York, Joseph Rowntree Foundation.

Wagner, G. (1988) *Residential Care: A positive choice (report of the independent review of residential care),* London, HMSO.

Walker, A. (1993) 'Community care policy: from consensus to conflict', in J. Bornat, C. Pereira, D. Pilgrim, D. and F. Williams (eds) *Community Care: A Reader,* London, Macmillan.

Walmsley, J. (2001) 'Normalisation, emancipatory research and inclusive research in learning disability', *Disability and Society*, Vol. 16, No 2, pp.187-205.

Wanless, D. (2002) *Securing our Future Health: Taking a long term view – final report,* HM Treasury, London.

Warner, R. (1994) *Recovery from Schizophrenia: psychiatry and political economy*, London, Routledge.

Watson, L. (1996) *Housing Need and Community Care*, London and Coventry, National Federation of Housing Associations, and Chartered Institute of Housing.

Watson, L. (1997) *High hopes: making housing and community care work,* York, Joseph Rowntree Foundation.

Watson, L. Tarpey, M. Alexander, K and Humphreys, C. (2003) *Supporting People: Real Change? Planning housing and support for marginal groups,* York, Joseph Rowntree Foundation.

Weaver, M. (2002) 'Friction slows New Deal', *The Guardian,* 20th February 2002.

Weaver, M. (2004) 'Sink or Swim', *The Guardian,* 14th January 2004.

Webb, A. (1991) 'Co-ordination: a problem in public sector management', *Policy and Politics*, Vol.19 (4), pp.29-42.

Welsh Assembly (2002) *Better Homes for People in Wales – A National Housing Strategy for Wales Action Plan*, Cardiff, Welsh Assembly.

Welsh Assembly Government (2003a) *Wales a Better Country: The strategic goals of the Welsh Assembly Government*, Cardiff, Welsh Assembly Government.

Welsh Assembly Government (2003b) *Strategy for Older People in Wales*, Cardiff, Welsh Assembly Government.

Williams, P. (1998) *Standing by me: Stories of Citizen Advocacy*, London, Citizen Advocacy Information and Training.

Williams, P. (2002), 'Residential and Day Services', in D.G. Race (ed) *Learning Disability – a Social Approach*, London, Routledge.

Wilson, D. (2001) *Contemporary Local Government – continuity and change*, Occasional Paper 63, Leicester, De Montford University.

Wing, H. (2003) 'Do the work or risk a fall', *Community Care*, 23rd October 2003.

Wistow, G. (1995) 'Paying for long term care: the shifting boundary between health and social care', *Community Care Management and Planning*, Vol. 3(3).

Wittenberg, R., Comas-Herrera, A. and Pickard, L. (2004), *Future Demand for Long Term Care in the UK: A summary of projections of long term care finance for older people to 2051*, York, Joseph Rowntree Foundation.

Wolfensberger, W. (1972) *Normalization: The principle of normalization in human services*, Toronto, National Institute on Mental Retardation.

Wolfensberger, W. (1973) 'Citizen advocacy for the handicapped, impaired, and disadvantaged: An overview', in W. Wolfensberger and H. Zauha (eds), *Citizen advocacy and protective services for the impaired and handicapped*, pp.7-32, Toronto, Canada, National Institute on Mental Retardation.

Wolfensberger, W. (1975) *The Origin and Nature of our Institutional Models* (rev. and ill. ed.), Syracuse, NY, Human Policy Press.

Wolfensberger, W. (1996) *A History of Human Services*, Presentation made at University of Cambridge, September 1996 (unpublished).

Wolfensberger, W. (1998) A *Brief Introduction to Social Role Valorization: A high-order concept for addressing the plight of societally devalued people, and for structuring human services* (3rd ed., Rev.), Syracuse, NY, Syracuse University, Training Institute for Human Service Planning, Leadership and Change Agency.

Wolfensberger, W. (1999) 'A contribution to the history of normalization, with primary emphasis on the establishment of normalization in North America between 1967-1975', in R.J. Flynn and R.A. Lemay (eds) *A quarter-century of normalization and Social Role Valorization: Evolution and Impact*, Ottawa, Canada, University of Ottawa Press.

Wolfensberger, W. (2000) '*Historical expressions of learning disability in language and art: Implications for our times*' presentation made at University of Newcastle, July 2000 (unpublished).

Wolfensberger, W., and Menolascino, F. (1970a) 'Reflections on recent mental retardation developments in Nebraska ll: A new plan', *Mental Retardation,* 8(6), pp.20-25.

Wolfensberger, W. and Menolascino, F. (1970b) 'Reflections on recent mental retardation developments in Nebraska II: Implementation to date', *Mental Retardation, 8(6),* pp.26-28.

Wood, P. (1981) *International Classification of Impairments, Disabilities and Handicaps,* Geneva, World Health Organisation.

World Health Organization (1953) *Third Report of the Expert Committee on Mental Health*, Geneva, World Health Organisation.

Younghusband, E. L. (1959) *Report of the Working Party on Social Workers in the Local Authority Health and Welfare Services,* London, HMSO.

Zarb, G. (1991) Creating a Supportive Environment: Meeting the needs of people aging with a disability, in M. Oliver (ed) (1991) *Social Work, Disabled People and Disabling Environments,* London, Jessica Kingsley.

Index

Notes:
1. The index covers the main text but not author information or the bibliography.
2. Acts of parliament are only included if they are referred to more than once in the text.
3. Proper names (e.g. of organisations) are generally only included if they are referred to more than once in the main text. Names of government departments are omitted.

accessibility (of housing to disabled people), 113-125

aids and adaptations (for disabled people), 22, 34, 67-68, 77, 113-125, 149, 158

alcohol problems, 9, 17, 29, 53, 64-65, 136, 164-166, 171-172, 177, 179-180, 184, 195

anti-social behaviour, 10, 53, 56, 146, 148, 157, 172, 185, 224

area based initiatives, 168-169

assistive technology, 116-117

asylum seekers and refugees, 5, 64, 83, 90-95

asylums, 20, 24-26, 30-34, 133, 136, 139

Audit Commission, 5, 12-13, 17, 42, 45, 49, 56, 83, 107, 117, 143, 145-146, 159, 204-205, 209

bedblocking, 48, 52, 156, 159

'Berlin Wall' (between health and social care), 59, 150, 201-202, 217

Best Value, 9, 49, 65, 77, 79, 196-197

Black and Minority Ethnic groups, 80-82, 88-96, 146, 154, 156, 177, 180, 192

capacity building, 89, 92, 95-97, 169, 173

charities, provision of services by, 24-26, 65, 173

Chronically Sick and Disabled Persons Act 1970, 21, 35

citizenship, 2, 6, 15, 125, 138, 167

co-housing, 162

Commission for Social Care Inspection, 65, 83, 159

Communities Plan (2003) (also referred to as the Sustainable Communities Plan), 68, 72, 171, 198

community alarms, 5, 52, 62, 68, 73, 116

community care
    assessment, 75, 77, 78, 207
    history and development of, 4, 24, 29-40, **46-61**, 63, 103, 106-112, 134, 149, 204-205, 215

housing's role in, 3, 5-7, 38-39, **41-61**, 62-63, 65, 67-68, 73, 77, 82, 104-112, 113-125, 139-141, 143-149, **153-162**, 175-186, 191, 201, 202-204, 218-219
    plans, 46, 48, 51, 189-193, 196, 199
    resources for, 4, 76, 78, 114, 149, 204

community cohesion, 91-92, 96, 164

community, concepts of, 164-168, 215

community development approaches, 37, 75, 77, **83-88**, 92-97, 183

community involvement, 76, 164, 167-171, 174

community plans, 49, 188, 191-2, 196-197, 199-200

compulsory treatment, 132

Connected Care Centres, 2

Conservative party and Conservative government policies, 46-47, 76-77, 127, 168, 180-181, 214

cost-shunting, 12, 49, 217

crime and disorder, 53, 69, 195

Cullingworth report (1969), 5, 29, 190

demographic trends, 39, 68, 143-147, 153, 161, 183, 208, 213, 216

devolved government, 14-15,

'difficult to let' housing, 21, 67, 139

Disabled Facilities Grants, 68, 73, 122-123

disabled people, 18, 21-24, 33, 35, 39, 65, 68, 76-77, 101, 109, **113-125**, 178, 182, 195, 203

discrimination (age, ethnicity, etc.), 22, 93, 153, 224

domestic violence, 9, 14, 53, 64, 177, 190, 195, 198

domiciliary care and support, 11, 20, 29, 31, 33-40, 45-50, 56, 62, 77, 149, 158, 161, 214

drug problems, 9, 12, 17, 32, 53, 64-65, 165-166, 170-174, 177-184, 195 exclusion (social) *see* social exclusion

ex-offenders, 6, 17, 53, 195

extra care schemes, 3, 10, 52, 59, 63, 67, 73, 142, 144-145, 149, 152-156, 159-161

floating support, 5, 9, 14, 34, 68, 73, 156, 166

focus groups, 90-91, 94

frail older people, 35, 66-67, 73, 142-162

health action zones, 51

health, impact of poor housing on, 21-22, 25, 41

health improvement plans, 51, 53, 188, 190-191

health policy *see* NHS, history and politics of

HIV/AIDS, 17, 195

homelessness, 5, 9, 22-23, 29, 34, 53, 69, 82, 139, 166, 171-175, 178-179, 184-185, 187, 189, 195-197

Homelessness Act 2002, 14, 53, 56, 189

home improvement agencies, 44, 68, 73, 144, 154

hospital discharge, 50, 52, 54-55, 151-152, 157-159

hostels, 7, 23, 34, 38, 62, 105-106, 108, 110, 166, 173

housing and health *see* health, impact of poor housing on

housing associations, role of, 5, 35, 44, 50, 52, 55-57, 59, 64-68, 81-82, 147, 171, 179, 183-185, 191, 203

housing benefit, 7, 12, 14, 62, 69-70, 82-83, 208

Housing Corporation, 52, 56, 64-68, 72-73, 120, 147, 162, 198

housing management, role of, 49, 55-56

housing needs assessments, 88-97

housing-related support services, 3, 45, 110, 208

Independence, Well-being and Choice (Department of Health green paper, 2005), 2-3, 13, 16, 61

independent living, 6-7, 16, 21, 33, 38, 41, 45, 62, 68-69, 111, 113-117, 148, 151, 154, 160, 215

institutional care, 29, 30-33, 36, 38-40, 51, 103, 105, 139, 143-145, 156, 158, 185, 210, 215

institutional racism, 80-81, 87

integration (of people or groups), 90-94, 96, 106, 112, 167, 171

inter-agency working, 42, 45, 48, 50, 52-60, 71-72, 154, 175, 184, 190

intermediate care, 10, 44, 52, 66, 144, **151-159**

joint commissioning (*see also* Supporting People, commissioning of services under), 17, 42, 142, 156-157, 217

labelling (of people), 33, 39, 60, 102, 105, 119, 129, 131, 136, 165

Labour party and Labour government policies, 2, 6, 14, 16, 41, 49, 66, 73, 75, **77-83**, 87, 134, 150, 164, 169, 180-181, 197, 207, 214

learning disabilities, people with, 5, 14, 19, 23, 30, 36, 53-54, 63, 66, **100-112**, 136, 195

Lifetime Homes, 68, 77, 117, 119-120, 195

Local Strategic Partnerships, 157, 168-170, 191-192, 196, 199

lone parents, 10, 14

long term care, 7, 15, 24, 28, 51, 66, 78, 136, 143, 145-150, 160, 161, 181

marginalisation, 6, 22-23, 33, 73, 138, 157, 164, 170-173, 189, 194, 197, 202-203, 206, 219

market-led approaches, 15-16, 47, 57, 77-78, 87, 107, 180, 210, 214-216 221

means-testing, 4, 56, 66, 72, 161, 181

medical model (of disability or mental illness), 33, 87, 128, 131-132, 162

medico-legal model *see* medical model

mental health problems, people with, 5, 14, 22, 24, 26, 28, 30, 36, 48, 64-66, 80, **127-139**, 157, 159, 172-173

mental health services, 34, 46, 54, 81, 128, 132-138, 184

mental hospitals, 25, 30-31, 34

mixed economy of care, 33, 36-37, 47, 138, 191, 204, 208

'modernisation' agenda for the public services, 2, 6, 41, 49, 51, 64, 69, 73-74, 138, 149, 165, 207, **210-216**

Modernising Mental Health Services (white paper, 1998), 132, 134-135, 137-138

move on accommodation, 8

National Care Standards, 11, 65-66, 111

National Service Framework for Older People (2001), 50, 138, 142, 144, **151-153**, 157-158, 161

needs assessment, 2, 9, 44, 48, 58, 60, 76, 86, **88-97**

neighbourhood renewal, 9, 53, 68, 88, 169-174

new technology, 2, 116-117

NHS

    delayed discharges from *see* bedblocking

    history and politics of, 28, 30-31, 36, 146, 207, 218

    housing, relation to, 110, 150, 155

    'internal market' in, 47, 211

    older people and, 152-153, 155, 213

    organisational change in, 140

    primary care emphasis in, 7, 135, 150, 207

    racism in *see* institutional racism

    relationship with other agencies, 36, 45, 48, 50-51

    resources and, 55, 78, 137, 140, 152, 207, 213

NHS and Community Care Act 1990, 9, **45-49**, 54, 64, 75-76, 88, 107-108, 149, 180, 190

NHS plan (2000), 50, 150, 152, 157-158

normalisation, 77, 100, 104-112, 115, 126

older people, services for, 5, 9, 16, 24, 27-28, 34-35, 48, 51-52, 63-64, 66-67, 72-73, 79, 92, **142-162**, 187, 195, 213-214, 224

performance assessment, indicators and targets, 65-66, 69, 78, 83, 123, 136, 159, 197, 213-214

personal care, 10-12, 45, 62, 66, 72, 78, 111, 143-145, 149, 157, 161, 209

personality disorder, 134-137

person centred planning, 13

physical disabilities or impairments, people with, 5, 34, 36, **113-125**, 132

pooled budgets, 50, 60, 67, 207, 216

poor law, 20, 23-24, 27-29

preventative services, 2-3, 5, 51, 55, 139-141, 144, 148, 154, 158-159, 203

primary care, 7, 38, 135, 138, 150, 207, 220

primary care trusts, 3, 14, 44, 50, 52-53, 150, 152, 156-157, 191, 199, 217

public expenditure, controls on and levels of, 7, 46, 146, 213

purchaser/provider split, 47, 57

Quality and Choice: A Decent Home for All (housing green paper, 2000), 9, 49, 147

refugees *see* asylum seekers and refugees

Regional Housing Boards, 68, 72-73, 197-199

registered care homes, 11, 65

residential care, 3, 7, 11-12, 24, 26, 30-34, 44, 46, 65-67, 85, 105, 107, 111, 142, 145, 147-149, 151, 154-155, 158-160, 204-205, 208, 215

residualisation (of social housing), 7, 21, 182, 203, 206

right to buy, 7, 82, 166

Robson Rhodes review (2004), 3, 5, 10, 16, 194

rough sleepers, 17, 64, 172, 195

schizophrenia, 32, 130, 136-137

Scotland, policy differences in, 14-15, 72, 78, 143, 161

Seebohm report (1968), 5, 29, 36, 38, 132, 139, 190, 211, 214

segregation (of people or groups), 30, 39, 102, 115, 134

service charges, 7, 55

service users, empowerment of, 59, 75, 79, 83, 87, 92-93, 101, 108-109, 129, 138, 140-141, 153, 158, 164, 167, 175, 178, 182, 203

service users, responsiveness of services to, 9, 17, 41-45, 49, 51, 57, 59-61, 63, 70, **75-87, 88-97**, 108, 111, 165, 168, 190, 226

sheltered housing, 3, 5-8, 10, 12, 26, 35, 38, 52, 55, 62, 65, 67-68, 72-73, 89, 142, 144-146, 148-149, **152-161**

single assessment process (SAP), 10, 50, 152-153, 160

social capital, 165, 167, 171, 201-203, 216, 218-221

social exclusion, 9, 15, 23, 39, 51, 53, 60, 76, 93, 114-115, 125, 132, 135, 141, 150, 158, 165-166, 170-173, 202-203

social housing

    residualisation of, 7, 166

    role in community care *see* community care, housing's role in

social model (of care or disability), 33, 87, 115, 128, 131-132, 138, 178, 215

social services departments
    directors of, 2, 36, 132,
    eligibility criteria (for services from), 6-7, 13, 17, 46, 48, 55, 76
    interrelation of other services with, 9, 14, 17, 40-41, 44, 48-54, 57, 109, 149-150, 154, 156-157, 190, 196, 207
    mental heath services and, 128, 140, 212
    modernisation of, 9, 73, 211, 214, 216
    organisation and role of, 36-37, 85-86, 107, 132
    resources for, 7-8, 46, 48, 54-59, 67, 69, 73, 105, 140, 158
    responsibilities of, 3, 46, 54, 146, 151, 157, 161, 191, 198, 211-212
    tensions with other services, 6, 40, 48, 50, 54-57, 139, 217
    service users and, 79, 122, 153

Social Services Inspectorate, 65, 153, 155-156

social workers see social services departments

'special needs' (housing, etc.), 21, 23, 29, 34-35, 38, 80, 101, 113, 116-119

spending reviews, 154, 160, 194

stereotypes (of people or groups), 80, 126, 128-129, 133, 139

stigmatising (practices, or forms of care), 7, 18, 20, 23, 33, 38, 77, 80, 87, 112, 133, 135, 137-138, 141, 165, 172, 174

strategic role (of local housing authorities), 3, 73, 183, 185-186, 196-198

substance abuse, 5-6, 10, 19, 136-137, 164-165, 171-174

supported housing, 3, 5-12, 14, 17, 19, **62-74**, 142, 147-148, 154-155, 157-158, 160-162, 167, 171

supported housing management grant, 64, 69, 208

supported living, 52, 109-111, 127

Supporting People
    commissioning of services under, 4, 14, 17, 42, 50, 53, 59-60, 67, 69-71, 89, 142, 151, 153, 156-158, 160, 214, 217
    community care and, 3, 5, 12, 64
    criticisms of, 10, 80, 82, 87, 111, 172, 208-209, 215
    development and history of, 8-9, 11, 17, 58-60, 69-73, 80, 206-206, 208-210, 220
    funding, eligibility for, 45, 70, 158
    inspection of services under, 70, 209
    resources for, 3-4, 11-15, 17, 59, 70-71, 73, 83, 157-158, 208-209
    reviews and strategies, 5, 13, 17, 53, 70-71, 80, **188-200**
    role of housing in, 58, 63, 69, 72-73, 129, 142, 209
    role of local authorities in, 5, 9, 53, 73, 195, 198, 209

Thatcher, Margaret, 7, 20, 101, 107, 109, 202

Travellers, 64, 83, 195

unfit housing, 22, 25, 28

unpaid carers, 76

'upstream' and 'downstream' services, 128, 134, 139-141, 204-210

voluntary sector, 24, 30, 35-37, 41, 44, 47, 50, 52-53, 57, 39, 65, 82, 95, 169, 177, 179-184, 202, 211, 214215, 219

Wales, policy differences in, 15-16, 161

wheelchair access, 23, 68, 113-114, **118-124**, 145

whole systems working, 5-7, 10, 16, 18, 41-44, 58, 60, 69, 141, **142-162**